# When Men Are Gods

G. Cope Schellhorn

Other books by G. Cope Schellhorn:

*EXTRATERRESTRIALS IN BIBLICAL PROPHECY*
*and the New Age Great Experiment*

*DISCOVERING THE LOST PYRAMID*

# WHEN MEN ARE GODS

G. Cope Schellhorn

HORUS HOUSE PRESS, INC.
MADISON, WISCONSIN
distributed by
INNER LIGHT PUBLICATIONS
NEW BRUNSWICK, NEW JERSEY

Library of Congress Catalog Card Number: 91-72270
ISBN: 0-938294-43-1

First Edition
First Printing August 1991

Published by
Horus House Press, Inc.
P. O. Box 55185
Madison, Wisconsin 53705

Distributed by
Inner Light Publications
P. O. Box 753
New Brunswick, New Jersey 08903

Printed by
Litho Printers
Cassville, Missouri

# Acknowledgements

The author wishes to thank the staff of Memorial Library of the University of Wisconsin; also professors David Michelson, John Kutzbach and Marjorie Winkler of the University for their kindly assistance. A special note of gratitude is offered to Marie Dvorzak, Head, Geology-Geophysics Library, also of the University, for her interminable efforts to supply the author with whatever he needed, and to my wife, Patricia, for her sound advice, proofreading skills and hours of manuscript preparation.

For Sarah and Kristian
and all cosmic questers
everywhere

# Table of Contents

Jesus answered them, 'Is it not written in your law, "I said, you are gods"?'

Jn 10:34


You are god but not God; and yet you have always been God, even from the beginning.

Chaka Tat

# CHAPTER ONE

## The Ultimate Game Parable

Once I met a man working on his game. He was earnestly hitting a tennis ball against a practice board. I noticed, however, that the board itself was unusual. It was divided in halves, with a vertical line separating the right side from the left. As I watched I could see that the man seemed to be aiming his strokes and the ball at the right side of the board.

"Excuse me," I said, "but why do you aim only at the right side of the board?"

"It's quite simple," he answered. "And really the ultimate. I pretend the board, both right side and left side, is life itself. The ball is me, my actions in this world. The strings of my racket, my will power. I try to hit the ball to the right side which I pretend is the area of positive experience and positive results. The left is negative experience, as you might have already guessed. Sometimes, as you can see, I hit the negative side even though I'm trying for the other. *C'est la vie*, you might say. But I am getting better with practice and time."

I looked around and saw that others were practicing, but most of them did not really seem to have their hearts in it.

Later I returned to the court and noticed many of the same people were practicing or playing but my friend was gone. I wondered if he had finally mastered his "ultimate" game and had left for elsewhere, some other world, perhaps, where the game is more difficult but the rewards that much greater.

As I was musing, a stranger approached and handed me a

1

note and a racket. The note was addressed to me from my departed friend. "Good luck," it said. "And don't forget, after hard use, to re-string."

# CHAPTER TWO

## The Making of Gods

If we as mortal men and women are to become aware of our godlike destiny — a destiny of which most of us are very unaware — we must learn to read the book of the past. Then we can enlighten ourselves about the now evolving book of the future, which is intimately related to the past, and the immortal role we are destined to play in that future, if we choose to do so. Most of us, once we become a little aware of our true potential, and the historical and prehistorical roots of that potential, are eager to learn more, all we can, about what we are and what we can be.

One key to an understanding of yesterday and tomorrow, and their relationship to us, can be found in the ancient clay tablets of Sumer, Babylonia and Assyria. Here quite succinctly in a number of different tales, is described the genesis of *Homo sapiens*, as crafted by the "gods." These tales considered in mass make one consistent, grand, total story full of much sound and fury, but pregnant with meaning, awe inspiring in suggestiveness, and filled with a great hope. How did these tales come to be and what do they really tell us?

The Sumerians of the Tigris and Euphrates basin, whose culture reached its zenith two to three thousand years before Moses, were well aware of how human beings came to be on earth. They were told of their true genesis by those who had created them after these creators, apparently cosmic space visitors, had brought civilization and the institution of kingship from heaven to earth, colonized the planet and set about improving genetically some of its indigenous life forms. Cultures as diverse as the Australian aborigines and the Mayas of ancient Yucatan, British Honduras (today's Belize) and Northern Guatemala, as well as many other cultures worldwide, have tales similar to the Sumerian-Akkadian-Babylonian genesis accounts. This should not surprise us. The Hebrew *Midrashim*, which are historical rabbinical commentaries on the Scriptures, tell us that all men everywhere were brought the knowledge of basic cosmic laws. It should not be too surprising, then, to find that they were also informed in time about their own creation into not only living but intelligent beings.

It would appear that the Sumerian space visitors, who bio-engineered *Homo sapiens*, imperfectly realized in the beginning the full implications of their biological experimentation and the true potential of their creation. The initial impetus for their project will become momentarily clearer. At this point, suffice it to say that, having made a slightly less perfect duplicate of themselves, they opened a window of opportunity for their hybrid earthly offspring which could ultimately allow these offspring to match the physical, mental and spiritual accomplishments of the hybridizing parents and, theoretically, even exceed them.

Thus the natural (and more or less Darwinian) evolution of *Homo erectus* (ape man) on earth was altered irreparably by the interference of the cosmic visitors. What might have been his future is impossible to say. *Homo sapiens'* future, however, thanks to that interference, seems limitless. Man's fate may now ultimately lead him outward in mind and inward spiritually until he becomes a true equal of those space "gods" who helped create him — a new "god" that life forms in some distant part of the galaxy may some day look upon with the same awe and wonder that *Homo sapien*, the new Adam, looked upon the *Elohim* and *Nephilim* who are the biblical versions of the Sumerian greater gods and the lesser gods, the Anunnaki and Igigi.*

*The *Anunnaki* are the lesser "gods" on earth; that is, the crew(s) of the visiting

4

It is fortunate for us today that the Babylonians and Assyrians, like the Sumerians before them, preserved the record of their (and our) past. It is also fortunate that so much of this record has been found and translated within the last century. It is not so fortunate, as the tablets prove, that by the time of the writing of the Judeo-Christian Genesis, the earlier, more accurate accounts of man's creation, or, more properly speaking, of this refashioning of an already extant biped, had become compromised.

The Judeo-Christian Genesis appears to be an abridged melange of several stories made most probably from several different sources, that is, from the styli, more than likely, of several different authors. Almost all biblical scholars are convinced of this. Moses *may have* pulled it all together. But Genesis remains a put-together synthesis, a stew whose ingredients have been gathered from a world which was, even at the moment of composition, far removed in time.

It is understandable, and forgivable, that the case should be such. It is much less forgivable to see so little effort being made by biblical scholars, theologians, Sumerologists and even celebrated academic mythologists, such as a Joseph Campbell, to cut through the pall of smoke of conventional interpretation and orthodox religious preconception which so confounds any serious effort to give the Sumerian accounts a fresh, open, unbiased airing — the kind of attention and the kind of credence they seem to deserve.

The ancient Sumerian tablets make several things clear. First, extraterrestrial visitors, "gods" from the sky, descended to earth and occupied it long before mankind, as we know it, was present. Secondly, because the lesser gods, the *Anunnaki*, were made to do the heavy, physical work such as building and mining in the various small colonies and cities under harsh conditions, they finally revolted. In the words of the epic *Atra-Hasis* (literally, "The Extraordinarily Wise"), the *Anunnaki* complain, "Excessive hard work has killed us/Our work is a

spacecraft of Sumerian times. The *Igigi* is a Sumerian term for those crew members who are working in space stations and spacecraft above the earth; that is, the lesser "gods" not on earth.

burden/our suffering great." Another text is simply and revealingly named, *When the Gods as Men Bore the Work*.

To solve the problem of these grumbling, rebellious astronauts forcibly turned menial laborers of the earth, a son of Anu (Lord of the Heavens), called Enki (literally, Lord of the Earth), steps forward. He has a solution to offer: Let the Birth Goddess create a *lulu*, a "mixed being." 'Let him carry the burden...let him carry the burden of the gods.' The offer is, which should come as no surprise under the circumstances, agreeable to everyone concerned, to greater and lesser "gods" alike. His name, the "gods" concur, 'shall be Man.'

In numerous texts, some Sumerian, some Babylonian, including *When the Gods as Men Bore the Work* and *Atra-Hasis*, the *Enuma Elish* and *Creation of Man by the Mother Goddess*, we find the biological experimentation that followed related in graphic detail. The "gods" found extant on the planet a hominid which they could utilize for their purposes. This hominid, *Homo erectus*, had been formed by the normal evolutionary cycle of planetary life.* Now the Sumerian "gods," the *Elohim* and *Nephilim* of later Hebrew texts, step in with the idea of altering *Homo erectus* into a new creature, Adamic man or *Homo sapiens*, thereby speeding up the evolutionary process. Thus we have Enki, Lord of the Earth, proclaiming, 'The creature whose name you uttered—it exists!' And he added, 'Bind on it the image of the gods.' We now have, as it is apparent, an infusion of extraterrestrial genes into *Home erectus* stock by these erestwhile bioengineers.

In the much later Hebrew version of the process, we are told in Genesis (1:24) that the *Elohim* (which is literally a plural form, meaning "gods") said, 'Let us make man in our image, after our likeness....'** "Make over" rather than "make" would be a more accurate translation of the original idea.

---

*This does not rule out, however, the possibility that life on earth may have been seeded from elsewhere earlier in the planet's prehistory.

**Voltaire, the French sage, said every educated man knew that Elohim designated plural gods—which should tell us something about the educational level in this country today.

What we have described for us in the Sumerian creation texts is a process, a project which supports both traditional scientific Darwinian evolutionary evidence and divine genesis by proclamation as well. As long as we understand what "gods" are doing the proclaiming. And as long as we are aware that each position by itself is only a half-truth. The real truth is a synergy, a synthesis of both. Neither theory—each of which has caused so much emotional contention—is shown finally to be an accurate account of what actually occurred. There is, we suppose, an irony here. After all the fuss, a compromise is called for—a truce dictated by evidence.

The tireless Sumerian scholar Zecharia Sitchin (*The 12th Planet*) has summed up the larger truth by stating, "the Sumerians described Man as both a deliberate creature of the gods and a link in the evolutionary chain that began with the celestial events described in the 'Epic of Creation' [*Enuma Elish*]."

This new man, this Adam, this evolutionary hominid which has had impressed on it by biogenetic engineering the "image" of its creators, raising it, according to the New Testament, to a status "a little lower than the angels"—it is this new specimen which was placed in the Hebrew Genesis in the Garden of Eden. It is this new specimen which, we are told, broke rules, wanted to know too much too soon, "ate from the tree of the knowledge of good and evil," and was eventually expelled from the immediate care and tutelage of its keepers. It is this creature, almost the very genetic image of its creators, which so angers them by its inquisitive actions as it is developing and learning, and by the mischief it is capable of fomenting, that causes these *Elohim-Nephilim* creator-monitors to decide to destroy the progeny of their hands, 'I have determined to make an end of all flesh; for the earth is filled with violence through them; behold, I will destroy them with the earth.' (Gen 6:13) It is also this specimen, whose potential and ambition was so troublesome, whose desire to imitate and emulate its creators was so worrisome, that finally led one of them in the course of events to exclaim in dismay, '...this is only the beginning of what they will do; and nothing that they propose to do will now be impossible for them....' (Gen 11:6) And our visitors scattered these Noachian survivors over the face of the earth.

But some remnants of mankind, no matter how terrible the catastrophe, whether it is accidental or premeditated by the "gods," always seem to survive. The Sumerian Ziusudra. The Hebrew Noah. The Greek Deucalion and his wife, Pyrrha. Man tenaciously endures.

What are we to think of ourselves, this creature for whom it has been said that 'nothing will be impossible' for us once we have 'imagined to do' it? What is an honest evaluation of our status? What is our true potential? We have been told by our Judeo-Christian scriptures that we are created "a little below the angels." Are we really gods in the making, if we understand human potential correctly? If we understand the term "gods" to mean extraterrestial visitors of a superior genetic and spiritual makeup, as well as an advanced technology — can we become like them? Can we develop mentally and spiritually to their level? Perhaps beyond?

The answer is yes. We are, in fact, "gods" in two ways. We are not only gods in the making, humans who can emulate and perhaps supersede the accomplishments of our extraterrestrial bioengineers; we are, from another perspective, gods already made but unfinished. The idea is best explained by a paradox. We are god but not God; and yet we are God and have been God from the very beginning.

First, let's look at the paradox from the human point of view. We are god (small g) because we are a part of God, the Creator. But we are not all of God, only a portion of the overall creation. And yet because we are a portion, we are God and have been God from the day that portion came into being. It is a matter, you might say, of perspective.

Now let's look at the statement from (theoretically) God's point of view. You are god (small g) because you are a portion of Me (God), but you are not all of Me (God); and yet because you are a portion of Me, you are God (Me) and have been God (Me) from the very beginning.

In both instances, a little thought will indicate to us that we are not completed, not perfected beings. We have not, in

8

the first instance, attained the accomplishments, mental, spiritual and otherwise of our extraterrestrial visitors. In the second instance, we are god but not God completely. Perhaps as we grow mentally and spiritually, as we perfect ourselves, we will become closer, more identical to the Godhead Itself.

A little more thought may lead us to an interesting conclusion. The metamorphosis of man toward the greater perfection of our extraterrestrial visitors is also a metamorphosis toward Godly (capital G) perfection, toward a future day, perhaps, when the little gods correlate one to one with the Greater God and become, are subsumed, in fact, into that Greater Godhead becoming as One, indistinguishable from It. Our extraterrestrial visitors, from this point of view, can be put in proper perspective. They are part of the hierarchy of all creation, moving, just as we are, toward a greater perfection, personally willing at times, or commanded from higher regions in the hierarchy, to assist by moral instruction and good advice their less developed cousins. Ancient man, not knowing the fuller story, called these extraterrestrial visitors "angels" (Gr. *angelos*, literally "messengers") and "gods." We would not be mistaken today to call most of them simply "friends."

To reach a greater perfection, we must have patience as well as the will power to raise up ourselves to become all we can be. What appears to be our future as a species will become our future only if we make it so. It does not necessarily have to happen. It probably will not happen for the great majority of mankind in this lifetime. Time, however, as a Zen Buddhist might say, is no time. There will be life upon life for us to continue the journey upward and inward as well as outward. But an important minority of humans is leading the way right now as they have always done. The membership of this small band changes with time but the minority, and its upward thrust, continues to exist and endure. It is the avant-garde, the herald of an increasing number (but still very much a minority) of humans who are approaching a state of development which will transform them and propel them to new levels, and new worlds, of development. These individuals are about to make the great leap forward and shuck off, once and for all, the inhibiting animal bodies which enclose them, with all the attendant restraining animal characteristics inherent in those bodies which make uplifting of the spiritual essence in man so difficult.

This metamorphosis is man's fate, his destiny, if he makes it so, wills it so. The *will* is the key. It *will* open any door. It is the magic word, if there can be said to be one.

We hold, each one of us, our futures, as the old metaphor says, in our hands. This is much truer than most of us realize. How we develop now and tomorrow, how quickly we as individuals and as a species can come to certain understandings — which can, by the way, once learned, alleviate almost all of the present social and ecological problems threatening the world — will determine our future. Like a Greek tragedy, our character is our fate. But we needn't have a tragedy, neither a personal one nor one that affects the whole species. We must remake not our "image" now (the "gods" did that for us) but our character.

How, then, can we grow in a way which will best use that potential which was bioengineered into us by our extraterrestrial visitors? How can we become "gods" like our cosmic progenitors?

The answers to those questions lie in a thorough understanding of our past as a species. We are quite clearly of a dual nature. Half of us is the evolutionary beast, the *Homo erectus* ape-man which preceded us and whose body and emotions we in large measure still carry with us. It inhibits us, restrains our growth and makes us dangerous at times to ourselves and others. The other half of us carries the genes of our bioengineers, as we have already indicated. That latter half opened a window of opportunity for us. If we do not acknowledge the window and "jump for it," we will remain prisoners of our lower selves, locked in to great limitations until the day we discover what we can truly be.

How divine these visiting bioengineers were (are) can be debated. But we had best recognize their spiritual as well as technological superiority then and now, for they are still with us. It was they, after all, who brought the Hebrews the Ten

Commandments and carried God's law (which was also their law) to the ends of the earth. They quite possibly engineered the appearance of the Great Nazarene. The evidence, if seen with an open mind, at least suggests so.* At any rate, whether that cosmic law brought to us was the absolute cosmic pronouncements of a Greater God of all creation or the interpretation of it by less godly and somewhat imperfect extraterrestrials, we have to admit, I believe, that whatever the case, the information, the moral instruction, the advice they gave us was much superior to anything in this world that then existed.

The jump from *Homo erectus* to *Homo sapiens*, which happened somewhere between 30,000 and 75,000 years ago, was quite sudden. The expansion in brain capacity (roughly from 1000 cc to 1400 cc) and the more agile body type has no compelling explanation in evolutionary biological science.** And it can not have. There is no biological "missing link." It can not be found if it does not exist. The most that could ever be found, and this is unlikely, are a skull or two remaining from unsuccessful, aborted biological experiments—and these would be, if found, approximately the same age as the earliest *Homo sapiens* skulls. The jump, the evidence indicates, from one species to the next was almost instantaneous, with certain minor fine tuning along the way.

Brinsley Le Poer Trench (Lord Clancarty) is well aware of this dual nature of man which so often put him at cross-purposes with himself. He names him, in fact, "Cross-Man" as a recognition of his two-branched genetic tree.

Le Poer Trench puts his finger squarely on the major problem in his work, *The Sky People*, when he states, "That is where Cross-Man begins—the fusing of the Serpent People [some of our extraterrestrial visitors] and Jehovah's animal-man creation...."*** He seems, however, sometimes more

*See my *Extraterrestrials in Biblical Prophecy and the New Age Great Experiment*, which analyzes this evidence.

**See John Philip Cohane, *Paradox: The Case for the Extraterrestrial Origin of Man.*

***Johovah is also recognized by Le Poer Trench as an *Elohim*, a leader of our extraterrestrial bioengineers.

aware, and sometimes less, of the previous mixing of extraterrestrial genes with ape-man to produce Jehovah's "animal-man creation," although when he does acknowledge it, he indicates that he does not believe the earlier, original, partial mix holds much hope for humanity. He calls *Homo sapiens*, bioengineered in the Garden of Eden Laboratory, Adam II and man who interbred with the "Sons of God" (Gen 6:4), just before and after Noah's time, Cross-Man, which is *Homo sapiens* with the addition of even more extraterrestrial genes. It is his opinion "when the sons of God came in to the daughters of men, and they bore children to them..." that the resulting gene mix positively reinforced man's heredity, making especially Noah and post Noachian survivors of a planet wracked by earth changes more adaptable and more malleable human beings.

The solution to the problem of this dual nature of man is, he feels, for those who are genetically "Galactic-dominant" to recognize their latent potential, if they are not already awakened. Those individuals whose genetic mix makes them what he calls "Adam II dominant" are still inherently slaves to their original nature. He realizes that we all have elements of both types within us, to be sure, but is convinced that wherever the greatest propensity lies, so goes the man today and the species itself over time.

Brinsley Le Poer Trench seems very close to adequately explaining the quixotic nature of human character — at its worst so base and animalistic, at its best so temptingly near what we have come to think of as noble, even divine. Without, however, a recognition of the real source of that nature — the cross between a genetically superior cosmic race and an earthly biped — man's basic character structure will remain to us a mystery, always baffling, sometimes extremely annoying, but a mystery nonetheless. All the research in the world into the DNA of chromosomes and genes will not suffice to thoroughly explain it. The problem of man's sociological adjustment — or maladjustment — and his perception of himself as an individual must remain incomplete until he recognizes where he comes from. Then he can begin to realize why he is as he is. Then he can begin effectively to remake himself through an act of will if he so wishes.

The problem with Le Poer Trench's understanding, if there is one, and I think there is, is his insistence on a genetic foundation to man's character problems. Genetics is only part of the problem. The great problem lies elsewhere — with the degree of spiritual evolvement that an entity brings with him when he "takes over" a genetic body at birth. More spiritually developed entities are entitled by cosmic law to embody themselves in a body more conducive to respond to their "Galactic-dominant" (to use Le Poer Trench's term) nature. Those less developed spiritually are relegated to bodies and brains that are suitable fits. These entities are more animalistically oriented in spirit *before* they ever take over a human body. They are given, or choose, a body appropriate to their nature.

Thus what seems to be basically a genetic problem isn't finally one at all. The genetic makeup of any given man, whatever it might be, is a symptom, not a cause of his spiritual condition, a reflection, not a source. To be deceived otherwise, is to begin again to approximate the errors of mechanistic Darwinism and orthodox Judeo-Christian theology which posits the possibility of only one human earth-life and rules out reincarnation altogether.

We need to understand, finally, that almost every human brain is large enough to respond to the growth capabilities of almost any human being, if nurtured and developed properly. It is not an accident that mortal man uses approximately only one-tenth to one half of his brain power. It is also not accidental that approximately one half to nine-tenths of all cosmic creation is beyond our instrumental-mechanical ability to register it. The two situations are intimately related. As man grows in spiritual capacity, larger areas of the brain respond. He becomes increasingly able to register some of that one half to nine-tenths of which he was previously unaware. Man at this very moment has all the latent brain power he needs to grow mentally and spiritually as much as he is able.

This does not mean that our extraterrestrial visitors have not improved on the *Homo erectus* physical body. They have.

As time has passed, a genetic strain, say a family line, will have more or less of this genetic improvement showing, depending on how pure the lineage—that is, how close that particular family line has stayed to the last extraterrestrial charge of new genes.* Interestingly enough, scriptures such as the Book of Enoch as well as Genesis 6:4 indicate that the interbreeding of extraterrestrials with man was frowned upon by extraterrestrial Central Command. We may be "better" than we were originally intended to be. Real demanding upstarts, posing a long prehistorical and historical problem for our bioengineers. That is what can happen when an experiment gets out of control. Out of control, of course, from the bioengineers' point of view.

Intermarriage between families could improve or debase the future genetic structure, depending on whether the line being married into was closer or more removed from the last extraterrestrial genetic charge. Now it so happens that mankind has so intermarried over time that, generally speaking, there isn't much genetic difference (variance) from man to man.** *But there is a difference.* What I am saying has nothing to do with race, color or creed. These considerations do not apply now, and there is a serious question whether they ever much did. I doubt it. What I propose is the idea that the slight genetic difference spoken of is, however, utilized by entities at birth. Who chooses what body, who gets what body, is dependent on where you are at spiritually and what is suitable to your needs. You get what you've earned, what you deserve. There is nothing to keep you from improving on what you have other than yourself. Improvement is, in fact, the very idea. To improve on what you've got using will power. That idea applies to all of us equally, from the slightly more spiritually and mentally advanced specimen to the one who has not come quite so far along. This is the Ultimate Game we are all involved in. It is a serious game but not without its moments of levity which, if

*The color of the various races has nothing to do with this gene-charge. The issue has nothing really to do with race at all.

**Actually, we are all approximately 50th cousins or less.

we are wise, we will learn to thoroughly enjoy.

What has been called "Galactic-dominant" humans, I would prefer to call cosmic-oriented people. These are cosmic questers, searching for self-knowledge and cosmic understanding. I will have much more to say about them later. What Le Poer Trench has labeled "Adam II dominant," and a large portion of his "Cross-Man" type, I would prefer to call earthbound-oriented people. We need to take a close look at the characteristics of each type but first, we had best consider the numbers of each type to be found in the world today.

At any given moment in earth's history during the past four thousand years both cosmic-oriented and earthbound-oriented types have been present. The earth is continually receiving new entities from other worlds who are transferring here and, in many cases, are "moving up" from less developed civilizations to the more developed situation of the earth-life dimension. Likewise, some entities transfer here from more spiritual and mental worlds where they have not completely assimilated themselves successfully. To say they have been demoted to prison-camp earth is inaccurate and misleading. Earth is not a prison camp for cosmic failures. In the scheme of evolvement, each entity tends to be placed (actually places himself) where he deserves to be, and where he deserves to be is where he can learn the most in an appropriate environment without too much stress. There are no dishonorable discharges as such meted out by unfeeling cosmic judges and inquisitors, no sentences to perdition. Entities who have spent all their lives, or at least many of them, learning earth's particular lessons of experience, are continually reincarnating into earth bodies. Each entity arriving on the earth plane, no matter from what point of origin, is given an appropriate genetic body, one that is compatible with his spiritual needs or suitable for the kinds of life experience he (she) needs to facilitate spiritual and mental growth. Many of these ideas are familiar to a great number of people and scarcely bare repeating. Sadly, the great majority of mankind is not familiar with them. These people are quite literally in the dark, a condition in which many of the people who control them and manipulate them would like to see them remain

An extended analogy at this point might be appropriate. Each individual genetic-body, including the mind of that body, can be conceived of as a protoplasmic circuit board. The boards are quite similar. Everyone has one. But some boards have more circuits wired in and consequently function better for certain purposes. It is well known, as we have already mentioned, how little of their indigenous brain power humans use. The "extra," unused areas of the human brain were a genetic gift of our extraterrestrial bioengineers who shared their genes with us. With them most, if not all, of the brain is functional and functioning. With humans, only those who are cosmic-oriented have begun to tap into this reserve. As they progress mentally and spiritually, more and more circuits are wired and become communication links — bands of contact with that large part of the physical cosmos that our scientists now believe exists but which does not register on their mechanistic instruments. Most scientists, of course, discount completely any spiritual dimension to the cosmos. Their instruments do not register it, ergo it does not exist. So they are failing to register not only the large missing matter — energy constituent of creation, which they admit, but the spiritual constituent as well, which they do not acknowledge at all.

Earthbound-oriented humans have the same circuit boards as do cosmic-oriented men and women but most, if not all, of the extra circuitry lies idle. It is not yet hooked up. This poses problems for the earthbound-oriented, some of which they are not even aware, and as well for those not so earthbound who are striving to break away from their fetters and fly free. We have a world filled with people at different stages of spiritual growth. The great multitude of humanity is at a rather low stage spiritually and yet, conversely, there is a growing number, still a small minority, who are opening new circuits of understanding every day. The New Age movement at its best has been celebrating that fact, recording it, and offering encouragement to those who are striving to develop their better self.*

*Each one of us must learn to remove mentally all the claptrap which has para-

Unfortunately, much of humanity insists on remaining at a low spiritual and mental stage, resists attempts at any kind of education which would raise consciousness, and is often willing to take violent action against those responding to their cosmic orientation who wish to grow. This is not a new state of affairs in the world. It is as old as *Homo sapiens* is new.

A close look at the character type of the earthbound-oriented reveals why he is often at odds not only with himself but with others, including the cosmic-oriented, who he vaguely suspects, without good reason, is a threat to him. What is more, his attitude problems in general immensely contribute to the tension and violence in the world. Most outstanding among his traits is his lack of an enhanced telepathic ability. He is a very limited receiver, most likely to garble any message received, and he does not understand how to "send." As Le Poer Trench points out, this psychic shortcoming contributes greatly to his basic paranoia. He never can know for sure what the other person is thinking. This makes him forever suspicious of the motives and actions of his own kind. It is not overall a state of affairs that contributes to mental health or world peace.

Man was given the scriptural dictum to 'Be fruitful and multiply, and fill the earth and subdue it....' He was also given 'dominion' over 'every living thing' on earth other than his own kind. Regrettably a great problem has arisen since ape-man was genetically improved into man as we know him. He carries latent genetic greatness but is unaware of the fact. Distrusting the motives of his fellow human beings, he finds it all too easy to consider his personal desires primary and to give short shrift to the needs of his neighbors. He is all too willing to impose his selfishness on those around him, sometimes with violence. Violence is a remnant behavioral characteristic common to pre-*Homo sapiens*. The carryover of this characteristic to the new species now threatens man's very survival in an age

sitically attached itself to legitimate New Age aspirations and threatens to undermine its spiritual objectives. The public at large does not understand even now what the real New Age is about and is continually being misled by the mass media.

of nuclear blackmail. If man cannot soon by reason and force of will either control or expunge this trait from his being, his future is dark. Needless to say, there may be no future for him on planet earth.

Add animal aggressiveness and violence to human acquisitiveness (greed) and subconscious (and conscious) paranoia to an already unstable character and you have an Attila the Hun, a Hitler, a Stalin, an Idi Amin, an Ayatollah Khomeini, a Saddam Hussein *ad infinitum*. All are authoritarian type personalities exhibiting in one form or another, or combination thereof, sadistic-masochistic tendencies. We might conclude, and rightly so, that earthbound-oriented man does not like his fellow man very well, or himself.

Until the world masses are taught how to recognize such demagogic temperaments, and what the consequences of such temperaments in positions of power invariably are, the world will remain a dangerous place. The solution, it would seem, is education: We must realize that we carry genetically within us the propensity to act violently, and we must learn to control, each one of us separately and all of us as a species, our lower nature; succeeding in the above, we must make certain that aspiring rulers are peace-oriented, peace-loving people who have conquered their own animalism and will not condone its display in any form in the conduct of their supporters. If these words seem idealistically philosophical, consider the alternative. The world teeters on the brink of nuclear and environmental destruction. It has done so now for over fifty years. How long can the player play Russian roulette and win? Regrettably, as anarchist Emma Goldman pointed out earlier in this century, it is often "organized violence on top which creates individual violence at the bottom."

Man was told to 'subdue' the earth. He proceeded to *conquer* nature, to dominate her, to wring from the planet, as if it were a wet mop, whatever golden drops were his momentary fancy. The difference is the difference between reasonable restraint and out and out police brutality. We need only take a passing glance at our daily newspapers to get a partial update on the continuing story of depredation, pollution and irresponsibility concerning the treatment of the only physical home we now have in the cosmos. A small but illustrative case in point: Honeywell Corporation is now accused of dumping approximately 1400 barrels weighing approximately 800-1200 lbs. apiece into Lake Superior 30 years ago. One explanation offered: The barrels contained secret information about an experimental grenade the U.S. feared the Russians might acquire. Logical question: If it was only information in these barrels, why the talk of potential radioactivity levels? Do the barrels contain radioactive materials? If so, did Honeywell consider how long it takes for a steel barrel to rust and leak? Did it care? Do other corporations and governments, including our own, who use the oceans of the world for dumping hazardous materials, including much nuclear waste, have an appropriate respect for the earth's ecology which, to be healthy, must be in balance?

We all know the answer to that last question. Governments like people can be paranoid and violent. Like people, they can also be self-serving and greedy and irresponsible. After all, they are made up of people and can be no better than them. It is at this time in the earth's history, and for this reason, extremely important that the cosmic-oriented individuals be recognized for their gifts and the potential salutary effect they can have on the present course of world events if they are allowed to, encouraged to, participate in public service.

The cosmic-oriented individual has a thirst for knowledge and understanding and a proper appreciation for the power of love which begets, among many things, peace among men. He (she) realizes that all understanding begins with knowledge of self and is aware that this is a never ending quest. Once an appropriate amount of self-knowledge is attained, however—after what could be called "inner path" exploration—greater possibilities of discovering even more about the outer creation in all its manifestations begin to appear. The old adage, When the student is ready, the master will appear, has a sound basis in fact. The cosmic quester of pure heart and true motives finds the knowledge he seeks becoming more and more available to him, sometimes wondrously appearing almost out of nowhere. A rare book, for example, is needed for study and, surprisingly, it is found in a used bookstore. Or a seemingly unsolvable problem presents itself and a "dream" offers a solution or insight.

The cosmic-oriented individual has now reached a point of spiritual development where more and more things are possible for him. His previous striving, his thirst for knowledge in this life and previous lives, on earth and elsewhere, has earned him access to a new knowing. More and more circuits on his "board" are opening. He is moving from marginally telepathic in his abilities to increasingly telepathic, *and his new talent can be used, should be used, in the service of others*. There are a few individuals, what Buddhists call *bodhisattvas*, who already being enlightened entities, have chosen to reincarnate on earth to spiritually uplift the life wave at large. Most cosmic-oriented humans, however, who are making the breakthrough to cosmic understanding today, are doing so for the first time. They are the biblical "first fruits." And they are very much a precious minority, little understood by the mass of men who feel vaguely threatened by them as they fear the loss of their materialistic fascinations. Yet this small minority of the newly enlightened are the hope, the future of mankind.

If the life wave that exists now on earth cannot rise to the occasion soon and by force of will become predominantly cosmic-oriented, the species of man as we know it may exterminate itself and physically destroy the planet at the same time. This does not mean that the spiritual entities that reside in these genetic bodies will be destroyed. They will endure. But they may well have to go elsewhere to continue their progress upward, to similar worlds with similar problems to reenact the same kind of drama all over again in the hope of getting their lines right and avoiding the destruction once again of the play, the players and the theater of operations. How unfortunate it would be if the genetic species *Homo sapiens* becomes extinct and takes along a world with it. It need not be. Nothing of the kind has been divinely ordained and written on indelible stone here or in the heavens.

There is some dispute in philosophic, theologic and occult literature as to whether *Homo sapiens* was ever intended to exist as it is constituted—that, perhaps, it was an unauthorized experiment which did not turn out as expected. We will forego adding to the controversy except to add the observation that it does exist, that it must be dealt with and that it must learn to deal with itself; that from a cosmic perspective, spiritual entities using material bodies as vehicles of learning do need some kind of intermediate form and that the human body, with all its shortcomings and imperfections, has provided that form. As the Great Nazarene indicated, the higher spiritual world is available to the "overcomers." We need to learn to use what we have as well as we can to get to where we wish to go. When it—our form, our vehicle—no longer serves us, we can abandon it. But gracefully. With some dignity. In proper time. Not violently. Not suicidally. Not in a holocaust.

The growing telepathic abilities of the cosmic-oriented, our cosmic questers, open communication not only with fellow humans who have a similar ability but also with a great many dematerialized entities of one degree or another of spirituality. This can be a great help to the quester, if he communicates with positive entities of high evolvement, and very dangerous to him, if he consciously or unconsciously gets caught up in the insidious evil of taking advice from an entity (or entities) which is not a positive spiritual influence. Some are quite negative. Possession does occur, much more often than the public suspects, if it suspects at all. Some of these entities are capricious. Some appear as know-it-alls and are really quite ignorant. Some seem lost in a limbo, displaced souls, many of them former earth entities. Almost all artificially-contrived attempts to reach spirits, such as Ouija boards and seances, will result in the calling up of "elemental," low level entities who can teach little and harm much or in outright fraudulent claims by the "seers" in control of such entertainments. Anyone who has had much experience with such goings-on will attest to this indictment. True meditation is the preferred, and least dangerous, way of possibly contacting an intelligence which is beneficial and loving. Many experienced people would say it is the only way.

Some of the beneficial, loving entities who are willing to communicate at times with us mortals are from extraterrestrial regions. Many of them have also had earth lives. Many have not. You name the possibility, it seems to exist.* Some who present themselves as your guides and friends do truly have your best interest at heart. Once one of these is found, if indeed it is found, it should be respected and cherished.

The best general advice that can be given to the first-time telepathic communicator is to "try" your new friend. Find out what kind of friend this is, if it (he/she) is a friend. Do what the disciple John suggested. Test it (he/she) thoroughly. First make sure you hear (or see) accurately. An entity that has your best interest at heart will *never, ever* give you advice that will harm you, those you love or anyone else in the world. It will never suggest acts of violence or aggression — not even for the grestest of causes. It will never encourage you to subtle scheming or revenge of any kind. If it is found wanting even once in these respects, you had best quickly abandon your communication with it for good.

The psychic world and the cosmos at large are filled far more than we sometimes think with a vast spectrum of life-energies that run the gamut from the divine sublime to the muddiest foul. Don't allow yourself to get stuck in your initial enthusiasm and false pride — because you have made a contact, a false one — and get sucked under, from which you may not emerge with your body and mind intact.

The threat the earthbound-oriented non-telepathic humans feel from what they consider the strange ideas and behavior of their cosmic-oriented cousins is illusory but nonetheless it has caused many persecutions during past history, even

---

*For a study of nonhuman entities which seem to be a part of our dimension, or to border on it, but who do not seek direct communication with humans, so far as we know, see Trevor James Constable's *The Cosmic Pulse of Life*.

when the cosmic-oriented were proportionately a greater percentage of the population than they are now, and may well do so today. The danger is real. If we are to believe Christian prophecy (and there is some very strong evidence supporting much of it), especially the Book of Revelation, then persecution in the near future seems imminent. If this potential persecution becomes a widespread reality, it is a great misfortune, a catastrophe as great as nuclear war and devastating earth changes.

It is vitally necessary now that the earthbound-oriented come to see the cosmic-oriented as way-showers, if such a prophesied future bloodbath is to be avoided. It is necessary for the earthbounds' own good. If they do not see the advantage to them of following the lead of the more cosmic-oriented, they impede their own growth, potentially destroying their own bodies and the earth itself through the nemeses of war, pollution, famine and plague. If the baser animal instincts of man are allowed to prevail, it will be, ironically, animal-man who pays the greatest price—the loss of the one thing he holds most dear, his bodily self, in addition to the materialistic accounterments with which he flatters it. The greatest misfortune is that he will have lost another chance to stretch and expand his soul-life, lost another chance to soar free of so much that constrains and restrains him; the greatest tragedy is that, through ignorance and prejudice, he may never learn what he has missed.

Finally, we return to the two large questions posed earlier: (1) How can we grow in a way which will use most effectively the potential which was bioengineered into us by our extraterrestrial visitors? and (2) How can we become "gods" like our cosmic progenitors? When questions like these are asked, people generally expect to hear startling information, "new," original answers, intriguing occult knowledge laid bare before their gasping gaze by a metaphysical Houdini offering the secrets of immortality. People like to be jolted out of their humdrum lives. They like to be entertained royally and yet, when all is said and done, they want their own prejudices confirmed. They don't want the apple cart upset too much, not to the point of having the apples spill all over them, making a mess.

People will drive hundreds of miles to listen to a guru who, they have been told (often by the guru himself), has the answers to the problem of earthly happiness, eternal bliss and maybe also how to solve the monthly shortfall in the budget. They are looking outside themselves for answers, quick and original and entertaining ones at that, as if they were on an Easter egg hunt and the game, what we have called elsewhere the Ultimate Game, could be successfully completed in a few hours if only one could find the right number of brightly colored metaphysical eggs.

Truth is, the Ultimate Game lasts forever. We also play forever. To infinity. Truth is, there is nothing new really under the sun and yet — here is a cosmic paradox — continual change is pervasive and eternal.

Truth is, our spirits grow in this world encumbered by these bodies for as long as the bodies endure. When the bodies fail, for any number of reasons (health, age, warfare), when they are no longer serviceable, the spirit migrates elsewhere where it continues to learn. These truths the "perennial philosophy," the mystery schools, the brotherhoods, the Ancient Wisdom of the world has continued to proclaim since time immemorial.

We play the Ultimate Game forever and we continue to grow forever, some a little more slowly, some a little faster. This growing, this learning about the inextricable, intimate interrelatedness of all things everywhere is not, however, a race. There is no laurel to the winner. There is no winner as such. There is movement, change. Of that much we can be certain. Change is a cosmic certitude. Growth is a cosmic likelihood.

What does the Force which placed in motion all this movement of mass and energy want from us? How difficult and presumptuous for us, for any of us, with our limitations of human mind and body to try to answer that question. We can, however, make several observations. This Force, of which we are a part, appears to desire us to experience its creation in all its magnitude, grandeur and variety at every level of its being. And the God-stuff of which we are made, it seems, is in the process, here and now, of doing just that. It is as if we are being asked to look in mirrors and learn to see — or see to learn — that whatever image appears, it is our face also. The face of It (our Ultimate Creator and Sustainer) and our face, no matter what form our "face" may presently hold, no matter how high or low our spiritual quotient, are the same face. So it would seem.

We are during every nanosecond mingling our atoms and "consciousness units," experiencing, learning, spiritually growing in a great cosmic dance.* All consciousness units, including subatomic particle units — the human form being composed of trillions of units just as the largest star is composed of immeasurably more — are communicating together in their own ineluctable and ineffable ways, or are at least capable of communicating. God, you might say, speaks to Itself in innumerable, mysterious ways. From the smallest to the largest unit.

Is the cosmic variety of matter and energy being inflated, multiplied during what the Hindus call the Day of Brahm when the universe, all creation, breathes outward in a great explosion-expansion of possibilities and realities? Perhaps so — that we may be able, have our chance to tell our stories, to share our adventures with each other and simultaneously with the Mother-Father of all beingness. *It* may already know the stories. And It may not. It may right now be watching and listening and feeling Itself as It undergoes a metamorphosis that amazes even It. Our human minds, even as small as they are, with all their limitations, can still conceive of many possibilities that fascinate and amaze us. Truly, there are more things in heaven and earth, Horatio, than thou has dreamt.

Ultimately, even with all the evidence of cosmic order and affection in the outer world, it is in the inner world, inner

*See Jane Roberts' *The "Unknown" Reality* for an instructive discussion of "consciousness units."

25

space, that we will find the greatest confirmation of order and affection. It is here also that we will find the greatest confirmation of the meaningfulness of our existence. It is here that we leave the mechanistic scientist behind because the limitations of his methodology cannot follow us. He cannot either, because of the inclination of his training, unless he is an exceptional being who can overcome the programming he has been given and the programming he has given himself. Each man's journey inward is surely different. What he discovers will probably be mediated by what he has learned before, who he has become, what he is essentially right now.

One thing, however, is most worthy of note. Those serious cosmic questers of now and yesterday who have been in the habit of journeying inward have reported, almost unanimously, not only the unity of all things but of a wondrous loving emanating from It and all It is. To get a chance to further explore this loving emanation, that seems to pervade essentially everything, is all that those who have felt Its currents ask.

If we wish to become "gods" like our extraterrestrial progenitors and are practical-minded, what can we do? The answer should not surprise us. Our own earthly human wise men have offered to us in the past many of the principles of successful living which apply as well to earth as anywhere in creation, as much to men as to extraterrestrial "gods." We must learn to live by these principles as well as by the precepts offered by the same extraterrestrial visitors who, so much evidence now indicates, programmed the Old Testament prophets and so many other leaders and shamans in various and sundry parts of the world long ago.* We must learn to recognize the Ten Commandments and the Golden Rule for what they are. Never anywhere has a more timelessly perfect formulation for both cosmic, spiritual growth and orderly, happy, successful human living been offered to man. But because this formulation is so much under our nose, we have often ig-

*See Extraterrestrials in Biblical Prophecy and the New Age Great Experiment.

nored it and even evaded it, thinking it would spoil our fun. Confucius said, "Do not do to others that which you would not have others do to you." The Great Nazarene improved on the phrasing by striking out the negatives, "do unto others as you would have others do unto you."

But the practical-minded moan, this is the same old stuff we've been getting thrown at us for centuries. True. This is the more or less Christian version, found elsewhere in the world in slightly different versions. It is not new, not flashy, not entertaining. But it is potent and necessary advice that all men everywhere must learn to respect. And practice. For this reason. Until earthbound-oriented man learns to honor the Creative Force of the universe and respect all of Creation, including his fellow man, there can be no peace and little love. It is as earth-shakingly simple as that. Thus the need for precepts and proscriptions to teach us that simple truth.

Once these basic precepts and proscriptions are learned (and the mass of mankind most surely has not yet done so) and the entity becomes convinced of their truth and proceeds to practice them diligently, then the entity, presumably earthbound-oriented at the time, has reached a transformational stage. He (she) has become marginally cosmic-oriented, probably without even knowing so. It is now his further responsibility to continue to exert his will power in his search for cosmic understanding. The more will power he exercises, the more circuits on his "board" will light up, the greater his capacity for communication and further understanding will be — on and on in a geometrical progression of growth. Theoretically, there are no limits to the potential extent of this growth. Quite simply, the sky's the limit.

Now that we have outlined the great godly potential of Adamic man and studied his early roots, both naturally and extraterrestrially bioengineered, it is time to take a closer look at more recent man to see if he is living up to his capacities and, if not, why he is not. First, however, let us look at him as a coalition of matter and energy which transcends, in some ways, any overt and direct biological engineering. Then we will analyze the spiritual and social malaise of the 20th century which has done so much to impede the development of both the earthbound-oriented and cosmic-oriented man. We will look closely at some of the influences now shaping him, everything from the movement toward a New World Order to the present-day extraterrestrial abductions, and attempt to demonstrate, as best we can, the interconnectedness of these many influences. We will also look at ancient and modern prophecies which predict and proclaim his difficulties and the dangers that may face him again soon from great earth changes which threaten to wrench and wrack the planet. Finally, we will try to place him in larger perspective once again, as the coming cosmic quester, as the potential god-in-the-making which seems his rightful destiny, if he will only find within himself the will power to claim that destiny.

CHAPTER THREE

## Star Stuff

Our destiny as temporary human beings is a thousand thousand transmutations — a milliard transmigrations. We are all accomplished chameleons, whether we know it or not, like it or not, fated to change and change again, not by choice necessarily but driven by cosmic necessity. We are essentially primordial extraterrestrials. This small planet we call home which, in the larger scheme of things, seems to us so singular, is not nearly as unique as we would believe — just as we as life forms are not nearly as peculiar, and as cosmically alone, as we so often think or are led to believe.

Earth is a way station for the continuing metamorphosis of the matter and energy which is us, which gives us form and movement, temporary shape and ephemeral exhibition of being. We may become more of each, or less, but we will never ever again be quite the same. Not even a nanosecond from now.

We need to never forget that we are star stuff. And more besides. Our bodies are marvellous compounds of matter and energy which have come into their present being as a melange of cosmic atoms, each atom having its own electromagnetic charge, each having its own peculiar group signature. Our sun, this solar system and planet earth are all similar coalitions of this basic cosmic stuff. We are star born right down to the salts and water and innumerable other elements that constitute our chemical makeup. And although we may be created out of the same elements, each of our bodies, whether sun, planet or individual human being, is somewhat different. The atomic carpentry, you might say, varies anywhere from a little to a lot depending on whether we are comparing apples and oranges, suns to planets or one human individual with the next. Each planetary body has its own peculiar atomic signature, as does each human being. And each body, whether planetary or human, does its own unique dance.

Too often, however, we human beings sell our specialness short. Our materialistic attitudes about things in general, including this shell we inhabit, blind us to greater insights about our selves and a greater understanding of our potential for self-directed change. We are not, after all, just a chemical broth jiggling about space but an energy vortex as well. Each atom in our body is immeasurably alive, its particles revolving at tremendous speeds. Electric currents surge through our bodies, along the neuron pathways of our brains, creating an electrical field about us that extends as far as twenty feet or more. That is the approximate distance outward Russian scientists have observed the field, they having shown more interest in measuring such things than have our own scientists.

We are, then, both matter and energy. As one scientific wag put it, parodying John Keats' "Ode On A Grecian Urn": "'Matter is energy, energy matter,'—that is all/Ye know on earth, and all ye need to know."

But is it? Most "hard" scientists, physicists, chemists and the like, including most of the "new" quantum physicists, seem to think so. Even those that intuit a reality not capable of being explored by scientific methodology and its instruments claim that if that reality does exist, it is outside the province of their interest. They will have nothing to do with a search for it. A critical pundit might point out to them that the Latin noun *scientia*, which itself was derived from the Latin verb *scire*, which means "to know, to discern, to distinguish" and which itself is derived from the Indo European base *skei*, which meant "to cut, to separate," suggests that *knowledge* and the search for it, was not always so departmentalized and overspecialized. The pundit might make the observation and get pie in the face for his efforts. Most scientists aren't interested in the generalized search for knowledge or truth, no matter where found. Most likely, our pundit, having made his observation to his scientific brethren, would be politely ignored. Such thinking, it is thought by many, is idealistic at best and in reality a quaint anachronism. Perhaps like the stubborn pundit, we interested observers need to be absolved, forgiven or politely ignored for our continuing assumption that a man interested in understanding reality, all of it, should not be willing to forego the study of so much of it simply because it does not fit the present popular methodology.

We are star stuff, all right. And along with the atomic star stuff, the stuff of our bodies, there is a spirit which infuses us that has baffled mankind for millennia and still baffles us today. It is something that is beyond simple discussions of matter and energy, although several of the more bold among us have even tried to photograph it and weigh it at the moment of death, and philosophers of the East and West have spent whole lifetimes meditating upon it, hoping to capture it in thought and experience, often with little success. We intuit it within us but it confuses us, escapes us easily like a snake in the grass or gas in the air. Often as not we hide from the idea that this indwelling spirit is there. We are taught in our schools that it does not exist. We are encouraged by mass media, politicians, economists, employers, personal acquaintances and others to ignore any thought of it. But we ignore it at our peril.

For millennia prophets, messiahs, teachers of righteousness and wise men here and there have proclaimed that this spirit indwelling in man, this *divinus inflatus*, certainly exists and needs to be listened to, studied and followed. As often as not, they have received, these teachers of righteousness, mud in their eye for their exhortations. But that really is beside the point.

The great religions of the world and the ancient brotherhoods, such as the Hermetic, Luciferian (i.e. Venusian), White, Rosicrucian and others, have taught that man is no biological accident. He is here, in this world, at this particular time, for a reason. He is here to prove himself. The world, with all its natural beauty and its distracting temptations of one kind or another, is a special testing ground or, if you will, a practice field. Man is here to "improve his game." While he is here, what he does and what he thinks becomes his Ultimate Game.

One possible philosophic definition of the Cosmic Creative Force (or Logos, the Word or God) is of an omnipotent, omniscient power that amuses itself with its creation, a sort of Ultimate Laughing Buddha who has given free reign and free will to Its creation, watching it unfold before Itself. This would create the Ultimate Godly Game, one might say, encompassing everything including our human games of learning and growing, which might seem rather puny and insignificant when compared to the greater Ultimate Godly Game as a whole.

What that Creator ultimately is up to, we cannot be sure. What Its purposes are, if any, we cannot be sure.

Yet the definition of God in terms of an Ultimate Laughing Buddha is not as strange as it may at first seem. Especially if we impute to that God an interest in at least a partial "hands on" approach to Its domain. It is as legitimate a mental construct as any other, and a seemingly less perverse one than many, and a far more meaningful one than most, when we come to recognize as human seekers of understanding that cosmic creation, by most evidence, indicates an ordering to it parts. In other words, the Game seems to have pieces, both material and theoretical, which would appear to fit together—a grand cosmic puzzle for us to put together mentally and spiritually if we feel so inclined. As we have already admitted, we cannot be sure of the ultimate purpose of this Cosmic Creative Force, if indeed there is any. But the ordering we do observe is encouraging to the human mind in a century which has had an increasingly difficult time in believing there is a purpose to human existence, other than the immediate objective of surviving bodily as long as possible.

Things were not always so. Before scientific empiricism and positivistic notions of reality began to dominate man's thinking, it was believed by the majority of Westerners that man was placed on earth to serve God and, as some of the more enlightened versions had it, to grow spiritually in imitation and emulation of the exemplary figure of the Great Nazarene, thereby qualifying oneself to move onward and upward into the "many mansions" of the greater creation, there to continue to grow spiritually until some undefined time. The basis for such a belief, with all of its various sectarian versions, was found, of course, in the biblical scriptures. Mechanistic interpretations of the universe have gone a long way, until recently, in quashing this earlier theologically based certitude that death of the body was not the end of all life.

But today simplistic mechanistic and atrophic theories of the cosmos do not hold much interest for our professional scientists. The physical sciences at the moment, with all their limitations, are finding, increasingly, cosmic laws governing cosmic unfoldment. The more we learn with instruments alone, the more interrelatedness, the more ordering there seems to be. The Ultimate Game seems to have rules. Although free will exists in higher life forms on earth, it appears to be governed by certain broad parameters — and it appears, perhaps, to exist for a reason. Social scientists are busy trying to understand that reason. If they, and their "hard" science brethren, insist on a narrow empirical approach to this question, and similar questions, we cannot hope for much enlightenment from their direction. The mention of the word "soul" or "spirit" to most of them is tantamount to invoking Voodoo gods.

Cosmic unfoldment, then, appears to have organization. It is not a helter-skelter process. But the big question, the one that interests human beings most, is this: Does it also have direction? Is there, perhaps, a Master Plan? And what is the reason for human free will if the answer to the previous two questions is "yes?"

The physical sciences and the social sciences as yet do not have an answer to these questions. Because of the limitations of method they have set for themselves, they may never have answers. Where then do we look for answers?

We can look basically in two directions. The first is outward—to our own worldly experiences and the knowledge gained by others. We can rely solely on what our senses teach us and what we learn from our interrelationships with other human beings. We could call this the look-see method or the school of hard knocks approach. It is a training we all need, but as time passes, its limitations become more obvious. It is basically subjective and the parameters are rather rigidly circumscribed, reduced to what we come in contact with, including who we meet.

We can escape the narrowness of this outward approach somewhat by including within it the influences of the spoken or written work of others. We can accept if we like the word, the explanations of reality and the meaning of life offered by great religious leaders, prophets, gurus, psychic sensitives and other spiritually interested parties who claim to have made contact with a greater reality than the mundane one we all face each day, who claim, perhaps, to have personally contacted the Cosmic Creative Force itself in some way or its representatives. They are, we might note, in basic agreement about the validity of their experiences although they disagree among themselves as to the best method or manner of achieving those experiences and often disagree greatly as to the particulars of those experiences. Unfortunately, there have been problems with the transmission of the teachings of the acknowledged great teachers of the past. By the time their revelations or teachings are systematized and passed on to the masses, who eagerly await their word, a great deal of warping occurs often obscuring the message, however true it may have been at the beginning of the transmission. We only have to look at early Buddhism, Christianity and Islam, for instance, and compare the original teachings of each to the smorgasbord of later interpretations of each to get an idea of the "noise" that can intrude to distort the original song.

There is, fortunately, another approach. This is the other direction of which we spoke, an alternative which can be used alone or, more effectively, in conjunction with the outward quest. It appears on first examination to be quite personal and intensely subjective although, somewhat surprisingly, on closer examination, its results seem to be anything but inherently egocentric and the knowledge gained is recognized as quite universal, applicable to both the microcosm of the individual and the macrocosm of the greater universal creation. This is the inward quest. We can direct our investigative energies to inner space, as the Essenes and Gnostics of the Great Nazarene's time once did to escape slick talkers and materialists or what they called "seekers after smooth things." We can seek, if it exists, the spiritual thread within us that binds us to the Cosmic Creative Force that gave us being. If it does exist, if we find it, we can explore it for evidence of direction. If it does exist, we can claim heritage with it. We become sons and daughters of the greater parent—the lesser gods of a Greater God. The world, the cosmos, does not become the hostile or indifferent or absurd existentialist universe we are so often taught, sometimes quite subtly, that it is. We find, at last, that we truly belong, that there really are cosmic paths (and natural laws) that follow a Great Plan. It is for us then to find one of these paths and follow it towards its source, whatever and wherever that may be. It would seem, from the accounts of many travelers, that the paths to this source are many and various which, like spokes of a wheel, lead centerward toward a greater revelation, a greater truth.

Ancient inner travelers such as the Vyasas, the Manus, the Zarathustras, the Thoths, Gautama Buddha, Jesus, Mohammed, and more recent travelers such as Meister Eckhart, Emanuel Swedenborg, G. I. Gurdjieff, Rudolf Steiner, Baba Ji, Krishnamurti, Paramahansa Yogananda, Maharishi Mahesh Yogi (and a host of others both ancient and modern) have ventured inward and found one or more of these paths and have returned to vouch for the legitimacy of the inner approach and the expediency of it as a method to achieve cosmic enlightenment and personal growth. When questioned, they have been quite adamant that the inner way is a more effective, and swifter, approach than outer-directed experience. Significantly, they have claimed that the inner-directed way can teach the traveler/quester much that the outer way cannot — primarily because out bodies and senses, being the inaccurate measuring mechanisms they are, do not fully register truth. Furthermore, they have maintained that the inner way can teach everything known about the outer way.

This turning inward, which does not, by the way, preclude learning all we can from the experiences of messiahs, prophets and sages of the past and present — this following "the still small voice" within can be done by anyone who is earnest and diligent and hungers for answers that science and secular leaders, because of their narrow focuses and vested interests, can not give. 'Ask, and it will be given you; seek, and you will find; knock, and it will be opened to you.' The advice of the Nazarene is still good even today.

The ancient brotherhoods were charged with the responsibility of bringing along those who were ready to ask the great questions and wanted answers. The members of the brotherhoods were the *magister ludi* teachers, the master-game teachers of their time who taught those who were hungry to learn answers to the great metaphysical questions. These questions concern us now and always as human beings. Questions such as, How was the cosmos created and by what or whom? Is there order and direction to creation? What is the place of man in the scheme of things? What is man's relationship to the Cosmic Creative Force? Is he perfectible? Is he godly? The brothers were guides along the way and still, to a certain extent, remain so. In this day of mass communication, which seems at first glance to promise so much — most of which turns out to be false and misleading noise — the individual finds himself offered great gobs of information, megabytes of data but few real answers to primary questions. Hermann Hesse, the great German novelist, once pointed out the irony of a future world in which information was plentiful but no one knew how to retrieve what he really needed. Perhaps we are there. This is that future. We must first learn that data is not necessarily knowledge and certainly not wisdom.

The individual truth seeker finds ultimately, and most

often after much pain, like Gautama under the Bodhi tree, that if he is going to get what he seeks, he is going to have to turn inward and explore the spiritual thread which attaches him to his true beginnings, to his original genesis. No matter how much he has learned from the outer world of personal experience, he will find it is not enough. No matter how hard he has tried to plumb the depths of physical reality and squeeze truth from it, he will discover he has come up short. He will discover he is driven inward, either willingly or out of exasperation with his struggle to understand external reality and especially those things beyond external reality. He will find inner space is his last great hope, and he will not be disappointed. Brian O'Leary, astronomer and former astronaut, after observing the failure of our human attempts to understand the total reality about us, both our inner and outer space together, with conventional scientific approaches, has lately observed, "I wonder if all of astronomy, astrophysics, and related science is not a protective decoy to keep us out of the 'real' universe until we are ready." The quester after truth will discover, finally, that the inward journey can be done anywhere by anyone, with eyes open or closed, in a parking lot or in the midst of the desert, as long as the quester is so willing.

Both paths, the inner and the outer, lead in the same direction of cosmic and worldly understanding—a cosmic paradox. If each were traveled till their end, they would presumably meet, conjoin. But the outer path is much narrower and filled with the illusions, the *maia* as Indian theology would say, of things in general. It is a tricky path for man to master, as his senses will deceive him and the machines he builds with so much pride to accurately measure reality, and which are in reality only extensions of his senses, will often be found, on closer inspection, to give him only the readings they have been constructed, programmed to offer. Readings of this kind are skewed and suspect.

The inner path is swifter. It encompasses all realities everywhere. It does not depend on the human senses for accurate readings but rather on the energy, integrity and diligence of the traveler. The greatest danger, if it can be called such, is the birth and growth of smugness, spiritual vanity, on the part of the traveler/explorer. This, however, is usually not a large consideration because most individuals who are ready to explore inner space have been seasoned by the pains and problems of outer reality and have developed some of the humility necessary for the successful initiation of the inward journey.

The New Age, if it is anything, is the desire of many individuals at one period of cosmic time to look within themselves for a spiritual thread(s) which, upon discovery, offers direction and meaning, a sustaining vision of the cosmos, the solar system, the earth and human life. The New Age quester has learned to recognize that all animate and seemingly inanimate objects are throbbing with life, that all are intimately related right down to their very atoms and the life force within them, that all are moving in a great cosmic dance of life, growing, intermixing, developing, metamorphosing—continually dying and being reborn—into something far greater than the meaning alone of individual parts. What does it *all* mean? Our understanding is not great enough to say. We lack certain kinds of experience. It may be eons before we have enough knowledge to hazard a guess. By that time, our human flesh will most probably have metamorphosed into a series of realities far beyond our present selves. By that time, we may not even care to question what we have then become. We may not need to. We may know without asking. What we will be then is unfathomable now. What is more certain is that in our present human state, once having chosen the inner path of discovery and having once tasted the fruit of that new land which promises so much, having heard a music which is both of this world and out of this world, we have become like Odysseus drawn to the serene song, only in this case we are assured from past experience that the song leads us to a revelation, rather than a rock pile, of the spirit.

What may the final revelation be? Only a fool would dare hazard a guess. But the signposts as of now give great encouragement to the inner space traveler, the quester after truth. We appear to be sons and daughters, one kind of progeny, of a great Cosmic Creative Force, a Greater God. We are in fact little gods—god but not God. The recognition of this cosmic paradox may be one of our first significant steps as we learn to work our way home.

## CHAPTER FOUR

## New Age Definitions and Cosmic Questers

If, like a Gallup Poll inquisitor, you ask the average man on the street to define the New Age, you will find, more likely than not, that he is nonplussed. Most likely he has heard of it, but he is not exactly certain what it is. Health foods, perhaps. Watching cholesterol counts. Saving the redwood forests. If that person happens to be a reader of the Bible or goes to church occasionally, he may say the New Age refers to the time after Armageddon when Christ claims his kingdom and his own.

If you were from, say, the Zeta Reticuli star system, just arrived and short of reading matter, and happened to pick up a sampling of New Age magazines at the corner newsstand, you might, upon opening a cover or two, come away with a peculiar idea of what planet Earth and the New Age is all about. The advertisements that caught your eye, assuming you had at least one good one, might make you think that the average man on the street, with his variable definition of the New Age, was correct. Here, for instance, is an ad for a health institute offering a "living food vegetarian diet and the development of self-esteem, cellular oxygenation and an enlightened awareness." Quite a mouthful—and oxygen as well.

Here's another offering, harmless enough and trendy in more ways than one—t-shirts with a star on them, presumably to give you that old cosmic feeling. Across from it is still another, a vitamin ad. Vitamins are, as anyone knows who does much reading of this sort, and as our Zeta Reticulian would soon learn, a staple of many New Age publications. They are, of course, in contradistinction to the philosophy of all those other ads encouraging us folks to "eat fresh" and never abide unnatural nourishment.

There are pages and pages of ads for tapes of one kind or another, regular or subliminal. One offers mysteriously to improve my vision, which I find momentarily fascinating. But you probably aren't as nearsighted as I am and might pass right over that one. There are subliminal tapes on almost every subject you could imagine and some you probably couldn't or haven't—anxiety, stress, sports, "enhancement," personal goals, professional goals, "whatever you need." That last phrase throws me a bit. After all, I could be mentally unbalanced. Can I have anything I want? What if I'm in training to become a Chicago "hit" man?

People who buy subliminal tapes must have unlimited confidence in the producers of these things. What is to keep an unscrupulous operator from subliminally directing me to withdraw my savings and send it to him/her as a donation for the cause? What if some maniac tampered with the signals and subliminally encouraged murder and mayhem? Can we really trust many of these purveyors, whose interest is often only money, not to diddle with our unsuspecting minds? How, after all, do we know for sure what is soundlessly, repetitively, being driven into our minds? I remember when they stopped theater managements years ago from subliminally sending me to the candy counter during intermission. Today any Tom, Dick or Harry can set up a studio and legally produce all the subliminal garbage he wishes. I want to warn my Reticulian newcomer to be careful. Use all the eyes you've got.

Here's an interesting ad promoting massage using "essential oils." One wonders what would happen if one chose to use a non-essential oil or no oil at all. And who, by the way, establishes whether an oil is "essential" or not? That gal, or guy, must have a lot of power and a lot of adoring groupies.

Here's another on firewalking for "spiritual empowerment." There's that "power" word again hiding between a prefix and suffix. But I wonder, is "power" what we're really after? Tony Robbins and his "personal power" tapes are doing real well. Maybe there's a side to the New Age I don't know about, but somehow, I always associated yearnings for power and money and success with gross capitalism, with the old order, the Old Age (that time of tyranny over one's fellow man), with materialistic greed and conspicuous consumption, with Donald Trump trading insults with Leona Helmsley while the growing numbers of poor and homeless marched in the streets.

A Tai Chi resort advertises, among other things, "strength through softness." Thank heavens for that last note. I was worried for a second they might be teaching folks how to bash each other senseless. But it occurs to me that studying the martial arts for any reason is a rather strange way to enter the Age of Aquarius. Kind of like George Orwell's "doublethink." I hit you on the head and tell you its "softness."

Zen Buddhism teaches us that we can master ourselves and life on earth, or come close, by learning to master thoroughly one aspect of life such as archery (see E. Herrigel's *Zen in the Art of Archery*), swordsmanship, flower arranging, even the tea ceremony itself. (See *The Book of Tea*.) Hopefully, that is what our Tai Chi people have in mind. There are, I recognize, many paths to enlightenment if one takes the outward way. You must forgive me for my tongue-in-cheek rendition of what can be discovered to be modestly associated with, tangentially touching or brazenly hanging to the coattails of the New Age movement. Even I know that if I ask any ten New Agers for a definition of the New Age or a definition of God, I am going to get ten different answers, although, hopefully, there will be some significant common ground among them, some thread or threads that run true and clean throughout this great mosaic known as New Age thinking. We need to look for these threads and hang on for dear life when we find them unless we wish to be inundated by, ah...waste material. Even the Great Nazarene, let's remember, made a clean sweep of the temple, driving the usurers out of where they did not belong. Each of us must learn to distinguish, each in his own way, what the true threads are and what is flossy dross.

But before we begin our search, I want to raise a caution flag, kind of like they do at Indianapolis when the boys in the big cars are in a hurry. I want to offer an observation which I believe is crucial to discovering what the New Age is all about and what it isn't, at least essentially.

In the magazine ads and hoopla surrounding "the movement," there is obviously a lot of time and money being expended in an effort to make even more money. Good old American entrepreneurship. This doesn't surprise me and shouldn't surprise anyone. It's been part of the movement from its beginnings in the early 60s just as snake oil was an early part of the western medicine shows of a century ago. Entrepreneurship attaches itself to movements as fast and as tight as a snake grows a new skin after shedding the old. One danger, of course, is that New Age thinking will become increasingly materialistic and hedonistic with only the outward trappings of real "soul." Some people would argue the ads already indicate this. So which comes first, the chicken or the egg? Do the ads reflect a materialism and hedonism already present or are they a cause of it, though perhaps not the only one, in themselves?

Whatever the answer to these questions, it is probably a good idea to recognize at least two New Ages: There is the spiritually intent one, without commercial overtones, and there is the sideshow New Age, which is sometimes fun but not very spiritually inclined, and definitely attracted to the greenbacks. The latter New Age, unfortunately and almost predictably, is the one that catches the public eye. It is the one that comes to the lips of the man on the street when he is asked for a definition of the New Age. If this kind of New Age becomes too dominant, it may swallow up the burgeoning potential of the more spiritual New Age like a snake swallowing a golden egg. That is a real danger. And if it happens, some of the opportunities for the more mature individual truth-seeker to raise his consciousness a notch or two will have been subverted, if not buried. And the young of the country and the world, who are just beginning to learn about New Age possibilities, will be lead by false pipers, like so many lemmings, to the sea.

I have no right to impose definitions. If I thought so, I would be a bigger fool than those who go no further than sun screen in their attempts at self-improvement. Ultimately, the New Age will define itself. The kitsch and hokum and schlock and schmaltz of these sideshows will be seen for what it is by those who look carefully. There is a kind of hierarchy which is already evident to a discerning eye, starting with the sun screeners and moving up through the mind improvers and topping out with those human beings making a more serious effort at spiritual awakening (and with those already awakened).

I'm afraid I've already given away the thread I spoke of earlier, the one that runs so true within many a New Age's definition of what the New Age is all about. It is quite simply the desire to improve the spirit and the mind of man, to push hard to the new frontiers of cosmic consciousness, to behold whatever there is to behold, which promises to be a lot, if reports by early returning scouts are considered.

One way of discovering what you believe, what way you wish to go, is to work backwards and begin by discovering what you don't believe, what ways you don't want to go. In a way, we have been doing that now. We have been attempting to sort the more fruitful paths from the thornier ones. We have not been promoting, I hope it is clear, a snooty New Age country club of the spirit that excludes from membership those who seem confused about what spiritual inquisitiveness is all about. There is no exclusive club. The doors are open to everyone. The individual defines himself by what he does and what he thinks, what he does not do and what he does not think. The individual must judge himself. Let God be the final arbiter. Any definition of the New Age must be large enough to enfold all sincere, diligent efforts to improve body, mind and spirit. Human beings need to be harmoniously whole, and it is the tragedy of our time that so few are. The old idea that a healthy body is the temple of a healthy spirit, at least in this world, is true enough. All we have to do is take a look around us to become convinced by the evidence that modern values and life styles have thoroughly unbalanced modern man, that he exhibits at any given moment a grave lack of coordination between spirit, mind and body and is, practically speaking, not in control of himself.

As the pace of life has become quicker in the Western World, peoples' lives have been fraying not only at the edges but at the very cores. A decade ago television advertisements for good mental health pointed out that one in ten Americans needed professional psychological counseling sometime in their lifetime. In the last decade that percentage estimate has more than doubled, to one in five. How many undiagnosed and unhelped people stumble through life needing counseling but never receiving it is anybody's guess.

What is wrong with the life style of America and elsewhere that is causing so many people to come apart slowly at the seams and, like a leaking damaged drum of inflammable fluid, carry about their explosive burden secretly — walking time bombs, consumed inevitably by internal fires that often as not leave them a burned out case and too often singe all those caught in their vicinity? The reasons are many, no doubt. The issue is immensely complex, granted. But a few general observations seem pertinent. Aside from the recent New Age idea held by many that the vibrational rhythm of planet Earth has for some reason risen (there is no particular agreement as to why) and causes the less adjusted among us to become even more maladjusted, especially if they are not making efforts to balance their lives, we need, perhaps, to look backward in time and see if we can identify any other reasons for the problem developing.

Efforts of this kind have been made. Robert Pirsig made the effort. His work, *Zen and the Art of Motorcycle Maintenance*, one of the more hip titles in the last few decades, may have come as close as any recent work has in identifying the causes of our contemporary malady. He argues that postAristotelian thinking in the Western World has made us divide ourselves against ourselves. We do not see clearly anymore how everything is intimately related to everything else. Instead, we are busy, in academia especially, pointing out that physics is different from philosophy, that psychology is separate from history and history from art and so on interminably.* We have in many ways become a civilization of niche-makers, categorizers and system analysts more interested in demonstrating differences among things than the great correspondences, affinities and connections between all these fields of human interest. It is as if we have taken the differentiating ideas of men such as Aristotle, Linnaeus, Lyall and Lavoisier and made them into a sacred ritual, and then become monomaniacal slaves to its practice. The idea of differentiating matter and ideas was intended originally only as an investigative tool, one among many available to the seeker after truth. I doubt if the above mentioned gentlemen ever expected the ritual itself to solidify intellectually into an idol to be worshiped.

Pity the poor modern college student. He receives four years of departmentalized education and is handed a baccalaureate degree. During that time he is lucky if any of his instructors have made him feel that there is a fundamental linkage between all the disciplines of knowledge. Just one example is illustrative. It is a rare science student who is taught that the atoms of all matter are very similar, whether they be found in animate or inanimate things, whether in a botanical flower or a biological bird, and that the particles of these atoms, whether of rook or rock, are moving at tremendous speeds, are indeed alive in their own way. The college student, and the high school and grade school student who precedes him, comes away from his schooling thoroughly unconvinced that subject areas are intimately related and wondering about the relevancy of his (her) education. Where, he asks, does all this fit into the "real world"? He is, unfortunately, turned loose upon

---

*Ironically, but not surprisingly, much of our best philosophy today is coming from our physicists. Things are happening so fast in this field that physicists have not had time to close their minds.

that real world as confused about its real nature as were his instructors, who long ago lost a feeling for the interconnectedness of all things, if in fact they ever had it.

One of the tiniest but most important threads that runs through, tacitly or explicitly, some of the more observant definitions of the New Age, no matter how stumblingly they may be offered, is a yearning to grasp the interrelated meaning of things and, indeed, of life itself—and along with it a desire to find answers to those related basic questions that some souls have been asking for untold millennia: Who really am I? Is there meaning and life of some kind beyond this life? Is there a Cosmic Creative Force? Can it be known? Can it be "communed" with? How do I achieve this communion? Are there other higher dimensions, planes of being? How do I improve myself spiritually and mentally so that I might enter them?

These and questions like them are ancient questions, as old as man himself. They are immensely old but always new, always pertinent, always vitally significant to an individual who seeks to fulfill himself. It is accurate to say that the New Age has existed as long as people were asking these questions and desiring, working on, answers to them. In this view the Age of Aquarius is one more growth cycle in which these questions stand eternally pertinent. It has been preceded by others and will be succeeded by still more, which does not in any way minimize the importance of the moment.

We don't really know how many ancient civilizations, how many life waves, have faced periods, perhaps towards the culmination of their being or at extremely stressful periods within their span of existence, when larger multitudes than usual were yearning for answers to such questions and working consciously to raise the spiritual essence of their being so that they might migrate elsewhere in the greater creation and continue to grow where conditions were more appropriate for them.

One thing we can be sure of is that these cosmic questers have existed in the past on earth, although we have no way of knowing the numbers involved. Suffice it to say that every age has had some, every future age will produce more. Another thing we can be sure of is that large numbers of people in the world today are asking the kinds of cosmic questions we have been discussing and desire personally to spiritually metamorphose so that they may satisfy a cosmic destiny that they intuit even if they do not completely understand it. They are truly cosmic questers, convinced that the body is only a cocoon, a temporary abode, from which they can fly away and become, like the emblematic Chinese butterfly, immortal. They wish no less than to re*discover* the immortality of their soul and to understand that soul better.

After all, didn't the Great Nazarene say '"Ye are gods"'? Didn't he also say, You can do greater things than I have done. The promise was large, so great that Christians haven't known in the past what to do with such talk. They have been afraid to take him literally, as he intended them to. Because of their confusion about God, gods and what is godly, they have been embarrassed to consider the possibility that they were really gods in the making.

When holy spirits do not understand their holiness, anything is possible. The present tumultuous world situation gives noisy testimony to that fact. The seeking of the more aware New Agers, the cosmic questers of today, proves that even in the explosive atmosphere of this mundane testing ground, where the game is rough, some souls will not let themselves be daunted and diverted. They will play until they have mastered themselves, mastered the game, no matter how long that may take.

# CHAPTER FIVE

## Revolt of the Masses

The 20th century seems destined to be remembered as a great pivotal time in mankind's history on earth, whether we are considering the spiritual tenor of the times or the overall state of man's physical existence. It certainly will be remembered as a time of great tumult — of much blood and many tears — even if humankind endures and succeeds in remaking itself into an image which is sustaining.

In some ways, among the social critics of the first decades of the century, none was a more astute student and perceptive observer of the great changes taking place than the Spanish philosopher José Ortega y Gasset. With suavely patrician yet realistically deft strokes, he marked for us in the 1930s and earlier some of the new directions the new century was taking in comparison with the past. Much of what he saw exasperated him and saddened him as well as forebode, he believed, a dark future for mankind. Much of that foreboding seems to have come to pass, as events since the end of World War II and today all too clearly indicate.

Ortega y Gasset, as he admitted, yearned for a sun of a different morning, a day when the world was more predictable, "I support a radically aristocratic interpretation of history." But before we discount him today as a hopeless reactionary out of step with the times, we had best recall as thoroughly as we can the larger substance of what he said, which seems in retrospect so pertinent to us now. Much of what he deplored, what he saw happening and gaining momentum in the early decades of this century, has come to haunt us, the monstrous problems whose hydra heads have grown terrifyingly larger with the passage of time.

Ortega y Gasset viewed society as a dynamic unity composed chiefly of two components, the minorities and the masses. In 1930 he published *La Rebelion de las Masses* which attempted to analyze these components at length.

What did he see happening that so vexed him? First, the minorities he spoke of were not what we usually define as such in these post-civil-rights-movement days. They were instead composed of individuals or groups of individuals who have special qualifications. The mass, he said, is made up of all those not specially qualified more specifically. It is not just or solely the working masses but rather the "average man." This average man, he concluded, through a kind of "hyperdemocracy" had usurped control in the Western World of all society. "The hour's characteristic is that the common mind, knowing itself to be common, has the confidence to proclaim the rights of the common and to impose them wherever it can. As is said in the United States, 'to be different is to be indecent.'" He felt, then, that anybody who dared not to be like everybody, ran the risk of being eliminated.

Our first reaction might be to dismiss such talk as elitist and Ortega y Gasset himself as a stuffed shirt, a monarchist out of step with the times. But things are not so simple. He may have been out of step, preferred doubtlessly to be so, but his sensitivity to the change going on about him caused him to miss little in the perceptible world and to register on a deeper psychological level, better perhaps than anyone else at the time, the early seismic tremors of the society-shattering events and changes of attitude which were then happening and would soon happen. Somewhat like a Japanese goldfish kept in its bowl to predict coming earthquakes, he knew the dimensions of his world and he foresaw well what was to come of it.

What Ortega y Gasset saw unfolding, at least in the Western hemisphere, was something far beyond the extension of the Bill of Rights to everyone. A kind of grotesquequerie was being created where the illusion of the extension of freedom to all was being replaced by a smothering mass conformity. What he was talking about is essentially in part what psychoanalyst Erich Fromm was writing about a decade later in *Escape From Freedom*. As Fromm put it, "The principal social avenues of escape (from the exercise of personal freedom) in our time are the submission to a leader, as has happened in Fascist countries, and the *compulsive conforming* as is prevalent in our own democracy."

We will return to a more detailed look at Fromm momentarily, but first, perhaps, it would be a good idea to consider whether Fromm and Ortega y Gasset were accurate in their more general observations when they made them, if the tendencies they speak of are greater now than then, and what all this means for the individual today. Is, for instance, our New Age man exercising his freedom to have original thoughts? Or has he tuned into a kind of Musak of the mind, passing time repeating propagandistic slogans he has heard at work or on television or read in the newspapers and mistakes for his own original thoughts? Is he really able and willing anymore to think clearly, logically, originally?

But before we even attempt to answer these questions, we had best hear the final conclusions of Ortega y Gasset. "This is the question: Europe has been left without a moral code. It isn't that mass man has overthrown an antiquated system in exchange for a new one, but that at the center of his life scheme is precisely the desire to live without conforming to any moral code." And a parting shot, "Though it may appear incredible, 'youth' has become a *chantage*.* We are truthfully alive in an age which adopts two contemporary attitudes, violence and caricature."

Does this sound familiar today? Doesn't our growing penchant for violence of all kinds in this culture, and particularly the escalating ridicule by youth and the masses of older as well

---

*Chantage*: Fr., lit., blackmail. Here "blackmailer" would be an appropriate reading.

as contemporary cultural institutions, social attitudes and mores, including earlier cultural "heros," suggest that our Spaniard saw our present social malaise already breeding its poison and beginning to fester when only a few other observers like himself had also taken notice and alarm? The rest of the world remained blind, deaf and intellectually asleep, as the greater part of it remains today, out of either preference, ignorance or stupidity. Meanwhile the festering sore, the social malaise, has become a raging cancer, threatening to consume the patient.

To be intellectually asleep, with one's head stuck in the sand, and to prefer to be so when your very being is threatened, is fine, perhaps, for the ostrich (this, of course, is debatable) but dangerous, even fatal, for men. Most thinking people will have no great difficulty agreeing that such action, rather inaction, is dangerous. The "asleep man," however, finds a consolation. By pretending to hear no evil, see no evil and do no evil, he can escape for awhile from reality, insulate himself from facing personal, national and international problems. He can pretend, when he admits to any kind of partial awareness, if he happens to do so, which he rarely does, that most problems are beyond his influence and, therefore, beyond careful consideration and action. Consideration and action, after all, are hard work.

The idols and fads that draw the devotion of the masses are, for the most part, shallow and fleeting. The Daniel Boones are surely gone, replaced by tinsel heroes with names like Donald Trump, Leona Helmsley, Jessica Hahn, Gary Hart, 2 Live Crew and Milli Vanilli. Is this the best that America can produce for others to imitate and emulate? Two decades from now, if the world survives itself, how many people will be able to recall much about these idols of the moment who have recently commanded so much attention? How much social energy is expended in the name of (or pursuit of) shotgunned jeans, frizzled hair, the acquisition of the latest bauble or style? Why are we so captivated by the lives of the rich and famous, often forgetting conveniently how that money and fame has been acquired? No wonder we have been considered a shallow culture by many the world over, concerned more often than not with our own selfish desires and acquisitions of "things." The image of early, frontier America, with its more solid values and ideals worth imitating, is not the image most people, either foreign or native born, have today of this land. And yet our influence as a nation has been lately great and, in many cases, most unfortunate. We have now successfully carried, with the help of electronic mass media, our materialistic habits and intellectual sloth aboard, seducing others to our own peculiar style, although many of those affected needed no additional encouragement, being in the early to middle stages of the same disease as ourselves.

Doesn't the gross conformity to mass culture that we see all around us, and that so smothers the expression of clear original thinking, indicate to us what Erich Fromm recognized: Most people proclaim an active desire for freedom so that body, mind and spirit can grow and realize themselves, and yet the great mass of us are too lazy to exercise that freedom, preferring to have someone else do our thinking for us. Freedom, we haven't learned well enough, is a demanding gift of the gods. Sooner or later, if it is not cherished and guarded, it is lost. To delegate it without thinking puts it at great risk.

The New Age thinker, if he is to survive, must realize that the integrity of his mind and spirit is in peril at every moment. His freedom to think clearly and originally is constantly being attacked and compromised by cultural forces which would either lull him to sleep like the serenes of Homer (many of them entertainment serenes with names like "Saturday Afternoon Football" followed by Sunday and Monday football) or tear him to pieces physically on the streets of America's (and Europe's) cities, streets which are becoming increasingly criminalized each day here and abroad. It is still a dangerous world, even more dangerous perhaps than in the rough and tumble past. Electronic media manipulators, both private and governmental, would rule our minds; street toughs and professional criminals (white and blue collar) would have our bodies and our possessions.

The New Age thinker, or cosmic quester, cannot retreat to the moralities of yesterday. There is no place to go. Yesterday's moralities have disappeared, vaporized out of tradition and out of mind. Some disappeared simply because they were not sustaining to the spirit or were inherently false. Others because they were artificially imposed. Still others, the great majority perhaps, because they got in the way of mass man's capricious, hedonistic exercise of his new found freedom. Ortega y Gasset admitted in *La Rebelion de las Masses* that his work was incomplete, that he had not attempted to analyze the defects of society which had caused it to change so much causing a concomitant loss of morality. Although such an analysis is an extremely difficult, almost impossible, thing to do (no one who has tried has yet even come close to a definitive study that satisfies a majority of the better minds around), it is necessary to make at least a serious, even though cursory, attempt to do so here, if for no other reason than to indicate that the New Man, if he is to exist, to survive today and into the future, must realize that he is mostly on his own. He must build from the rubble of a worldwide system that has failed itself, look beyond it and discover new sources of inspiration and enlightenment. He must take the best from the past, including its hard lessons, learn to discard all flimflam, and then learn, finally, to look searchingly inward to discover the most eternal verities which can sustain him in the future. After all is said and done, after all is observed and correlated, he will learn that the world of men can only teach him so much; his inner world, properly explored, can teach much more, as much as he is capable of absorbing.

Both Ortego y Gasset and Erich Fromm, though they can teach us much, were used to looking at, as are most men, the outer world. They were disappointed, each respectively in his own way, at what they observed, as have been all thinking men. The experiential world, what most people call "reality," isn't nearly the totality of beingness that most think it is. It is, rather, a very small part of what is and of what is possible.

Anyone who mistakes our dimension, and what can be observed of it with our human senses, as all of creation is doomed ultimately to disappointment (which, paradoxically, will turn out finally to be a happy readjustment in thinking). Human beings will find in time that what appears to be the imperfectibility of man at the present moment isn't imperfectibility at all. Many already suspect the truth. It is the idea of imperfectibility which is an illusion. Humankind will likewise discover ultimately that many of the postulates of science, everyday thinking and much of church dogma are based upon the faulty human postulate that man's senses and machines can give a true and accurate reading of all beingness. Unfortunately, man may have to leave his body and this earth before the greater truth becomes evident to him, unless he makes a special effort at understanding, while his mortal peers continue to yield themselves to their misapprehensions and pet illusions.

The great religions of the world have failed us as trustworthy registrars of what true reality is. More accurately, it is the exegetes, the interpreters of the essences of Hinduism, Buddhism, Islam and Christianity who have failed us. This failure was almost inevitable and somewhat predictable—too many fingers in the pie, too many prejudiced cooks, really, in the kitchen taking the initially accurate reports of extraterrestrial messengers (call them "messiahs" if you like), taking the essences, and trying to tell us what they tasted like *to them.* Or what we *should* taste if we were so bold as to do our own sampling. What we have ended up with is an abomination of differing opinions, commentaries, exegeses, sermons, papal bulls, ecclesiastical encyclicals, catechism ad infinitum all defining and redefining how and what the little man in the street is to think. One man's orthodoxy has become another's blasphemy. And the little man, God's lamb, who historically has often been illiterate, has often tried desperately, nevertheless, to understand the truth, tempted by whatever piece of the theological smorgasbord has been passed his way. Thus have the cooks poisoned the diners, the wolves in ecclesiastical garb devoured the sheep.

Even in these fairly literate times, the masses of mankind have tended to look, when they did look, to the orthodox clergy for their spiritual direction. What they have been told has often as not confused them, angered them or left them nonplussed. Nevertheless, they have been patronizingly patted on the head and told to follow along ritualistically, whether they understood or not.

Those who have taken their chosen religion seriously have often found themselves pitted against their fellow man. The idea of *jihad*, holy war, is not solely Arabic. The West knows the idea well. We have practiced it in one form or another with the early persecution of Gnostics, with the Crusades, with the 16th and 17th century European and colonial witch hunts, ideologically with Luther and Calvin, in the past and present with antisemitism and with more subtle variants throughout modern times. The scale of such activity is not always the most important thing. Any time religion is used to make a man feel he is in possession of holy ideas which make him superior to his fellow man, we have a kind of holy war going on. The step from a holy war of ideas to a holy war complete with armaments is often a very small one.

The great religions of the world have betrayed us either consciously or unconsciously, often both at the same time, one suspects. The exegetes have taken control. But the problem is basically our fault as human beings because most of us have let this state of affairs come to pass. We have not insisted on going to the source of these religious structures personally, hearing the original messengers directly, reading the original texts, even if they must be read in translation.* We have not taken the time as individuals to plumb the depths of these religions carefully, slowly, looking for eternal verities. Nothing that applies to all men everywhere would ever set men against each other. We have let our religion and most of our other ideas be passed down the table to us already precooked and predi-

*Unfortunately, many of the translations are grossly inadequate, further stymieing the truth-quester.

gested. The cosmic quester rejects such dangerous, divisive ideological pablum. He wishes to discover eternal verities as best he can wherever he can. Thus he is willing to expend whatever energy is necessary to do so. And having done so, he finds himself ridding himself, emptying himself, of food that he has come to recognize as bad fare.

In fact, wholesale but thoughtless rejection of the religious ideas, customs and mores of the past is one of the most distinguishing characteristics of 20th century man. Thoughtless, across-the-board rejection, however, is as self-defeating mentally and spiritually as is too eager an acceptance of prepackaged ideology. Both tendencies are emotional and mindless.

Regardless of the causes of this mass rejection of the religious ideas, customs and mores of other ages, and they are many, Ortega y Gasset recognized that it was occurring at an accelerating rate. Soon others would echo his observations, adding their own, as they watched erstwhile followers and believers drop their allegiances quietly and slip away into the darkness to brood alone on their confused thoughts. Others, like the Nihilists and Anarchists of the late 19th century and early 20th century, influenced by cynical philosophers like Dmitri Pisarev ("What can be smashed must be smashed"), Pierre Joseph Proudhon, Mikhail Bakunin, Prince Petr Kropotkin and Emma Goldman, have been much noisier and even quite violent at times. Whole political systems such as Bolshevism and Nazism have been erected more by rejection of contemporary morality than by the offering of anything new. Hitler's philosophical ideas were in many ways a simple return to a vision of a "purer" primitivism where individual egoism could reign unrestrained.

Why, again we ask, this mass revolt? Why has the vast multitude of souls in the West, after shedding so much that was traditional, become slaves to a new conformity, to ephemeral fads and fashions of thinking and behavior which have little to do with religion or politics or even economics? Why have men become such predictable changelings? Why, as

Ortega y Gasset noted, the two predominant "attitudes (of) violence and caricature"?

Perhaps the answer to these questions lies in simple human nature, the same human nature which can be so lazy and gullible. Something in man smelled a rat in these bygone moralities. Something in Western man told him that the edifice of morality which he had allowed others to create for him, and which he had heretofore steadfastly supported, was built on quicksand. The increasing complexity of living in the highly technological 20th century, with so many kinds of disparate information bombarding him daily, made him begin sniffing about. The smell was wrong. The words of the script he was expected to speak everyday, the scenario of life he was expected to follow, did not fit the ethical and moral job description his culture and his employers gave him. Somebody was lying. But who to believe? What to believe? Could a man believe in anything anymore given "the way the world is"?

The void had to be filled. Desperately, he snatched at an unrestrained freedom which seemed to be the rightful natural possession of all men everywhere. Unrestrained, angry and confused, he mistook license for freedom. He would do as he wanted, what he could get away with. But because he was constitutionally lazy and no great thinker to boot, he settled for chasing material dreams of riches and fame. His rulers and employers, quick to sense his mood, much quicker in fact than the professional philosophers, played to this newfound weakness and pumped up his dreams of "things." If he wanted things, let him have things. If he wanted circuses, or other forms of entertainment, let him be entertained. Fads and fashions have flourished. Entertainment is offered in abundance. And 20th century man has become a slave to fads and fancies, albeit an increasingly violent and surly slave as he has discovered gradually the unfulfilling and unsustaining nature of such a quest. His anger has multiplied geometrically as he has come to suspect more and more his slavishness. Now he does not like himself, and he has lost respect for his rulers and employers. Now he wishes to strike out, at what he is not sure. He has become, by default, more and more not a man guided by principles, even if they were principles conceived of by other men, but a dangerous animal reverting backward to more primitive biological behavior.

The great religions and the great governments have failed him, this mass man, who has not found anywhere alternative spiritual sustenance. It is true that man does not live by bread alone — or baubles or circuses. How true is everyday becoming more apparent.

Christianity has demonstrated its pettiness by the perpetual wrangling among its sects. The Catholic Church, which has traditionally insisted that only through it could God be interpreted to the individual soul, has rejected itself by its exclusivity and feudalistic paternalism which seems so out of date in a century where mass man wants to believe in at least the illusion that he is a freethinking soul, whether he is or not. Hinduism and Buddhism are awash in interpretations of interpretations and variations upon variations. The exegetes definitely are in control. Orthodox Islam has failed in human compassion, insisting on injecting a strain of messianic violence into scriptures that support no such interpretation.

What we have here, as already indicated, are original religious ideas which are valid enough in their own right but which have been, with the passage of time, taken over by the expounders, the multitudinous interpreters who breed like flies. They have succeeded in confusing men with their babble of tongues, often setting them against one another and, in the end, causing an increasing number of them in all faiths everywhere, especially in the West, to reject religious inquiry, and the eternal verities it might uncover for them, as an unprofitable venture. The great religions today in their present form show no appreciable respect for and tolerance of the conceit that the *idea of God* can come in many forms, all potentially valid.

Man smelled a rat. The rat was real enough. Hidden within the cupboard of tradition, it nibbled at the sustaining cheese of ethical principle and right action until almost none was left. And, unfortunately, no new sustenance is easily at hand to take its place. The unfortunate discoverer of this phenomenon often, interestingly, blames himself. He blames himself that no new sustenance is available. He becomes even more confused, indifferent or hostile. Often he is filled with self-loathing which is, potentially, the worst possible attitude, and the most defeating one, for the seeker after eternal verities to have.

# CHAPTER SIX

## The Man Who Ate Himself

By the late 19th century the suspicion had begun to grow in the mind of mass man in the Western World that the new religious, political and economic freedoms won in the preceding several centuries were not all they at first seemed to be. What he had gained did not always seem to outweigh or equal what he had lost—a confident sense of self in a measured, orderly, though always dangerous, world where he had presented to him his duties and his faith by higher authorities. Soon prescient observers of the new century on the Continent, in the British Isles and America, were commenting on a profound sense of social lose that permeated the atmosphere even while the new powerful industrial engines of mass production were growing in might and material output.

The American expatriate writer Gertrude Stein once stated that post World War I youth were a "lost generation." It was at the time a most extraordinarily appropriate epithet as it applied well not only to the privileged youth of the day but, as became increasingly obvious, was also an apt description of the attitude of the working masses.

The poet T. S. Eliot penned an even darker picture of the Western moral landscape in his well known work "The Wasteland." By the end of the first three decades of the 20th century, mass man had become more than vaguely aware that, as far as a sustaining morality was concerned, including an undergirding of imperishable mores and customs, he had lost seemingly forever far more than he had gained from this new world order. Gradually a great malaise of spirit and will descended over Europe and the New World. Soon both were suffering economically and socially as well from a devastating worldwide Depression which compounded the psychological effects of this new disease.

The new world order seemed to be made of two worlds; the world of commerce which grew and grew and appeared unstoppable until the hiatus of the Great Depression, and the world of morality and traditional customs which seemed to be ever shrinking, ever diminishing. Could the go-getter thrill of business compensate for the emptiness that those like Sinclair Lewis' Babbitt, the epitome of middle-class American success, felt gnawing at the core of their being? Even Babbitt, who was no great thinker, might have asked aloud, "Is this all there is?"

Now youth, the middle class and mass man all began to perceive that they had somehow been disinherited from the values of their fathers. What after all could one believe in, what could be found to hold to, in a world whose practices seemed to confirm a heartless scientific positivism, a stark functionalism and an everexpanding amoral relativism and nothing more? If man had become the measure and master of all things, it was a hollow, disillusioning victory.* As he looked in the mirror at his own image, it was becoming apparent to him that he did not like very well the image of himself. If there were no such things as eternal verities to strive to understand, and by which one might guide one's life, and by which one could be made to feel as a whole integrated being with a purpose, what was the meaning of it all? To many there seemed to be none. As one British film of the 60s, and its accompanying theme song, put it, "What's it all about Alfie?"

By the end of the 19th century, man was quickly discovering that the Industrial Revolution, which needed his labor, could squeeze the spiritual life out of him — this despite the

---

*The poet Alexander Pope looked smugly from the vantage point of 18th century British culture and imagined "Man is the measure of all things." A typical view then and now.

quixotic economic security and freedom it seemed to offer. The cry of Russian novelist Fedor Dostoevski's "underground" man (See *Notes From The Underground*) is the cry of dispossessed, 20th century man making his debut on a stage upon which he is certain he does not fit comfortably, in a play which is not of his choosing. Stephen Crane's short poem "In the Desert" (1895) gives us a cameo view of what is to come — the subjective, egocentered state of the socially and morally dispossessed mind that narcissistically feeds upon itself for sustenance. It is a little morality play about the disillusionment of modern man that leads to self-loathing, despite the protagonist's claims to the contrary:

> In the desert
> I saw a creature, naked, bestial,
> Who squatting upon the ground,
> Held his heart in his hands,
> And ate of it.
> I said, "Is it good, friend?"
> "It is bitter — bitter," he answered;
> "But I like it.
> Because it is bitter,
> And because it is my heart."

This desert, one has to believe, is the modern social landscape, Eliot's "wasteland." Man has been reduced to a "creature," an animal, and the "heart" of him has been plucked out either by himself or by forces beyond his control. Here is the picture of a desperate creature, not a human being who has found happiness and mental and spiritual sustenance in the new economic world order, an industrial Golden Age.

The rise of capitalism spurred the birth of nihilists and anarchists, as I have already indicated, men who were convinced that modern industrial society was scavenging the worker while pretending to feed him. The simple-minded nihilist-anarchist solution was to tear down the works and start over, although there was little agreement as to how to structure a new

65

social order. Leaders and followers of both movements were like so many crows arguing over prospective scraps of dead meat. Prince Kropotkin called himself an anarchist communist, but his communism was not the thoroughly thought out system of "scientific socialism" offered by Marx and Engels. Communism's appeal, as a solution to capitalism's tendency to make man a slave to the machine, replaced subserviency to the employer with subserviency to a larger employer—the state. All of these observations are not new. They are well known and generally understood by those who have taken a little time to study the social landscape of Europe and the United States in the latter decades of the last century and the early decades of the 20th century.

What seems most relevant about these social and asocial movements, and others coexisting in parallel time with them, and what is not nearly as well understood, is the terrible failure of governments in theory and practice to have themselves and their programs accepted by mass man as a comforting alternative to the more cohesive systems of customs, mores and values—total cultural morality—which supported pre-20th century living. What has generally been offered as a replacement, no matter the name, has been generally found wanting and been rejected, sometimes sooner, sometimes later. In the main, the social programs of governments, and the programs of scientific research sponsored or encouraged by those governments, have almost invariably been materialistically oriented. Economic security and a steady stream of new available goods was supposed, according to bureaucratic governmental rationale, to make people happy. Chasing goods, however, often called popularly "seeking a better life," has made the individual, in competition with his neighbor, a selfish and frustrated predator-consumer. He thinks first of himself and his family, only vaguely if at all about ideas of universal brotherhood and the material and nonmaterial needs of common humanity.

As long as man keeps rising to the proffered bait and insists on injesting the lie that economic security is happiness, he is going to find himself both trapped and poisoned. As long as he insists on being a modern day Sisyphus, mesmerized and deadened by his own daily struggle to command uphill a larger and larger economic burden of his own making, sometimes perversely relishing and bragging about his own pain, he is asking for disillusionment. So long as he allows himself to be led by the nose by commercial advertising and public opinion, including family members and friends, so long as he lets electronic and written media program his brain and his reactions, he is destined to be disappointed ultimately in what life can offer. If he does insist on tuning out and turning off the critical faculties of his brain, of which every human has a fair share, he is denying himself the opportunity to push beyond the distracting flak and obscuring trappings of everyday living to discover himself as a meaningful player in a cosmic drama that most probably will astound him. He is forfeiting his right to truly understand himself and his place in the larger scheme of things. Until he comes to this greater understanding, his is like a wolf in a trap who must gnaw away his own leg time and time again to free himself.

Governments and ruling economic minorities spend much energy, time and money devising ways to keep the populace amused, controlled and materially satisfied (at least satisfied for the moment). Subjects are most amenable when their minds are either brainwashed or kept in suspended animation. The last thing in the world most governments of men want is a thinking citizenry, especially one interested in cultivating within itself a spiritual dimension which could free it from its trained compulsive attachment to this world and the things in it. It would be wise for all New Agers and cosmic questers to remember this. They will never be thanked by the governments of men for their efforts to free themselves or others. And their presence in numbers in any country will ultimately be perceived as a latent threat to the established powers, even though the quester is by his very nature a peaceful being.

The rapidity of the growth of cultural despair and disillusionment with reality in the Western World can easily be tracked from its pre-World War I roots to its post-World War II flowering. No better early declaration of that despair can be found anywhere in literature than in Ernest Hemingway's short story "A Clean Well Lighted Place," written shortly after the end of the Great War. Here we see a direct shift away from and rejection of traditional values given added impact by the choice of subject matter used to express religious apostasy, the Lord's Prayer: 'Our nada who art in nada, nada be thy name....' But the spiritual malaise of many of Hemingway's more youthful characters seems to pale in comparison with the absolute total rejection of conventional morality—at any rate, what was left of it—and traditional social customs we find in the post-World War II existentialists and, especially, in the philosophy of its two greatest proponents, Jean-Paul Sartre and Albert Camus.

A whole generation, my generation, grew into maturity facing a world increasingly at odds with itself. We were, not surprisingly, extremely uncomfortable with the tenuous balance of terror that existed during the Cold War period and very anxious about our prospects of survival in a world which seemed to increasingly nullify those prospects. The macabre image of nuclear weapons and their destructive potential was forever before our eyes. We had the memory of Hiroshima and Nagasaki to contend with, even if we had been too young at the time of the conflict to have participated in it. It is important to realize, however, that the negative philosophy of life known as existentialism, specifically French existentialism, which so influenced a generation or more of college students and young, thinking adults after the war was in large measure conceived and rhetorically deposited in manuscripts of one name or another *before* the actual testing and use of nuclear weapons. The malaise we have spoken of had been growing and spreading and eating up the patient long before the first flashes of death appeared above the practice site at Alamogordo, New Mexico.

In retrospect, it now seems clear that the spiritually depressive philosophy of existentialism would have dominated

Western philosophical thought even without "the bomb." The nuclear age, with its promise of a worldwide holocaust beyond all conceivable past holocausts, added a dimension of horror, a surrealistic nightmare of death, to man's existence that had not been there before, not quantifiable in megatonage, anyway, but it did not definitively define the malaise itself.

Existentialism was one version, the most distinctive and perhaps the most representative version, of the general malaise. More accurately, it could be called a symptom, probably the most noticeable symptom, of the disease itself. It certainly was not a cause — a version, a symptom, a reflection but not a cause. If we owe any gratitude to Sartre and Camus, it is for putting into clear words what was troubling so many of us. They did what Ortega y Gasset had not done but recognized must be done. They analyzed in dramatic and narrative forms some of the causes of the malaise, and they did an impressive job of demonstrating how the disease crippled the ability of man to live happily and express himself, his feelings, effectively and cathartically. They held up to us a mirror of what we were becoming.

Satre, in his first major work, the long, turgid, almost unreadable dissertation called *Being and Nothingness* set the early parameters of definition and gave an early diagnosis of the malaise. He redefined Hemingway's "nada" — nothingness — into a mental emblem that youth could use to describe the desperate feeling of disassociation it felt with the values, customs and mores of their parents' generation or what was, properly speaking, still left of those values and mores.

In the existentialist view, man exists in a hostile or indifferent universe. He is fundamentally helpless, a victim, a rat caught in a trap. And this trap is not necessarily, as a Greek tragedian would have it, of his own making or a reflection of temperamental flaws. Life is often absurd; it seems seldom to have a real logic to it. The good do not always prosper in this world. When they do, it is by accident. The choices man is offered (Satre's *No Exit*) are most often contradictory or really no choices at all. Man becomes an accidental victim simply by being born (Camus' *The Stranger*). Fate plays with him, laughs at him, scorns him, ultimately kills him. The man who thinks he is in control of life is a fool. If he is so unwise as to believe that conventional morality or piety or anything will save him from the predations of others and from his own illogical actions or from death, he is not being realistic, a careful observer of what is going on about him. There is no confidence in the idea that man has an immortal spirit as well as a mind and a body, and that his spirit can be enlarged, can grow in cosmic awareness, that it can find a purposive meaning in this growth and can come to take consciously, knowingly, its place in an ever changing but ever evolving cosmic scheme. The existentialist thinker really does not believe in the mind, much less the spirit. And the body is no sacred temple, enclosing the spirit, by any means. It is a bag of bones that fails you sooner than you might think.

Notions of an evolving immortal spirit and of objective meaning to life here on earth or elsewhere seem to the existentialist point of view like the foolery of a fantasizing mind. To both Satre and Camus, the mind is basically subjective, illogical and relativistic in its meanderings. The body is a lump of animated clay until all the air is squeezed out.

The nadir of existentialist despair is recorded by Camus in *The Stranger*. Meursault, the main character, does not believe in anything. He acts from the beginning like a walking dead man, although his mind continues to manufacture thought from observations as his legs carry him about. He is accused unjustly of murder and watches with detached emotion as he is arrested, tried and found guilty. His spirit is comatose. His life-force depleted. He does not care whether he is found innocent or guilty. He is beyond caring—about anything, even himself. He has become the epitome of 20th century *insouciance*, indifference to his fate. This indifference is the flip side of 20th century man's hyperactivity, mental anger and violent behavior.

Meursault's mother dies. He does not care. The woman who loves him sits watching the courtroom drama. He does not care. Her pain and suffering does not affect him or concern him. And, it almost goes without saying, he is not concerned about his imminent death.

What is wrong with Meursault? Obviously much. He has rejected his culture, its values and beliefs — all of them — and has made himself a walking zombie. He is also, obviously, psychopathological. He is a classic case of a nonviolent psychopathic personality. He appears amoral and asocial and is basically irresponsible and without remorse or shame, all classic symptoms of this particular type of mental disturbance. He is quietly dangerous to himself, covertly depressive and suicidal. Theoretically, he could commit any act, any crime whether violent or nonviolent without remorse *if he cared to*, which he does not. He is the epitome of noncaring and nonfeeling, as if all feeling has somehow been surgically removed from him. He is beyond everything or it is now beyond him. He exists as if in a dream-like vacuum where whatever is happening seems insulated and removed from him no matter how close or personal. Reality impinges and the subject feels nothing. The Pavlovian dog refuses to register stimulation.

And here is the clincher. Although Meursault is fictional and was created as a literary device more than three decades ago, in many ways he is very much alive. Our cities and the countryside today are filled with an ever growing number of Meursaults. At their most violent worst (the other side of the coin), they shoot and stab and maim indiscriminately. They are the Mansons and Bundys and Squeaky Fromms who register no remorse and feel none. They roam among us doing as they please on Wall Street and in Washington, in industry and our neighborhoods. When they are least noticeable, they simply move about silently among us slowly dying inside, their feelings shriveled like so many dried cornstalks, their spirits as desiccated as parched stream beds, their bodies the shells of Eliot's "hollow man" looking for a place to give up the ghost.

Before I take up the question of what is the greatest failure, the real tragedy of the Meursaults among us, we need to take a look at one of Camus' later creations, the character

Dr. Rieu of *The Plague*, because with him we are offered an alternative attitude to the existentialist dilemma that all actions in life are meaningless, futile or absurd. There are, for instance, some significant differences between Meursault and Dr. Rieu. Rieu is not without some attachments—he has, for example, a wife who he seems to value in an unemotional, abstract way. She is, however, conveniently in Europe, at the time the doctor must face the challenge, in an unnamed North African city where bubonic plague has erupted, of either taking some purposive course of action, however limited, or letting events totally dictate his fate. In other words, the choice is between either becoming some kind of active agent in the unfolding of his destiny or allowing himself to be passively acted upon. It is made abundantly clear that whatever he choses to do or not to do, he may, nevertheless, become a victim of the epidemic.

Rieu is, at least in the beginning when we meet him, a Meursault in essence, quite beyond whatever motives may have inspired him to take up the practice of medicine in the first place. He is not compelled, despite the mandate of the Hippocratic oath, by any humanitarian motive to alleviate suffering. Not at first, anyway.

Rieu doesn't attempt to flee the plague city but lingers on. He has no particular will power in him to make the necessary effort to escape. He stays, rather, from an inability to motivate himself. A great lethargy seems to possess him. He is close to becoming, like Meursault, one of the walking dead. Even when he mentally explores the possible reasons for staying on, he cannot come up with any that are personally compelling. He is simply there, and being there, in possession of certain skills, he decides to remain and do what he can. He is well aware that may not be much.

This is no great humanitarian, this Dr. Rieu, although some critics, so used to existentialist neurasthenia and depression, applauded loudly, as if they were witnessing the reincarnation of a selfless physician the likes of the colonial Dr. Benjamin Rush or a Walt Whitman caring for the wounded amid the carnage of some Civil War battlefield. His decision to remain and alleviate what suffering he can, is done by default. He simply cannot think of any alternative to remaining which appeals to him. His wife is not a strong magnet drawing him away and infusing him with the will to carry one.

Rieu decides to serve his fellow man in a hostile environment because he is so indifferent to his fate. Nothing really matters to Rieu, certainly not people, just as nothing mattered to Meursault. If he had not had certain skills which were desperately needed, he would have sat on his hands. It is hard to believe that if this human being were starting out again as a young man but with his present attitude, or lack of attitude, that he would ever bother with the stress of medical school. Not for love of money. Not because of human compassion. Not for status. Not for power. None of these things interest him. He has gone beyond them. He has become a denizen of a strange land where nothing is important, nothing impelling, nothing even appealing. It is a land where few decisions are ever made. And he has become *almost* incapable of making any. His final one is, in fact, an easy one for him to make. He will do what he knows how to do simply because he knows how to do it.

Rieu's "choice" has been called an example of "humanistic existentialism." It has been praised as the ultimate choice, this decision to use one's skills, if one has some in this absurd, hostile world, to alleviate the suffering of one's fellow human beings. All very praiseworthy stuff, on the surface. But let's look at Rieu's "choice" and what it means a little more closely.

Rieu had just as soon be playing ping pong. He isn't really committed to what he is doing. I find that idea a hard sell. Do you want this physician, who is not a caring human being, working on you? Especially if you have a choice yourself? Can the world function if everyone reduces himself to doing his job, a job, any job with only marginal commitment and no feelings to speak of? What kind of world is that?

Camus isn't offering us a positive or even hopeful picture of the world or mankind. That much should be obvious. There is no underlying thread to his philosophy which gives human beings any kind of dignity or hope for it. Man at best just muddles through, if he makes it at all. The value placed on human life in this philosophy is zero, zilch, and there is no respect for an idea such as the possibility of spiritual growth. This system or way of looking at things does not recognize human improvement of any kind.

The characters found in existentialist literature act as if they are devoid of spirit or any inklings they might possess one. There is no recognition that there is any discernible order to the cosmos, certainly no conviction that a Great Force, Prime Mover or God has orchestrated a vast, multifarious creation in which expansion and growth of all kinds play a large part.* The true existentialists would be the last people on earth to believe it possible that all living beings, no matter where they reside in this vast creation, may be growing continually, mentally and spiritually, coming ever, progressively closer to a greater understanding of themselves and their relationship to the creative energies — including the Prime Mover Itself, whatever it may be — and closer therefore to the meaning of their, and all, existence. They are disbelieving of such a possibility. They have rung hope from their consciousness like dirty water from a rag. There is no feeling in them that man is a worthy specimen capable of becoming whatever he imagines. They would find, what is more, the idea that the depressive funk which now rules and drains them is only a temporary passing phase of a greater learning process, as quite improbable. Bosh, they would say. And baloney.

There is no point to the existentialist world. Just as most scientists in the past decades (but fewer and fewer today) have postulated a cosmos without a Primal Creative Force, existing with no rationale, order or cosmic law to guide it, the existentialist sees no persuasive design or direction to anything. Man is tantamount to a thinking insect in their eyes who sometimes has delusions of grandeur, delusions which are all part of the

---

*As do their needed counterparts, decay and death, the great recyclers.

absurdity of things. Anything goes. Nothing counts. We have a kind of nitty gritty social Darwinism here — the stronger may eat the weaker but it really makes no difference because nothing is important. Unless you're the insect. But even then, if you could care less that you are being eaten (Meursault), perhaps the feeling of teeth biting into your flesh won't matter either and will only hurt momentarily.

The existentialists, it would seem, have anesthetized themselves against the game of life. But then they don't recognize earth life as a serious learning game, an extended growing experience, one proving ground among many cosmic alternatives for the spirit in its upward spiral of evolvement through the dimensions of time and space. Earth life to them is not a stopover on an immense, almost endless journey. It is "the end" to them and they don't like it. Their view is the exact opposite and a parody of the medieval conception, and some of the more ancient ideas, of man. Man is not the center of creation. That's absurd to them. But logic does not stop them there. Man is just a thinking animal, a cosmic oddity, who, filled with contradictions and muddy cross-purposes, had just as well repudiate those contradictions and cross-purposes, withdraw himself from active participation in them and wait stoically for the appearance of the grim reaper, in whatever form he may appear, to take them out of their consciousness, their psychopathological, repressed misery.

The appeal of French existentialist thinking to youth in my generation was exceedingly strong. Its appeal to youth today is obvious, if we take a cross-sectional sampling of youth's attitudes about life and human values. Existentialism mirrors a denigration of the value of human beings and human striving that has been going on in Western culture, as we have already seen, for some time. Western man has had great difficulty discovering new values to take the place of the old ones he has been so ready to discard. Indeed, there is a serious question whether he has really wanted the old ones replaced with anything. Recall Ortega y Gasset's statement that mass man has a strong desire "to live without conforming to any moral code."

Could it be that the existentialist dilemma is now the bastard child of the coupling of mass man's desire to be free of any moral code with the reality of what a world without one is like? The evidence would seem to indicate this.

There is a dangerous illusion that it is easier to be lawless and codeless than to submit outselves to a controlling morality. Unfortunately, the moral codes of man in the past have been imperfect and inadequate reflections of cosmic law. Their imperfections are in large measure responsible for their rejection. A more universal moral code reflecting cosmic law better than the ones we have had in the ancient past and more recently would have made the growth of the present social, political and economic inequalities in the world quite unlikely if not impossible. Existentialists have been quick to pick up on the gross inadequacy of the old moral codes. They have not, however, recognized the logical possibility, in fact the necessity, of replacing the old codes with new ones which better reflect cosmic law. They have been taught, or have come to believe individually on their own, that there is no such thing as cosmic law to begin with. Nearsighted science and its teachings and the manipulations of worldwide megalomaniacal power brokers, who have a vested interest in controlling mass man, have been chiefly responsible, it would seem, for encouraging such disbeliefs in modern man.

Mass man does not know who he is. He has stripped himself in exasperation—and been stripped by the manipulation of others—and is running loose, naked, terrorized and terrorizing. A Frankensteinian monster has been created who threatens to destroy the connivers who disinherited him from what heritage he had and then to destroy himself either furiously (by drug addiction, crime etc.) or quietly (the existentialist way).

We can, if we follow our present course of thinking to its logical conclusion, see the existentialists of the past, the neo-existentialists of the moment, today's rising drug addiction problem, the ever increasing rise in violent crime, the growing suicide rate among the young and many other aspects of the cultural disintegration going on about us, as all interrelated phenomena. They all, people and problems alike, reflect lack of belief in or respect for guiding forces or ideas. They reflect also a great lack of respect for self, and the extension of this lack of respect to other things, whether they be people, animals or property.

The tone of the times today is basically negativistic and fatalistic and, on a practical, active level, it reverberates to the selfish pursuit of personal wealth, public notoriety, and power. This negativism and fatalism have blossomed forth like deadly flowers to fill the vacuum left after mass man rejected traditional morality. We have already considered some of the reasons why he did so. He is both victim and perpetrator of his own predicament. Nevertheless, he has been taught falsely by historians, been lied to profusely by his political and religious leaders and yet been quick to assert his freedom from traditional constraining influences. The problem is, he does not know what to do with his newfound freedom. And he has recognized with a certain perspicuity that, although he is free of much of the old morality, he is not as free as his leaders in the government and the marketplace tell him he is. It would appear governments and employers are quite willing to suffer their citizens' and employees' amorality as long as that amorality does not interfere with their objectives. In fact, sometimes, as with the use of drugs in the inner cities, it can be used as a literal opiate of the people.

Youth today has in some ways attempted to fill the moral vacuum. It is quite often the maker of its own code. Two of the more remarkable attempts in this area are "peer morality," where the pack an individual runs with develops its own rules of behavior to which the individual feels constrained to abide, and what has been called by sociologists "situational morality," a state of affairs that depends on individual caprice and the leanings of the moment. Members practicing "peer morality" can be most ruthless in their treatment of someone outside the "gang," as any teenager can well vouch. Situational moralists probably fulfill the call of humanistic existentialists who maintain that each individual human being must choose what he/she wishes to commit themselves to (the French idea of *engagé*), that each individual must accept total responsibility for his/her actions. The only problem here, and it is a great one, is that most individuals do not seem self-confident enough and philosophically strong enough to make these kinds of decisions very well. It takes a strong person to develop an individual moral code and effectively follow it. And, needless to say, the possibility for unique, dangerous aberrations from normal human behavior is very great.

If the above kinds of behavior are very prevalent in a society, an astute observer might speculate, then, that society is close to a state of anarchy. And so we are. Moral anarchy, not political anarchy. Governments usually have an overwhelming confidence in their ability to control populations by such means as promises, social welfare, entertainments (legal or illegal, the latter being "winked at") and, at the worst, by such expediencies as direct threats and detention. The latter two means are usually to be avoided if at all possible because they are an *ipso facto* admission of at least partial failure.

If Western official governments continue to close their eyes and pretend their respective cultures do not have serious moral problems with which they must somehow contend and work to alleviate, they should not be surprised if their unruly children become progressively more violent and uncontrollable. In a society where "anything goes," everything usually does sooner or later; first convention, then law and order and, finally, even the last smatterings of civilized conduct.

As I think has been clearly indicated, this tone of the times — these fatalistic leanings observed in the first half of this century by Ortega y Gasset, Heramnn Hesse, Louis-Ferdinand Celine, Jean Genet and others and given more careful elaboration directly before and after the last great war by Satre and Camus — has become even more pronounced in the intervening decades up to the present moment, which threatens to be willy-nilly overwhelmed and possibly destroyed by it.

These leanings can plainly be seen in the men and women who were a part of the Beat movement beginning in the late 40s and continuing throughout the 50s, and in the influence this movement, and especially its writers, had on later generations of disaffected youth, in particular the "flower children" of the 60s, the Vietnam War protesters of the 60s and 70s and many youths and adults today.

The Beat generation was led principally by Allen Ginsberg, Jack Kerouac, Michael McClure, Gary Synder, Peter Orlovsky, Philip Whalen, William Burroughs, Gregory Corso, Lawrence Frelinghetti, John Clellon Holmes, Kenneth Rexroth, and, a bit later, Ken Kesey — all either writers or poets.* Although relatively small in numbers, this group was great in influence, the precursor and father of far larger groups of disenchanted youth that were to follow.

The term "beat" was, according to John Clellon Holmes, first used in a definitive context by Jack Kerouac. It reflected a life style that turned its back on what was left of conventional Western morality shortly after the war ended in Europe and the Pacific. Although native-born Americans, the Beats preferred to think of themselves as culturally rootless, as citizens of everywhere and nowhere. They found American and Western materialism as crass, spiritless and dehumanizing. To be "beat" was to recognize the loneliness of one's position, but there was always hope for communion and camaraderie with other like-thinking souls. While rejecting conformity, the Beats did not feel especially persecuted and did not have the streak of violence in them that characterized many of the earlier, politically-interested nihilists and anarchists. They did enjoy giving the raspberry to society and making a party of it in the process.

A more important characteristic of the Beat subculture was its attitude toward orthodox religion, especially conventional Christianity. Conventional Christianity was rejected as

*To these names we might add the "half Beats" of before and after World War II, such writers and poets as Henry Miller, Norman Mailer, Chandler Brossard, Robert Lowry, Robert Duncan, Charles Olson....

a sham, a magic show full of sound and shadow signifying little except hypocrisy. An equally important characteristic of the Beat personality was the attitude toward work. The last thing a Beat wanted was a steady, conventional job serving Moloch, god of materialism. This was slavery and demeaning to the human soul. It was a fate to be avoided at all costs. Allen Ginsberg, in his well known poem "Howl," takes American materialism to task for failing its youth and sums up well the Beat attitude, "I saw the best minds of my generation destroyed by madness/starving hysterical naked/dragging themselves through the negro streets at dawn looking for/an angry fix...." More than anything else, Moloch and its adherents were to blame, "Moloch whose mind is pure machinery! Moloch whose blood is/running money!"

It was, more than anything else, their minds and souls that the Beats were most concerned about but, having in the beginning no alternative spiritual system to replace what they perceived as having been lost, they at times slipped into despair. To soothe this despair, alcohol and marijuana and, to a lesser extent, hard drugs such as heroin, and later LSD, were seen as a palliative. The Beats were the first primarily white subculture in America in this century (other than a few musicians) to experiment heavily with drugs. For this reason they are seen by many as the stepfathers, if not the fathers, of the present drug culture running out of control today.

There is in the Beat literature much hard drinking which accompanies the camaraderie of these social apostates. In fact, drinking killed Kerouac before he reached fifty and drugs and alcohol almost killed Ginsberg before a *satori*, a moment of enlightenment (which may have been a gradual moment), caused him to ease away from his more frantic earlier behavior.

Many of the Beats, having rejected popular Christianity and the work ethic and other traditional social values of industrial lower and middle-class America as enslaving and debasing, were in time attracted to several non-Western thought systems, especially Zen Buddhism. Zen offered the hope of a practical philosophic and religious answer to thinking and moving in this world which, if it is not absurd and inherently hostile or indifferent, can be a pretty depressing place in which to find oneself reincarnated. Zen Buddhism, as they perceived it, offered a *modus operandi*, a program of learning to confront and overcome one's lower self so that one might learn how to effectively and harmoniously interact with life and life's forces. Such interests are reflected, for example, in Kerouac's novels, *The Dharma Bums* and *Satori in Paris*, and in the title of Ginsberg's poem "Sunflower Sutra."

Kerouac's best known and most important work is *On The Road*. This may not be great literature, but from a sociological point of view, it is extremely interesting material. The work mainly describes a group of young Beats traveling in automobiles at great speed back and forth across America. There are no particular destinations to these hegiras although there is always a sense of urgency to get to the next stop along the way, an excuse ostensibly to see friends and party and renew old personal bonds. We are treated to a prolonged description of a footloose cultural drama free of Western conventional morality, not a particularly happy play in all its parts but acted out by characters who refuse to knuckle under. Money isn't important to them. Power isn't important to them. And political thoughts of any kind are the furthest things from their minds.

What is most important in the Beat style of living is experiencing the moment as much as possible. A simple *carpe diem* philosophy. Americans have always had a tendency, one that does not ordinarily run very deep, perhaps, of seizing the moment and trying to squeeze as much out of it as possible, going for the gusto on weekends before returning tamely to work on Monday mornings. European intellectuals have long snickered at this kind of mindless American indulgence. But there is an important difference between what the Beats meant by squeezing the moment for its life juices and what yuppies, at one end of the spectrum today, and street hoods, at the other, expect from their respective displays. Yuppies today want to do it in style. They milk the moment as a smooth, fated offering, a moment and an offering deserving to be indulged.

The street hood does it fatalistically, violently, "drink and be merry (if possible) for tomorrow night we create mayhem and may die as a result." There is no expectation on the part of either the yuppie or the street hood that anything mentally or spiritually might be gained by their displays. This was not true of the Beats, however. Behind their insistence upon living the moment to the hilt lingered a yearning to learn something new, to add to the stock of individual perception and observation, a thirst, finally, and a hungering to replace the void created by what had been rejected with some new mental or spiritual insight which would seem, at least for the moment, to make *all the difference in the world.*

Even in their despair, the Beats always seemed to be searching. It is a characteristic which, in retrospect, makes them now, probably, more sympathetic and definitely more tolerable, even with their acknowledged excesses. This striving for new sustenance is not as noticeable, I believe, with the "flower children" movement of the 60s and even less noticeable with disaffected youth today. Granted, the Beats were not mental and spiritual giants by any means. But the crassness of contemporary youth culture, its hedonism and its ultra subjectivity, seem to indicate that today's youth are much more materialistic and much less interested in things of the mind and spirit than the Beats were.

Today's hard metal rock, rock culture generally, and particularly street "rap" have a hard negative edge. There can be no doubt that the theme of "violence" that Ortega y Gasset saw developing in Western culture is increasing in incremental leaps. The cold statistics of violence compiled by the FBI and local police departments tell us that.* And the tendency of youth to "caricature" that he also noticed has accelerated and dropped downward a notch, to out and out debasement of anything that does not please them. With many young people

*A few statistics to unnerve the nerveless and shake the unshakable: 1.1 million Americans are behind bars. America now leads the world in the rate at which it incarcerates its citizens. Out of very 100,000 citizens, 426 are in jail. Contrast this with the South African rate of 333, the Soviet rate of 268. Then consider that most offenders are not jailed in America but walk free.

overt debasement of self and society has become standard operating procedure.

We are at a point in Western culture where nothing, absolutely nothing, is considered sacred by a majority of people any more. Our traditional morality isn't slipping away, eroding slowly (but at an ever increasing pace) as it did during the first nine decades of this century because of the simple fact that there isn't much left now to erode. What we do have left is lip service to a tradition we don't find credible at the moment. In spiritual as well as material matters, it is catch-as-catch-can and watch out for your rear, because someone else may be coveting the prize of your eye. And, frighteningly, the overall sense of despair that accompanies individual self-seeking is turning to anger and violence, as might be expected in any society where almost everyone is thinking of number one and few give a thought to their neighbor's needs. Some animals when cornered attack their perceived assaulter; others turn on themselves and bit their own tail.

If we are not to be reduced to a kind of societal animalism today, and become in our despair like Stephen Crane's "creature" who ate his own heart, what are we to do? What is the human being to do who wishes to rise to the great challenges of the moment without falling into despair and a life style which is either manifestly or tacitly destructive? How can we be cosmic quester when the world in which we live seems to be collapsing about us? Can we ignore the collapse? Should we turn our heads away? Then what?

Each of us must find our own answer, the one that is right for us. That much seems certain. No one can present an answer to us. No book is so full of wisdom. No guru so wise. Too many students believe that you pay your tuition and teachers supply the education. Neither the best teacher or mentor in the world, nor a whole university of them, can lead the individual human quester down the road each individually must travel alone. The best teacher can only be a momentary guide pointing out, with gentle loving advice, a few observations and guideposts along the way. He may have traveled a similar road himself, but it was not the same road as yours because each individual's road is somewhat different. All, however, have their own special deadfalls, pitfalls and sharp stones that the traveler-quester must learn to pass by. The good teacher, no matter how competent, can never be sure that the advice he offers is perfectly matched to the unique road that is yours and to the special problems it holds in store for you alone. If he is worth his salt, he will be the first to admit his limitations, especially as they apply to you.

In an age which has repudiated so much which formerly sustained it as a social group, the individual quester who wishes to understand himself and his relationship to the greater cosmic reality and all that implies, can still borrow from the past the best that former spiritual traditions had to offer. He would be making a mistake not to do so. He must sift and sift carefully. He will find, I think, if he is diligent and bold-hearted, some nuggets which will glitter so brightly that it does not matter in the least from which particular traditon they originally came. The really great ideas that are universally applicable, and follow closely cosmic law, can be found again and again from one culture to the next. This should not, if we stop to think about it, surprise us.

The Great Nazarene had much advice which seems particularly pertinent in an age which has lost not only its sense of self but even the ability to recognize and respond to the grandeur of creation and especially the Great Force out of which that grandeur — earthly, solar and cosmic — emerged. We have already mentioned elsewhere the best advice of all, how to offer the ultimate appreciation, "Love thy God with all thy heart."

People are so busy nowadays (like the character in Saint-Exupery's *The Little Prince*, who is always 'busy with matters of consequence') looking for a particular key, a magic word or some other device which will suddenly enlighten them. They pay extraordinary amounts of money for magic talismans of various kinds which they think will bring this enlightenment, this new secret knowledge to them. *But there is no new knowl-*

84

*edge.* And no secret knowledge that will instantaneously transform a human being into something other than what he has already become. The great moments of enlightenment usually do not come in one fell stroke but are made up of many small enlightenments which have occurred over a lifetime. What we need usually can be found at our feet, while we are busy straining our eyes trying to see off into the distance, where we have somehow convinced ourselves that the answers to our questions and our dreams lie.

The advice to love the Force which created us and our fellow man, even if we do not thoroughly understand It, or him is not new advice. It is foolish, however, to think this is simplistic, old-fashioned or impractical advice. It is the best advice we can start out with in our search for greater understanding. We could do much worse with our lives than to come to our deathbeds with this love still intact and flourishing in our hearts. I wrote earlier that there is a great failure, a real tragedy connected with the Meursaults among us. I did not at the time try to specify what I think it is. But I will do so now. It is the failure to love. To love God. To love creation. To love the great teachers of humanity. To love one's fellow man. To love onself. The failure to love and the failure to allow oneself to be loved.

If we are to grow as spiritual beings, and keep growing long after our flesh has withered and we have shed this skin, then we must never let ourselves become unloving. If we have forgotten how to love, we must learn to remember. We must struggle, if necessary, with all our might to maintain our ability to recognize ourselves in everything—everyone. For we are all the corpuscles of one great vessel—and if we are to look inward into that vessel with the hope of learning more about it and ourselves, we had best approach it, all of it, respectfully and lovingly. To be able, then, to look upon ourselves in all our glory is, I would guess, to love ourselves absolutely as we are loved by that which created us.

CHAPTER SEVEN

# The Threatening New Tribalism

One day several months ago I picked up a copy of the August 27th *Newsweek*. It is a habit of mine, as it is with many people, to read a daily paper to keep up. Then I read *Newsweek* to catch up with whatever the dailies missed, or I missed, whatever the case may be. That way I can assuage my conscience if it starts nagging me about the necessity of being a well-informed citizen, although often a more skeptical voice in the back of my mind keeps whispering that Henry David Thoreau, from whatever dimension he now inhabits, is watching and laughing. I know what Thoreau thought of newspapers and I cringe.*

Right there on the front page was the big show all laid out, complete with helmeted GIs walking down a Saudi runway, "WILL IT BE WAR?" I paused to marshal my evidential thoughts, the pro ones that said, "Yes, war is coming," and the more careful ones that argued, "But not right now. Later, when we let our guard down. Then the king of the north will wrathfully descend."

Just shows how wrong a guy can be when he tries to think carefully. It did not take long for war to come. I got the "coming" part right. But the "guard down" business was all wrong. Some people might say on the first score that I was playing with a loaded deck. After all, in these times, one kind of war or another in the Middle East is never far off. And if they

*In a nutshell: If you've seen one, you've seen them all.

wished to be particularly annoying, they might argue that we let our guard down before Saddam Hussein invaded Kuwait. But at that I would have to draw the line. In my own self-defense, I think it fair to point out that the world continues to plunge headlong like lemmings toward potential worldwide genocide because everyone insists on keeping their guard up. We as a nation have been on guard, like most of the world, since before the end of World War II. A strong argument can be made for the case that this planet has long been, and is now, a violent place, especially for any unobtrusive soul who has a desire to dwell on its surface, raise a family and live in peace.

I continued on that day several months ago thumbing my way through the pages of *Newsweek*. Soon my attention was drawn to three separate successive articles. One was a summary of the court verdict of the first of the "wilding" trials. You will remember that coined word was applied to the extremely brutal beating and gang-rape of a Central Park jogger on April 19th, 1989 by a band of maurauding young black and Hispanic men. They raped and beat, so they admitted, for kicks, hence the idea of "wilding" violence. The newspapers and other mass media picked up early on the story and it became headline or feature material, despite the fact that countless similar acts of violence happen in America each day and are relegated to the back pages, if they are covered at all.

The second article carried the lead "BLACK ON BLACK BLOODBATH" and described, and attempted to analyze, the bloody confrontations in South Africa between the Xhosa tribe, which supports the African National Congress, and the Zulus, which do not.

The third article carried the title "Thwarted Hopes in the Koreas" and addressed itself to the urge many North and South Koreans have to unify their respective governments. The idea of unification, as the following analysis revealed, has proved to be an elusive goal. On this particular day "...South Korean riot police battled thousands of protesters who had hoped—but never dared believe—that progress toward a unified Korea was finally at hand."

As I put down the magazine, I had an unsettling thought. Actually it was a train of thoughts that started with a crucial question, "Are these articles related in any way other than by the theme of violence?" As I began to sift through satellite thoughts, thoughts which generated questions and questions which generated more thoughts, I came to a disturbing conclusion. These articles and the incidents which they described were related in a most fundamental way. They were, each in its own right, examples of a new tribalism in the world today which sometimes seems tangentially related to the old nationalistic impulses but as often as not knows no boundary of race, color or creed. Significantly, similar "news" can be found in abundance in a variety of media on any given day underscoring the reality and the widespread existence of this new tribalism. What is more, it is a growing phenomenon which feeds on itself and which, if not controlled, threatens the survival of all men everywhere. It directly menaces lives and the desire to live in peace. It also compromises each individual human being's ability to develop to their potential fullest by destroying the kind of atmosphere which nurtures such personal growth.

As a young man I was taught in school that individuals, families and tribes came together into a cohesive unit called a nation for certain primary reasons such as mutual protection, economic advantage and increased ethnic sociability. This was called the "social contract" theory and it seemed, then, a reasonable way to explain how nations came to be, a reasonable justification for their existence. Of course, it was a grossly simplistic view, and, admittedly, I have stated here a bare bones version. The theory didn't much concern itself with more complex issues and motives; for instance, the idea that the larger the band, or nation, the easier the maurauding. It was taught by teachers and accepted by students as an inevitable social movement that developing *Homo sapiens*, that sagacious son-of-a-gun, had *known* in his bones was best for him, his family and those around him. The birth of nations soon followed. Or so we were taught.

It occurred to me as I picked up the magazine again and reread the articles carefully that the self-interested individualism and tribalism that led to the birth of nations/states is now leading us often the other way. Not to a true benign nationalism. Not necessarily toward a one-government world and a more homogenous and harmonious humanity which recognizes the need to shed narrow personal and nationalistic ambitions. Quite the contrary. This new tribalism places individual self-interest and group or gang interest above all else, even when masquerading itself often as ethnic or nationalistic impulses and using acceptable, approved passwords like freedom, democracy and home rule. Legitimate urges for freedom and democracy in the world do exist and should be supported. But today it is becoming increasingly difficult to separate the legitimate urges from the spurious ones. The new tribalism is looking for license, not freedom, and has as subscribers to its inherently selfish actions both individual beings and subcultural groups, the latter often coalitions of self-interested individuals out for all they can get.

What motivates this new tribalism? Often personal frustrations, materialistic greed, the will to power, hate and a bevy of lesser emotions and baser desires. It is, as one might guess, a very destabilizing influence in the world today, even more so, in some ways, than traditional nationalism. We must ask ourselves if we can afford this kind of thinking and these kinds of actions, whether they are originated by individuals or groups in whatever masquerade — with the specter of an overcrowded, polluted planet facing us and the possibility of a nuclear Armageddon hanging over our heads or, perhaps worst yet, a slow death by suffocation as we lay buried under our own garbage.

First, let's look at some of the manifestations of this new tribalism on the international level, then on the subcultural and individual plane. Then let's ask ourselves what in particular caused this state of affairs to be threatening the world as it is. Finally, we will look for possible solutions to this problem and see if some can be conjured by logical thinking and common sense. If ever there is to be a New Age on earth, a world in which each individual being is free and able to reach the maximum flowering of his or her self, then this new scourge, this reversion to more animalistic impulses, must be recognized for the danger it is and be removed once and for all from the face of the earth, no matter how long it takes, because it is a blight upon men. This cannot be done with a scalpel or achieved with force. Somehow, some way, individuals everywhere must be made to realize, if they do not already, that individual welfare is intimately connected with worldwide human welfare and vice versa. We must also learn to recognize that the good of any nation, and its ultimate reason for being, if nations are to survive as distinct entities, is intimately related to how much it encourages, fosters and nurtures both individual and worldwide welfare, each of which must finally be seen by the state as inseparably linked, as indeed having the very same objectives.

What is the hallmark of nationalism in the world today? Gross self-interest. As Daniel Patrick Moynihan has observed about Marxist predictions made earlier in the century, "The second Marxist forecast was that ethnicity, nationalism if you like, would disappear as a force in world affairs. The attachments of language, religion, region were seen as preindustrial remnants soon to disappear. Well, of course, they have not disappeared and are today the very forces that beset the Soviet Union." Few would argue, I believe, that the nationalistic problems besetting the Soviets are many and are, furthermore, in large measure legitimate expressions of the Soviet republics' and satellites' desire to be free of a repressive yoke, or that it is in the Soviets' self-interest (and so they believe) to keep the dogs chained, even if the leash must be extended. Several large questions, however, immediately loom up at us like Shakespearean ghosts, demanding to be set at rest, if possible. *How many* of these nationalistic urgings are legitimate expressions of the desire for freedom and how many are a desire to grab a new personal or tribal license to dominate one's fellow men? How strong is the impulse to *equitable* government, how strong toward greed and hooliganism? Returning Europe to post-World War I self-governing nationalistic enclaves will not

91

necessarily make a better world. As long as people value the "attachments of language, religion, region" *above* the need for universal thinking, human beings will never achieve peace on earth. The Marxists were right in recognizing that raging ethnicity must go, must be supplanted by a thinking which is kinder and more equitable. But they were right for the wrong reasons. Scientific socialism, as they called it, has proved it is neither kinder nor really more equitable than what it replaced. And capitalism, while offering more license than Marxism, has not proved an especially kind or equitable system either. To be poor in America, as in most democracies, is to survive on a thin crust of kindness and public welfare payments. How thin? Ask the poor and dispossessed. They will gladly tell.

Hardly a nation, and certainly no major power, has demonstrated by policy or overt action any consistent ability to put the world's welfare before its own. It can be argued that this state of affairs has always existed and should be expected and that it is naive to expect anything else. I would counter such an argument with the thought that the historic record does indeed indicate nations almost invariably place self-interest above all else — that it has been the nature of societal man to do so. But the dangers of such behavior in the past were not of the same magnitude as they are today. If nationalism is not soon transformed, alchemized into something radically different, it will consume us with the flames of its selfishness. If individual members of society and the leaders of society, wherever they be found and of whatever ethnic background, do not redirect their thinking to the greater concerns, to the safety and welfare of the greater family of man, if they cannot find some way of overcoming narrow ethnic and nationalistic self-interests, find a way of rising above those interests, if for no other initial reason than to save themselves, then we will not long walk the earth as a species.

When Alexander the Great conquered the known world in 331 B.C., his conquest did not threaten the survival of the human species or the ecosystem of the earth. It is plain to see that the problems facing us today, such as food supply, population density, dwindling resources and pollution of land, sea and air grow geometrically with time. Today, one great accident or one malicious purposeful action of a biochemical or nuclear nature, committed by a nation, group or individual, can fatally contaminate the planet for everyone. The Chernobyl accident was just one foretaste of a bitter harvest. The biological, chemical and nuclear arsenals that exist now among the first level and second tier powers alone, make it mandatory that we redirect our thinking quickly toward survival. Real survival. Not lip service survival. This means condemnation of any act however large or seemingly small which compromises the health in any way of the earth's greater ecosystem and of all its creatures, including ourselves. We have gravely threatened our habitat as we have threatened each other. Simply put, without a healthy habitat, we ultimately die. Unless we overcome our temperamental aggressiveness and desires for narrow self-aggrandizement, we die. Or our children die instead.

What are some examples of the kinds of specific behavior that will make the world a safer, more desirable and healthier place to live, behavior that is necessary if the species is to survive and thrive? Nations must quit manufacturing armaments and selling them to any buyer with the wherewithal to purchase them. The United States, the Soviet Union, China, France, England and Germany are outstanding examples of larger nations guilty of this practice.* Too large a share of each of these nations' gross national product depends on direct armament sales or related manufacturing. Karl Kolb chemical company of Germany, for instance, had much to do with supplying the technology and hardware for Saddam Hussein's chemical warfare industry; Gildemeister Projecta helped Iraq increase the range of its Scud missiles by over 300 miles. America sold Iraq munitions. France planes. The Russians tanks. All of these nations contributed greatly to the horror inflected by the Gulf War.

*It is a disgusting reality that the Security Council members of the United Nations are the world's foremost arms merchants.

93

Armament manufacturing and sales are, however, the tip of the iceberg. Large corporations, many of which are international players, must become more responsible—and must be made accountable for their mistakes. Every precaution must be taken so that disasters such as the Bhopal, India gas leak will not happen again. Or a disaster like the Exxon Valdez oil spill will not be repeated. Paper mills must quit using mercury in their slimming process, which has polluted the Mississippi and its tributaries and many other rivers and streams as well as the Gulf of Mexico. The use of pesticides and herbicides must be drastically reduced and curtailed where at all possible.* Then the world's ground water and the planet's land can have time to recover from poisoning *where this is still possible*. Slash burning in the Amazon Basin, and the resultant air pollution and land erosion, must end. Likewise, factory emissions of all kinds must be greatly reduced. Every effort must be made to stop the spewing into the air of compounds like dioxin and heavy metals. Emission of such pollutants as sulphur dioxide and carbon dioxide must also be curtailed. They have the cumulative potential to change the planet's temperature disastrously and may have already begun to do so. All dumping of hazardous wastes into the oceans of the world, including nuclear wastes, must be stopped immediately.

The list goes on and on. At first glance, it seems any effort to halt the madness, and repair the damage, is a hopeless task. But that is only an illusion. Once people come to understand that their personal well being is directly threatened by such actions, they will be more willing to demand that these actions be stopped. What man's hand has done, man's hand can undo—up to a point. We must make sure we do not pass that point. We are, by all evidence, very close to doing so. Hopefully, in time, man will act not only out of personal self-interest but also because he has learned that what is in his brother's best interest is also in his own. Then he will, hopefully, learn something even more precious—the joy of working together and sharing in the great learning game that is life on this poly-

*Just one example: In some Wisconsin counties, 3 out of 5 wells are polluted by insecticides, herbicides, fertilizers or a combination thereof.

chrome, polysyllabic earth.

The first halting step toward working together in the modern world was made when the League of Nations was formed after World War I. The idea of a League was a noble and practical one, actually an American idea (Woodrow Wilson's). When the chips were finally laid down, and the League became a reality, America, ironically, refused to ante up and join. The League languished and soon folded but the idea of an international forum to address world problems persisted and found its reincarnation with the birth of the United Nations after World War II. Yet we can clearly see today that the failure of the United Nations, like the failure of the League before it, to bring peace to the world is a result of individual nations refusing to relinquish enough of their traditional sovereignty to the organization to make this new attempt at world government successful.

Today, however, there are some promising signs that nations are increasingly beginning to recognize, at least at particular moments of grave international crises, the need to cooperate. There seems to be a growing sense that the human species, the safety of man and the resources upon which he depends, are threatened. The United Nations embargo of Iraq, and the marshaling by it of an international force made up of troops from 29 nations to coerce Saddam Hussien into relinquishing his claim on the small emirate of Kuwait, is a case in point. What the long-term outcome of this particular crisis will be still remains very uncertain, although the events in their unfolding seem to confirm uncomfortably the progression of events as described in the Book of Revelation, events leading to a bloodbath finale called Armageddon.

Significantly, although we see international cooperation in an attempt to leash Hussein's delusions of grandeur, we do not see the United Nations condemning the very idea of war itself. Interestingly enough, there was never during the course of the mass media coverage of the Gulf War, as far as I am aware, a news service comment about the parallels of the situation with scriptural prophecy, with "end time" holocausts and Armageddon-like scenarios. Only a few Sunday preachers marked the parallels from their pulpits. The question might well be asked, Has the separation of church and state, of religion and government, become so complete, so thorough, that neither cares what the other does or is thinking? Are we asleep to the implications of what is happening around us? Are we hiding our heads like ostriches in the sand, afraid of what our eyes might tell us, if we take a good honest look, and what our brains might conclude, if we address the issue(s) head on?

There are some other positive signs of a world changing for the better. *Perestroika* and *glasnost* have allowed an invigorating breeze carrying with it the breath of hope to blow through the Soviet republics and satellites. If this hope is allowed to wean itself and grow strong, without the Kremlin reverting to old habits of dictatorship when under stress, Europe and the world will be much the better for it. Another positive sign was the tearing down of the Berlin wall and the reunification of Germany. And the movement of EC nations toward ever more common ground, and away from narrow self-interest, bodes well for the future—provided, of course, that the EC does not become, if it has not already, a reincarnation of the Roman Empire, fostering as Revelation suggests, the "beast" of the biblical Latter Days.

There is also more to the darker side. Any perceptive observer who thoughtfully scans the globe cannot help but be disturbed by what he sees. In an increasingly cosmopolitan world that likes to think of itself as having made great gains over disease, illiteracy and the narrow parochialism of past centuries, there is every indication that old-fashioned, fervid, self-centered, jingoistic, bigoted nationalism is not only alive but has in fact increased since the end of World War II. This kind of reality is extremely destabilizing to a world increasingly beset, because of its increasingly cosmopolitan nature, by problems that affect everyone, everywhere.

The early success of Saddam Hussein, just as that of the Ayatollah Khomenei and Ysir Arafat, represents an upsurge in Arab nationalism and Moslem fundamentalism which have, unfortunately, become inextricably mixed and equated as being one and the same thing in many Arabs' minds. Arab nationalists, more antagonistic each day toward the West, have found it not only expedient but quite effective to tie politics to the apron strings of religion (as has, for instance, the Moslem Brotherhood) to confront, if we accept the propagandistic pronouncements of its leaders, the great satanism of Western interests. Like the German Nazis of the 30s, they have cleverly tied their delusions of personal and ethnic power to a fervid cause, not Aryan destiny but its twin sister, *Jihad*, holy war, and have manipulated the masses as effectively as a Joseph Goebbels or a Machiavelli. The Middle East has remained since the Crusades (which were themselves the result of successful propaganda manipulations) a powder keg. What the actual flash point will be that may finally set off the region into a genocidal frenzy, which may take the West and the rest of the world with it in the resulting explosion, is anyone's guess. Perhaps it has already been reached and we have seen the first lurid flames with the Gulf War. Perhaps true ignition took place earlier, somewhere in the indefinable past of the 1973 War or the 1967 War or with the establishment of the State of Israel in 1946. Perhaps the spark occurred even before that, in the still more murky ancient history of the region. Never in the world's history, it would seem, has there been a better example of how imagined differences between men based on false ideology and ignorance can cause so much grief to human beings over so long a period of time.

Since the breakup of the British Empire and the retreat of European colonialism, the world has been awash in new nationalism. Now *perestroika* and *glasnost* have encouraged many Soviet republics and satellites, caught in orbit at the close of World War II, to unfurl their ethnic banners and threaten secession from the Soviet Union. The Baltic republics of Lithuania, Latvia and Estonia have made such moves, which have been resisted, as have Soviet Georgia's. In Yugoslavia the republics of Slovenia and Croatia threaten to withdraw from the greater union. The ethnic hostility between the Armenians and Azerbaijani is one more example of the deadly mix of old ethnic animosities coupled with desires for local autonomy; as is the Kurdish problem within Iraq. It is sometimes difficult, if not impossible, to differentiate false claims for freedom from legitimate yearnings whether we are considering nations, ethnic enclaves or individuals. Freedom for many is a license to run rampant, to impose a new order of repression in the name of change. As one of the mottoes of Rabelais' Abbey Thélème wisely proclaimed, "La plus changez la plus meme chose."*

The passing, not always peacefully, of colonialism and the corresponding rise of independent states in Africa, Asia and South America, states which were formerly firmly yoked to and rigidly controlled by European powers, has created many fledgling political entities (for instance, Ghana, Angola, Zimbabwe, Sudan, Sri Lanka, Pakistan, El Salvador, Nicaragua), some democratic, some autocratic, some not sure of what they are. The withdrawal of the Europeans, however, much justified and little missed, has created in many cases administrative vacuums. Where there are vacuums, exploiters are soon to follow — and have. Political exploiters, religious exploiters, corporate business exploiters, criminal exploiters. Every kind of human weakness exploiter known to man. Old devils have been replaced by new devils, each new nation often becoming its own worst enemy (such as Tanzania), sometimes even with the best of intentions (as Tanzania).

Can any nation in the world today, given the magnitude of world problems which affect everyone either directly or indirectly, claim it is truly free? Is any nation really in control of its own destiny? To believe so is to deal with chimeras and chameleons and to think like a sophist. Haven't these world problems, running the gamut from ecological pollution to the threat of nuclear genocide, which plague all of us been created by diverse but inevitably narrow national interests, interests often at odds with the interest of neighboring states and the welfare of humanity at large? What we have with this particular brand of new tribalism — and make no mistake about it, the

*I.e. the more things change, the more they remain the same.

old-new nationalism is a part of it, on a scale one step removed from purely ethnic interests and two steps removed from selfish personal interests—what we really have is institutionalized selfishness, along with despair and anger, raised to levels of national policy. Never before in the history of the world is an individual standing in one hemisphere of the globe so likely to be the victim of the greed, despair and anger, and problems in general, of someone or group of beings standing in the opposite hemisphere. We have come to breathe directly on one another. Will we learn to breathe life into each other, incinerate ourselves in one sudden, grand holocaust or, perhaps worse yet, suck the life out of each other slowly until we are no more than the shells of certifiably hollow man? "And that's the way the world ends, not with a bang but a whimper." (T.S. Eliot)

The new tribalism can be found, as we suggested earlier, on levels much lower and in numbers far smaller than purely nationalistic ones. And yet it should be realized that this lesser tribalism not only feeds the greater monster but has a life of its own. It can be found wherever two or more individuals set up camp and decide that their particular ethnic, racial, cultural or ideological ideas, programs or life style are superior to other peoples' way of living and conclude that they should have preferential treatment. This is not an argument against cultural diversity and the appropriate recognition and celebration of it. Anything but. It is, however, a call for recognition that there are many groups of people in this culture and other cultures who wish to impose themselves and their ideas on others.

A healthy nation is one in which the citizens can support diverse subcultures, respecting their uniqueness but never forgetting the greater importance of the larger, more comprehensive, more cosmopolitan matrix of which it, the nation, is made. This does not mean the subculture or the individual must be dominated by the whole or that its (or his) freedoms are necessarily circumscribed. They need be circumscribed only to the extent that the subculture or individual seeks to impose his will on others who do not wish to be imposed upon. We have here a paraphrase of one of the basic definitions of the freedom of the individual—and a clarification of the moment when social law must be called upon to restrain the individual.

Unfortunately, what we see today, especially in Europe and America, with the collapse of traditonal Western values, and morality generally, is an increasing willingness of the small "tribe"—whether it be a street gang, a political party, a religious organization, a racial group or the like—to assert its will in an aggressive attempt to dominate others, often as many others as it can. Sometimes, as with street gangs like the Cripes or hate groups like the Skinheads or Neo Nazis, physical violence is the means of first choice. The amount of violence precipitated by the drug trade, and the violence generally found in American culture today, would probably have surprised even Ortega y Gasset. It might even surprise a Wyatt Earp, were he raised from the dead.

What does this "little" tribalism have in common with the new tribalism or world politics? It is as the son to the father. Nations today as well as individuals are not subscribing, or willing to submit, to any mutually understood and agreed upon set of basic standards for human conduct to save the world from destroying itself. As a first step, nations must come to realize quickly that a few basic rules of conduct are necessary before it is too late. Recognizing this need, Daniel W. Fry, founder of the international peace organization, Understanding Inc., has long advocated the calling together of a world congress, "to determine, through mutual discussion, and to document, through the minutes of the meeting, all those principles, postulates and rules or methods of procedure that are found by *all* of the delegates, to be generally accepted as valid principles of the social relationship of mankind." Once the principles are agreed upon, it is Fry's wish, as it is many of us, that they can be used to bring equitable treatment to all men and equanimity of being to this troubled planet.

I am not, in all truth, optimistic that the mass of mankind or its leaders will realize the need for calling such a congress and recognize the necessity of agreeing upon such universal principles of behavior. Or, if they happen to do so, that they will actually put into practice the accepted principles which would, in all likelihood, guarantee world peace. It is, however, the world's best chance. The alternative is nuclear war, an Armageddon, or simply a world gone mad from greed, over-population, food scarcity and pollution.

I am not a complete pessimist. I do believe that mankind, at least some of it, will endure even the worst future events, survive to become all it can be. William Faulkner summed up my own feelings in his eloquent acceptance speech for the Nobel Prize for Literature, "I decline to accept the end of man. It is easy enough to say that man is immortal simply because he will endure; that when the last ding-dong of doom has clanged and faded from the last worthless rock hanging tideless in the last red and dying evening, that even then there will still be one more sound: that of his puny inexhaustible voice, still talking. I refuse to accept this. I believe that man will not merely endure: He will prevail. He is immortal, not because he alone among creatures has an inexhaustible voice but because he has a soul, a spirit capable of compassion and sacrifice and endurance." The greatest need, of course, before all others, is for man to discover in concert as quickly as possible that "compassion" without which he denies himself the *immediate* hope of his future days. Given the present threats to world life forms and the rapid deterioration of earth's ecology, I am very concerned about the *quality* of his endurance, that man may "prevail" but do so overburdened with problems for which there are even today immediately available solutions, solutions which have far more to do with attitude than action. Attitude must, after all, precede action.

What, then, are some of the basic truths, principles and rules nations and individuals must recognize and adopt if the world is to stabilize itself and each of us is to get a chance to develop fully according to our talents? First, it would seem, we must come to realize that nationalism is obsolete and dangerous. Nationalistic self-interest, when it is only that and nothing more, must go the way of the dinosaur. This may mean the establishment of a world government. At the very least, it means that nations must drop their adherence to narrow self-interest in the name of the greater good of all—for humanity's sake generally and, in particular, for the sake of each individual entity that makes up the mass. We must burn the corpse of nationalism before its fetid body has a chance to continue to spread its plagues and poisons among us, which are, in the long run, quite fatal.

Secondly, we must recognize that each world citizen needs to be guaranteed an international Bill of Rights, which will protect his freedom and the sanctity of his uniqueness. Thirdly, we must learn to value more greatly each human life and all human potential; to recognize a human soul dwells within each human body and that it is sacred and inviolable. (This is obviously a religious idea but one, unfortunately, that major religions selfishly claim as solely their own.) Fourthly, we must learn to recognize that we are creations which are part of a larger Creation and that there is cosmic order and meaning to existence. Fifthly, we must realize that the Prime Mover or God has many possible definitions and various possible manifestations and that there is no place for religious intolerance in the New Age. Lastly, and perhaps most difficult to realize, we must come to see ourselves as essentially no different from our neighbors who are involved, just as we are, in a great cosmic learning game which happens to be playing at this moment, for all of us earthlings, right here on *terra firma*.

What can the individual, who believes in the above truths and principles, do amidst today's chaos of change, much of it negative, to help this New Age world order come into being? He (she) can support such truths as remarked above and many other self-evident truths of like kind that the "still small voice" within encourages him to uphold. As for checks and balances to an overeager reformer, the reformative-minded individual needs to ask himself one primary question: Do the actions I take and the programs I support uphold the idea of the dignity of all life and the right of each individual soul to the freedom necessary to develop itself to its fullest? And perhaps he might add one further question: Are my actions and programs nonviolent? If he can answer yes to these counterbalancing questions, he can probably proceed on his course with a clear conscience, in spite of the resistance to such ideas around him.

And what can the individual do amidst the negative governmental, societal and individually-inspired actions, many of them violent, he sees taking place around him? One course, other than pitting oneself directly against the bull, is to become the consummate "conscientious objector": to be willing to state one's opposition to anti-life actions and policies where and when one sees them while refusing to take part in them. This is, of course, a version of passive resistance which Gandhi and King and so many others after them have used so effectively to draw attention to social injustice.*

Henry David Thoreau, while pondering the authority of government and the foundations upon which government stand, made some cogent remarks at the conclusion of his essay "Civil Disobedience" which are as apt today, possible even more so, than they were when he took pen to paper:

> Is it not possible to take a step further towards recognizing and organizing the rights of man? There will never be a really free and enlightened State until the State comes to recognize the individual as a higher and independent power, from which all of its own power and authority are derived, and treats him accordingly. I please myself with imagining a State at last which can afford to be just to all men, and to treat the individual with respect as a neighbor; which even would not think it inconsistent with its own repose if a few were to live aloof from it, not meddling with it, nor embraced by it, who fulfilled all the duties of neighbors and fellow men. A State which bore this kind of fruit, and suffered it to drop off as fast as it

---

*Gandhi, when asked where he got the idea for passive resistance, said he had read Thoreau. We must recall, however, that Thoreau had read heavily in Hindu literature. It would appear that Gandhi was suggesting with quiet humor that we all inevitably influence each other.

ripened, would prepare the way for a still more
perfect and glorious State, which I have imagined, but
not yet anywhere seen.

# CHAPTER EIGHT

## The Wine of Life Parable

There was a hedonist who wished to experience the greatest pleasure of life. He was young and had means and therefore set about to satisfy himself.

He spent years searching for what he would have. Convinced his own city could not produce such a pleasure, he went to Chicago and became for awhile a great lover. But women soon disappointed him, proved to him too fickle. Or so he said. He decided to move on.

He became an investor in New York City and amassed a large sum of money. But one day, as fate would have it, he lost most of it. By that time, however, he hardly cared. The burden of large sums of money, he decided, was no great pleasure. He was tired and bored and, after resting himself, decided to seek elsewhere for what he needed.

He went to Las Vegas and learned to gamble. But the excitement he felt, which at first was very great, soon paled. He lost more money than he won and, in disgust, left the bright lights for a quieter place.

One day he found himself sitting in a park in Los Angeles. As he sat pondering his dilemma and trying to decide what to try next, and where to try for it, a stranger took a seat beside him.

"I see you are perplexed," the stranger said. "Perhaps I can help. The greatest pleasure is not to be found in any city per se but in the wine of life."

"Thank you," said the hedonist. "It seems I've been looking in the wrong place for the wrong thing."

He then rushed off and booked passage to Paris, thence to Bordeaux, and began with great enthusiasm tasting the local wine. But he found it for some reason lacking a certain...what? So he tried the wines of Alsace-Lorraine, but they were no better, actually a bit bitter. He then set out for the Mosel region of Germany, but there, too, he was disappointed once again in what he was offered.

In some desperation, he returned to his own country and traveled in haste to the Napa Valley of California, speculating mentally that he had overlooked his own fine national stock. But it wasn't long before he was in despair again having concluded that even the best of California was somewhat flat.

Once again he sat down to ponder his dilemma. And once again the stranger appeared, the same one as before.

"Why are you so dejected, my friend? Have you considered that the finest wine comes only from the finest vineyards?"

"Ah!" said the hedonist, jumping to his feet.

He rushed off immediately and purchased for himself the finest vineyard money could buy. Or so he was told.

But he was no farmer and he was no vintner. Consequently, his crop was average and his wine quite ordinary. One day, no longer a young man, having wasted his funds and weakened his body in pursuit of his passion, he slumped to the ground in despair.

Once again the stranger appeared as if out of nowhere.

"What more can I do?" the man asked, his face contorted with anguish. "I'll never experience the greatest pleasure in the world."

"Whoever said the greatest pleasure of life had anything to do with wine?" asked the stranger. "I first spoke to you in a figure of speech. It was only your foolishness which made you take me literally. Listen closely. Out of the vineyard properly prepared and lovingly tended comes the grape. The wine of life is no better than the grape from which it comes. And the grape no better than the soil from which it springs that has been faithfully, carefully prepared. The greatest pleasure which you seek and wish to experience does not exist by accident. First the tilling, then the toiling, then the squeezing and finally the wine."

But almost before the stranger had finished, the man jumped up and hurried off.

"Once a fool, sometimes always a fool," observed the stranger, watching the man disappear into the distance. "I wonder what he's up to now."

CHAPTER NINE

# Quiet Desperation: The Snare of Attached Loving

William Wordsworth was right, "The world is too much with us; late and soon/Getting and spending we lay waste our powers." Most of us are so busy, so attached in our daily living to material and immaterial things, including our friends and loves, that our spiritual nature is allowed to languish from inattention. And time, that terrible capricious abstraction, seems to mock us in our frustration as we more and more become thralls to our habits.

We have become marvelously adept at discovering ways to hold ourselves in psychological thralldom to our attachments. We pine for our desires and demand our wants be fulfilled, convincing ourselves, or being convinced by advertisers and other manipulators of public consciousness, that if we cannot have our attachments, whatever they are, or if they are not in great enough supply, we cannot live a happy life or even at all. Conventional wisdom teaches us it is smart to be avaricious, that instant gratification is not only possible but in our own best interest. Who knows, after all, what the morrow may bring? A parody of one of Winston Churchill's more famous remarks might be raised upon a standard as a motto of the times, "Never have so many owed so much to so many and been so ungrateful." The great irony of the present is the hard lesson it teaches, that attachment, whether to physical things or immaterial egocentered desires, brings with it disappointment, even pain, sometimes death, but always a selfishness that constricts and binds.

It is not surprising, then, to discover that the intensity of our feelings toward these attachments often is accompanied by neuroses and even pathological behavior. Henry David Thoreau remarked that the mass of men of his day lived "lives of quiet desperation." If the observation were true then, how, we wonder, would he be inclined to describe these present, space-age, hectic, avaricious days? Would he recognize that amorphous middle-class lump that has been called the Silent Majority as the proper inheritors of this "quiet desperation"? How would he react to the more recent cacophony that is a new lower class and lower middle-class addition to this "desperation?" What would he think of the increasing violence that accompanies it? Would he be struck deaf and dumb by this nightmare of our own conjuring that has come to life in the light of day to haunt us in all our waking hours? How close the shores of yesterday's Walden Pond seem today and yet so very far from Chicago's Cabrini Green, Los Angeles' Watts and New York City's Bedford Styvesant.

In the past, when obtaining adequate food and lodging were the undeniable foremost human considerations, and when putting in a full day's labor without the assurance that the effort would supply life's basic needs was a large issue, Thoreau's observation seemed apt enough, even if it were intended only as a recognition of the difficulty of obtaining sustenance and shelter. But Thoreau meant to suggest much more. He recognized even then a spiritual deficit in the lives of most of his countrymen, a deficiency which compounded the difficulties of living peacefully as well as fruitfully no matter how lavish the accomodations or how plentiful the victuals. If solving basic subsistence problems brings the "good life" in abundance, then how do we explain the spiritual malaise that infects both Europe and America today? In both, the majority of the population has achieved a level of material abundance beyond the dreams of their parents and grandparents. Why do we find the majority of these people still so internally "desperate?" Why have a good number of them begun resorting to violence, both planned and haphazard, to demonstrate their displeasure with their lot in life? Why do we at so many moments now approach the thin red line separating relative stability from social anarchy, many of us pretending all the while that we do not see the line, that it, in fact, does not exist, just as UFOs do not exist because our government tells us so, even though our own eyes may have seen them?

We have already observed elsewhere in this work the obvious crumbling of traditional values and morality in the 20th century, values and morality which had guided human conduct in Europe and America for almost two millennia, although significant identifiable alterations of both occurred occasionally during that time. Surely this is part of the answer. But it is most certainly not all of it.

One of the most identifiable of those alterations occurred with the Reformation and its revisions in the thinking and actions of men. Primary among those revisions were the changes in theological thought initiated by Lutheranism and Calvinism and, a little later, by other Protestant sects that added their own unique interpretation to many of the old dogmas of the Catholic Church. Of all the influences on values and morality during the Renaissance and Reformation, and indeed well into the 19th century, organized religion was by far the greatest. It was early Lutheranism and Calvinism that laid out the tenets of hard work, soul-guilt and redemption and salvation that so greatly affected a middle class then eager psychologically for reform because of anger at certain real and imagined prerogatives of the Catholic Church and also because of a justifiable fear of the consequences of a new economic order which was adopting methods of production different from the old guild system. The old system was perceived, on the one hand, as comfortable and unthreatening. It had maintained the social status quo for centuries, which alone seemed a large recommendation. On the other hand, the idea of social flux was threatening. Change itself was to be avoided at all costs. The rather rapid demise of the guild system, discernible to all those bold enough to look about them and wise enough to acknowl-

111

edge the obvious, was the beginning of a new order which ultimately would come to be called, in another day, the Industrial Revolution. As the system crumbled, mental stress grew apace and spiritual unrest and dissatisfaction increased.

Hard work as an ethic was both religiously satisfying and practical. It increased material property while saaving, and saving, the soul. This ethic was not, however, peculiar to only the Reformation era. It had been part of the Western mind since Moses and was reflected in classical Greek and Roman culture, both of which affected deeply, from the Renaissance onward, European attitudes generally.

By the time of Luther and Calvin, the burghers were thoroughly ready to accept the idea that they could save themselves and the life style to which they had become accustomed by taking matters into their own hands, shrugging off the overseeing and constraining influences of the Catholic Church, and working through — hard, if need be — to their own worldly success and religious salvation. It was a program which offered great appeal, double victory. A kind of eleventh Commandment came to be acknowledged, "That shalt work hard."

In Luther's and Calvin's time and long after, it was established that idle hands made trouble in God's kingdom. The good Christian strove to exemplify his goodness by the sweat of his brow. Had not God said to Adam as he drove him out of the Garden of Eden, 'In the sweat of your face you shall eat bread till you return to the ground'? The work ethic, or Puritan work ethic as it often came to be called, established itself with a vengeance in Europe and especially in the American colonies. Well into the 20th century, people would say with grudging respect for a neighbor "He worked himself to death."

The change in attitude toward work in the 20th century, especially in America, and particularly since the end of World War II, is noticeable and in many ways disturbing. It was also in many ways predictable. Along with the erosion of belief in traditional theologically-based morality, and a parallel weathering away of respect for civil authority, which has so often and in so many ways proven itself incompetent and corrupt, the masses have begun to doubt the truth of the idea that work for work's sake is an unequivocal goodness or that it leads inevitably to the "good life." Stripped of allegiance to a demanding God and his rules, mass man finds the temptation of a "free lunch," if it can be had, or of a welfare check which pays more than regular wages, hard propositions to resist. Many do not try. They embrace the ideas wholeheartedly.

We live in an age when the populace at large wants greater material prosperity, having given up on the idea of heaven and salvation. "Things" are desired, but the desirer does not want to be bound, and refuses to be morally bound, as Ortega y Gasset made clear, by past rules of acquisition. Threats of hellfire and damnation fall on deaf ears and are seen by the street-wise as rather quaint attempts to instill fear and conscience.

The drive for greater and greater material prosperity, while demanding a seemingly perpetual expenditure of energy, is often found to be discouraging and, even when successful, is discovered most often to be unsatisfying. Yet alternative motives for working and living are found lacking. This leads almost invariably to frustration and anger, to the kind of "no exit" mentality described by Jean-Paul Satre, where every choice seems an impossibility and a disappointment. A vicious circle is created, and morality-shorn modern man, like a rat in a maze, becomes temperamentally more and more dangerous as he scurries about in his own peculiar *cage de folles*, driven increasingly mad by the failure of his dreams. Hence, the rise in mental illness which covers the whole spectrum from neurasthenia through psychosis should not surprise us today. It should be expected.

Recently a West German economic analyst, commenting in the *Wall Street Journal* on his country's prosperity and the chance for further development of its economy, remarked, "Yes. We are doing well. But just how many VCRs, cars and television sets can a man use?" Could it be that no matter how much men have, they are never satisfied; they always want more? If so, the accretion of material wealth is a treadmill. We would be correct in drawing the conclusion that, more often than not, the process leads to mental and physical exhaustion, not satisfaction and happiness. The fear is always lurking in the shadows of the mind that inflation, revolution, natural catastrophe or some other cause, foreseen or unforeseen, will come along and rob us of the honest or ill-gotten fruits of our labor.

The 17th century English philosopher, Thomas Hobbes, was convinced that the drive for material prosperity was just another of man's passions which creates "a perpetual and restless desire for power after power that ceases only in death." Lust for power causes universal competition, a "war of all against all." It also leads rather predictably to the kind of life that Hobbes called "solitary, poor, nasty, brutish and short" (*Leviathan*).

But wait. Wasn't the industrialization of the West, according to its boosters, supposed to have raised the poor, and the rest of us, above such a state? Economically, we are assured, the average wage earner is better off than he has ever been.* Then why doesn't he feel more free? Why does he feel he is held hostage to the conditions of his employment? Why isn't he happier than he has ever been historically? Why doesn't he feel safer, more secure? Is it because he is now bereft of reasons for living, other than basic survival? Having so willingly shucked off his heritage and the guiding principles which were a part of it, he now stands naked, exposed and fearful. He fears the motives of his neighbor, not knowing what drives him, as he fears himself, knowing full well what he himself is capable of in the pursuit of his desires.

Why hasn't social violence abated in this new economic order that has promised us so much?** Perhaps it is mainly

---

*Yet we are also told 1 in 8 children are living in poverty and not getting enough to eat and that, officially, there are now 3,000,000 homeless Americans. This is not, obviously, a utopian situation.

**Homicidal violence, as almost everyone knows, is escalating each day. With nearly a month left in 1990, 12 US cities have already broken their annual homicide record: New York, 2000 deaths, up from 1905; Washington, 434, a new mark.... Police in the nation's 20 largest cities have recorded 7,647 murders so far in 1990, up about 3 percent from a year ago.

114

because of the laissez-faire, go-getter, catch-as-catch-can attitude that is very much a part of the philosophy of this new order. Where anything goes, everything eventually does, and stability of any kind is cast to the wind as a sacrifice to the ideology of the "main chance." Why is violence, by all reckoning, on the increase, far beyond what it was even in Ortega y Gasset's day? Why shouldn't it be? What is to impede its growth? All barriers are down and the tiger is on the loose. When one lives by the laws of the jungle even while masquerading as a civilized being, he should expect himself to be maimed and clawed. We have returned to the half-civilized state of "an eye for an eye and a tooth for a tooth" although the weapons of choice are vastly more potent than in Moses' day. Ortega y Gasset's judgment has been vindicated in a fashion, and to a degree no doubt, that would have surprised and saddened even the most stoic heart of his day.

Is it surprising that the existentialist view of the post World War II world describes that world as "solitary, poor, nasty, brutish" and often "short"? Albert Camus added the observation that it was "indifferent" as well. And it became, finally, to Camus' Meursault, who is the epitome of the existentialist type, also absurd. No traditional morality lingers here. The birthright of positivism and scientific functionalism has become Hemingway's *nada*. Moral *nada*. No God looks down laughingly at his miserable offspring. There is no God to look down. What remains is a piece of real estate in space, without prime causes, without truly meaningful effects and definitely without any real direction. Absurdity. *Nada*. Unfriendly. The catch-as-catch-can place. Where the tiger lurks in darkness.

The world has lately been turned on its ear. As we have already indicated, another kind of desperation, neither quiet nor unassuming, has stolen our repose, turned our days into watchful vigils and denied us the peace of our evening slumber. It is altogether different from the simple panic of the over-extended middle-class manager who discovers he has overspent his credit card limit by several tens of thousands of dollars. Quite unlike the shock of losing illusions about apple pie, Uncle Sam and General Motors. Unlike the quiet despair of losing the innocence of youth and being denied the luxury of nostalgia for times past. Unlike even the surprise of seeing confidence and respect and compassion and hope for the future slip slowly away.

As we continue, it is necessary to make an increasingly large effort to understand the great complexity of this new kind of desperation, to try to define it, to break it if possible into its component parts, and to analyze them if possible. All of this is no easy task. And we are never assured of plumbing the problem to its depths and to our satisfaction. There is really little hope of that. What is more, there is a paradox here. Several in fact. Seldom is something so simple yet at the same time so complex and baffling. That is the first paradox. But there is at least one more. The line separating quiet desperation from active, violent demonstrations of desperation is a thin one. Sufferers or practitioners of both kinds are thoroughly intermixed in our society. Sometimes one becomes the other, like Jekyll and Hyde, although almost all evidence suggests that when a human being crosses the line to "noisy" desperation for any extended period of time, he (or she) tends to remain in that camp for the duration.

This new desperation of the noisy, violent kind is very much like, as we have already indicated, the flip side of the old hippie-existentialist indifference. It is fury and it is rage. And it intends to eat us alive if it can, when it is not preoccupied with feeding on itself.

We cannot hide from this fury, this rage. It surrounds us. It is worldwide. There is no place to go to escape it. We inherited it in great measure because of the illusions we insisted upon mentally constructing, because of our belief in the false promises were made to ourselves or others or that we made to us. Now we must suffer the consequences of the dispossessed and the disillusioned. In many cases we must suffer the company of our own selves.

The American dream, the Horatio Alger-type success story with its many verions, has proved to be a fake. It was sold to us by glib vendors on the installment plan as a material Valhalla which everyone would (or could) reach if they worked hard enough and maintained their integrity of character. And now the lie has been uncovered. The dirty truth is out. Integrity of character has become a rare commodity. Those that have in great abundance are not truly happy. Those that bought the lie and have not are not happy. Ask the overextended burghers and watch their faces closely. Ask the homeless wandering the polluted streets of New York, Los Angeles, Chicago, Des Moines.... Ask the young jobless and the untrained, white, black, red or yellow, about their prospects for the future. Ask them all if their booty, their things, if they have accumulated some, have made them happy, brought them to the shores of paradise on earth. Ask the commuter how much he loves the treadmill which spins him. Ask the child of the one-parent family how close the American dream of material prosperity is, how much money is left at the end of the month, after groceries, car payments, rent or mortgage payments, to fulfill it. Ask the country club matron how fulfilling the life of the rich and not so famous really is. And watch her face closely. Check the eyes.

America, in fact no place in the world, was ever so rich in resources that it could provide a penthouse, a maid, a Mercedes and a carefree life to everyone, as Hollywood and Washington so long pretended. Disillusionment, whether conscious or subconscious, was bound to be the result of such promises. And disillusionment, disappointment with the never ending stream of mass-produced gadgets, with things to which one could attach one's heart, one's longing, has come, often with a vengeance.

Those with everything money can buy are left to remorsefully contemplate their spoils, spoils which break and rust and are soon outdated by new gadgets with limited warranties. All that is left for the consumer beyond the first thrill of possessing something new is the burdensome task of trying to protect it, if he can, from the perpetual threat of depredation. Most consumers will admit, if pressed, that their attachments inevitably fail them. Yet they cling to them, for want of something more satisfying, like survivors of a sunken ship cling to a buoy awash in sea foam.

Those with nothing often brood — unless they explode. These are the bereft, the dispossessed, the unemployed, the mentally ill. They suffer quietly in degradation but they have few illusions. They know all about the American dream and they won't buy it any more. If they had it and lost it, they know now how ephemeral it is. And how hollow. Ask them about the beauty of their attachments, how fulfilling they are, with what happiness they make the soul burn. Ask their opinion about the largesse of Uncle Sam and General Motors. Give praise before them of apple pie and wave the flag if you dare. Then watch out for the spit in your eye.

Not only has the dream of material success and happiness failed the poor and dispossessed (40 to 50 million of them, by a conservative count), it has failed the middle class and even the rich. It has been a long time since Nathaniel West wrote *A Cool Million*, a caustic little indictment of the naive belief in the Horatio Alger myth, of the American dream of success and plenty. But the circumstances which inspired such a satirical vision have not changed. They have multiplied like a virus, and the results are of the same kind only worse by degree. These can be partially summarized as general social nervousness, anguish, a vague sense of betrayal, many forms of mental illness and a simmering, uncomfortable feeling that social chaos lies just around the corner. Where the violence is. Where the fury is in full force. Just around the corner.

Some of those with nothing never bought the dream. They could not care less about it. They are the predators and scavengers of society once found only in the cities, where their numbers grow larger daily, but now found everywhere. They are the lawless and the merciless, and they roam about singly or in groups hunting their prey. Other people's attachments to them mean money — and quick money is chiefly what they are about. They know things do not make for long term happiness. They have never been so foolish. Things acquired are momentarily flaunted, used or sold for instant gratification which soon wears off, like a cheap drunk or quick fix. Life to these human predators is a never ending round of instant, hedonistic indulgence. They are in some ways the epitome of the conspicuous consumer, a parody of the corporate customer, a caricature of materialism. They know of no other life style, believe in nothing but themselves, and that barely, the fleeting loyalty of their companions always suspect and on trial. Talk to them of traditional morality. Speak to them of the need for a new morality. Hear what they say. You will find they do not know what you are talking about. You might as well ask an untutored child his opinion of subatomic particle theory.

We have, unquestionably, lost what held our passions in check and gave us purpose, what kept us at the time from becoming amoral beings — and potential monsters. We have lost the vision of the endless green vista of a pristine America pregnant with the possibilities of human growth that a James Gatz could feel as a young man. Scott Fitzgerald long ago offered us a cameo portrait of visions betrayed in *The Great Gatsby*. The hope of those earlier visions has been squandered in the building of a Babylon West where money, power and things, and their conspicuous display, metamorphose the James Gatzes of the land into the Great Gatsbys — a transformation of character without character growth, a moral sellout leading to despair and death. The old morality is cold and lies amoldering. More dead than dead meat. As dead as such a thing as an idea, a system of controlling ideas, can be. Kaput! The guiding head of statescraft, of moral human conduct in general, has been severed and flung afar to rot. The politicians and priests, those self-interested sycophants, are hiding from the stench or whimpering somewhere or smiling mendaciously, still looking as one might expect for a handout. But who cares. No one is watching them. Meanwhile, the headless run amok, maiming and killing, while the frightened survivors quietly try to make themselves inconspicuous, invisible men, pretending to themselves that everything will be all right, if only they can hold out long enough. Such, it would seem, is the illusion men insist upon to keep their sanity for a little while longer.

Nevertheless, for want of a better philosophy, or any at all, many human beings still pursue the evils of power, money and fame. The desire for such attachments (and power and fame are abstract attachments) have always existed in the hearts of many men, even while some quietly suspected that they would eventually be betrayed by them or the pursuit of them. But discretion is not always the better part of greed, seldom in fact is. Never have these attachments seemed to so dominate the conscious activity of so many men as they do today. Never have they seemed so close, so teasingly near the reach, of the common man as they do today. Never has the programming of such false ideas been so successfully orchestrated by those who have something material to gain from other peoples' follies. Never has there been a time in history, perhaps, like the present when so many disillusioned materialists were treated to the spectacle of so many as-yet-to-be disillusioned hedonists, gold-diggers and power-seekers thrashing about, willing to die for and to kill for the successful acquisition of what their greedy hearts desire. Interestingly enough, and hardly surprising, few of these seekers, though willing to admit the gravity of the social problems existing around them, are willing to sign up for a moral crusade to rid the planet of such menaces as hunger, homelessness, pollution and disease. Neither are they willing, for the most part, to donate much of whatever money or power or fame they have accumulated to redress such problems. The great law of attachment intervenes to stopper the flow of generosity: He who has keeps what he has until he loses it or it is taken away from him.

Hobbes believed man could be rescued from this "war of all against all" mainly by three forces to be found in human nature: fear, hope and reason. Reason, he thought, could finally be counted on to suggest "articles of peace" or natural laws. The problem of the New Ager, the cosmic quester, sickened by the sight of the cultural mayhem about him, depressed by the lack of moral direction exhibited by the mass of men around him and the shallowness of their personal motives, is to discover these natural laws, these "articles of peace." Until he is able to do so to a degree which puts him internally at peace with himself and the world, until he has learned enough about cosmic law to have a reasonably strong understanding of what is happening in the world and why, and what position he should take relative to world events which would be most fruitful for his own personal growth and at the same time most consistant with the best interests of the human race — until that time, he needs to develop a *modus operandi* to carry him safely along the main road through the proving ground of earth life. He has to learn as soon as possible to avoid the temptingly disguised by-paths filled with land mines which will cause him all manner of injury. He may conclude, and quite rightly, that a continual war is going on about him — that those who are carrying it on wish to draw him in and make him a participant. It is, he may perceive, a war conducted by the confused, the ignorant and the selfish among themselves for imagined power and glory. If he is wise, he will soon learn to avoid this war, and all physical warfare, as much as possible. It does not make souls shine; it tarnishes them and slows them in their ascent to a more knowledgeable, more perfected state. And as far as earth life is concerned, it often destroys the body before the mind, led by spirit, learns better.

If our quester is observant, he will soon abandon fear, which has no saving virtue, and impedes growth, but never hope, which, as Paul noted in 1 Corinthians 13:13 ("So faith, hope, love abide...") is an essential characteristic of the Christian. But any man, Christian or otherwise, must have it in plentiful supply if he is not only to "abide" but to grow and reach out toward his potential.

If our quester is perceptive, he will develop his reasoning powers as well. He will soon discover, if he has not already, that consciousness without mind control and reason, makes him the tool and toy of fate. He will learn that the corporate world of business, as well as religious institutions in general and the governments of men, would prefer him to be a non-thinking customer, member or citizen. They would have him

121

malleable and docile, willing to follow instructions, forego embarrassing questions and do as he is bid to do. That is how the shepherds of this world train their flocks.

Every man must find the path, the main road that is right for him and him alone. But if he does not learn to intuit at the outset (and few of us do), or soon after, the abiding spirit of life within all things, animate and seemingly inanimate, even within the mean and violent, and come to value it, no matter how hidden or corrupted it may seem at the time, he will never succeed in his quest as he would like to. To learn to value this abiding spirit of life is to learn to love selflessly. "So faith, hope, love abide, these three; but the greatest of these is love." And herein lies for the quester another of the many paradoxes of life. To make it safely and effectively along the main road he has searched out and found, he needs to discover this abiding spirit of life and to develop the capacity within himself to love it. To discover this abiding spirit of life and the capacity to love it, he needs to find his main road.

There is a solution to this delimma, and we are going to return to it shortly, but first we need to discuss one attachment which many crave and believe to be essential to their happiness, believe is a solution to all their worldly problems. This is the human attachment to a kind of "love" which has no relationship to the disinterested, selfless love that we have just considered.

Let's begin, then, an overture to love and leave the larger and longer great opera of love, which has many acts, to a later time and a different kind of discussion. Let us consider love in the context of attachments, which has been our focus up to now. This in itself is a large order, and we can only hope to sketch the basic melody of our overture, which itself is so often misplayed, misheard and misunderstood.

The word "love," especially in the combination "love of," is used commonly almost like a prefix. Phrases such as "love of money," "love of power," "love of fame" serve as weak idioms linguistically. They do serve a useful purpose, however, by suggesting strong attachment to whatever noun follows the preposition "of." They are really nothing more than simple descriptions of attachment and have nothing to do, which should be obvious, with expresssions of erotic or platonic love or the more abstract love of God. They are, as phrases go, as significant as their usage is commonplace. In this material and power-oriented culture, they are, needless to say, used a great deal.

The Greeks used several different words to describe different kinds of loving; for example, *agape* for brotherly love and *eros* for sexual love. The American Zuni Indians, like many other cultures, have made a particularly strong effort to distinguish between various kinds of love and loving and recognize a dozen or more possibilities, each with its appropriate word or words. The French, however, masters of verbal simplicity with a correspondingly compact language, use only the verb *aimer* and let the context of the sentence and the situation speak for itself. When we consider love as attachment, we will find it most profitable to do likewise and let context and situation lead us.

Both context and implied situation would suggest that the man who loves money, power and fame is not having an affair of heart. He is seeking to possess what he desires because he feels that satisfying his desire will magnify his being in a number of possible ways: control, status, hedonistic pleasure quotient.... He becomes greater in his own eyes and greater, he imagines, not always inaccurately, in the eyes of other like thinkers. We need offer only a few examples, and some of the words out of their mouths, to suggest something of the basic ludicrousness to be found in the thoroughly committed materialistic view of life. Donald Trump, the wheeler-dealer financial tycoon who enjoys an exhibitionistic delight in making headlines, exemplifies well the individual who feels that attachments — money, yachts, personal mansions, tall towers and casinos — are the proper accounterments of the successful man. He has made his fortune with his gambling willingness to take risks and use leverage, which is another name for borrowed money, to finance most of his deals. Recently, as lady luck turned against him, he remarked soberly, "I don't need necessarily to live like this. I can be very happy living in a one-bedroom apartment, believe me."

Michael Milken, former head of junk bond trading at Drexel, Burnham, Lambert, the man credited with turning the use of junk bonds into an art (some say, black art) and fueling the corporate leveraged buyouts and takeovers of the 80s with them, until he was convicted of fraud, wrote to the judge who sentenced him, "I never dreamed I could do anything that would result in being a felon." As a counterpoint, James Dahl, former Drexel bond salesman and co-worker with Milken, testified that during a bathroom meeting at Drexel, Milken told him, "Whatever you need to do, do it." Ivan Boesky, convicted of making tens of millions of dollars through insider trading, said of his stay at Lompoc Federal Prison Camp, "There were a couple of chaps, and I gave them a few quarters to do my laundry." Charles Keating, formerly head of Lincoln Savings and Loan, and indicted for massive fraud, now claims he is the victim of "malicious bureaucrats," yet not long ago his own savings and loan bureaucrats, representing his interests, sent a memo which read in part, "Remember the weak, meek, and ignorant are always good targets."

Women are as likely as men to grovel before the false gods of power, fame and fortune — and to look just as ludicruous when trying to rationalize their way of life. Leona Helmsley, New York hotel magnet sentenced for income tax evasion, had this advice for Saddam Hussein, "I know something about how one is supposed to treat guests, Mr. Hussein." Imelda Marcos, former first lady of the Philippines whose shoe collection rivaled Marie Antoinette's and whose spending habits could justify transferring the old queen's nickname, "Madame Decifit," to herself, said not long ago, "It is so petty — this talk about a million here and a million there."

The follies of individuals such as these are plain to see, if we are willing to look at their lives objectively and are not smitten by glamorous superficial appearances. The terrible flaws inherent in their philosophies of life then become obvious. Yet the mass of men never cease to marvel at the presumed success of their more illustrious countrymen. For each tinsel "hero" who falls, another arises. It is a sad commentary on our age that modern heroes have in the main ceased to be men and women who have accomplished, often through herculean effort, great social or spiritual achievements — a Pericles, for example, or a Jesus, a Jefferson, a Lincoln, a Madame Curie, a Martin Luther King — and have become instead rock and roll or rap heroes, movie and television "stars," petty politicians and assorted male and female "pretty people." We see here the replacement of figures of substance, who have made real contributions to society, with those that only glitter. A large media has been created to market this glitter. It is fed by public relations firms investing great sums of money to pump up their human products and foist them upon the public. The tabloid press and many popular mainstream magazines owe their existence to this kind of advertising. The excuse proffered by the media, when one is, which is seldom, for the low quality of contemporary social models is that what the public is given is the best available substitute for more deserving cultural heroes, which have failed as yet to materialize. The public is therefore given what is available or what the public wants. Discussions over the question of who or what really creates public taste and public adulation for formulated idols, whether in fact it is not the media itself, is most of the time conveniently avoided, as we might expect. One conclusion remains obvious: Both the worshipers and the worshiped remain fascinated by the attachment of power, money and fleeting worldly fame.

Those who love power more than anything in the world are themselves fascinating to anyone with an interest in personality types and their relation to the troubles of our times. They often are willing to forego wealth, anything, to obtain and keep it, although wealth is commonly seen as a means to achieve it just as, conversely, power is quite often recognized as a means to wealth. We might think logically that even a brief perusal of the history books, and a quick look at the "powerful" among us today, would dissuade the mass of men from having much admiration for most of these figures or any keen desire to imitate them. But that is not the case. Mass man lives in the present. Devoid of what he conceives of as real power, he is fascinated by the idea of it, even more by what he fancies as the near presence of it, which helps explain why he can become so fawning and mindless when in the proximity of it. He has, unfortunately, no great interest in the lessons of history. He is led by the spirit of the times, and is its dupe.

Even if he were a reader, there is little that should encourage mass man in the Greek myths like that of Midas or the history of Croesus, last of the kings of Lydia. In fact, stories such as these, true or mythological, were related in ancient times to discourage man from repeating such follies if possible. There is little encouragement, for instance, to the megalomaniac in the story of Alexander the Great, most powerful man of his day, conqueror of the known world but victim of his own weaknesses, as was Julius Caesar, Atilla the Hun, Ganghis Khan, Lucrezia Borgia and others, as the saying goes, too numerous to mention. What could be found appealing to a realist, we might wonder, in Alexander's drunken death scene in Babylon, the picture of a sick and dying king surrounded by all his squabbling generals? Granted, he was a magnificent figure when he was upright, wearing his white plumed helmet, sitting astride his magnificent white charger, Bucephalus, dashing into the midst of the enemy. Yet the greatest enemy lay within him and bid its time. And it did not have long to wait. Not all the ambition for power in the world could save him, not even having someone like Aristotle the wise as tutor. If you cannot hear truth speaking to you from your own heart, your ears will not hear it when it is spoken by others.

How can we forget Hitler, that great exemplar of the pathological authoritarian personality type? He teaches us, we should hope, the ultimate lesson in the abuse of power—and yet for a large majority of Germans he became a modern god on earth. Reasons have been offered for such a phenomenon. Some historians like to refer to the economic problems that threatened to overwhelm the German Republic. Others, more psychologically inclined, like to blame the peculiar German temperament in its historical and modern versions for the appeal of a Fuhrer (G. "leader"). Whatever the reasons for his attraction and his popularity, the fact is a large majority of Germans fell at his feet and a still larger lot silently and hypocritically genuflected obediently in the wings, transmuting in their minds, like clever alchemists, the idea that silence and noninterference with madness was not really cowardice but the better part of quiet, long, suffering valor.

We have had our share of big and little tyrants since Hitler left the world: the Stalins, the Papa Docs, the Amins, the Pots, the Pinochets, the Daniel Ortegas, Castros, Ceausescus, Saddam Husseins.... At any given moment, the world is full of dictators, autocrats and megalomaniacs convinced that power over their fellow men and their fate is desirable. At the same time there are always men willing to throw in their lot with such barbarians, to be toadies to their deeds of terror, convinced that there is some personal advantage to be had hanging on to coattails. Sometimes it is fear and cowardice within men that calls forth their begrudging support; sometimes grovelling admiration. The motives of men are many and various, but almost always predictable, when it comes to selling their integrity and compromising their self-respect.

How much admiration can we have today for most politicians among us? Is politics a calling which now appeals to the best and brightest among us who have a selfless desire to serve society? Cynics would say the motives of politicians, whether now or anciently, were never selfless and that we are naive to ever think otherwise. Perhaps they are right. Is there one in twenty today who has maintained the integrity of his being? Of his office, if he has one? Professional politics in this day and age does not attract the idealistic, compassionate social reformer—the Jeffersons, Madisons, Lincolns, Wilsons, Roosevelts.... Or so it would seem. Politics has become, if it were not always, a profitable business with the dual glamour of money and power. Constituencies are cultivated, then milked. Great moral fiber is found lacking at crucial moments. Examples abound: Richard Nixon during Watergate; Edward Kennedy at Chappaquiddick; the Keating Five senators (Glenn, Cranston, DeConcini, McCain, Riegle) during the national savings and loan debacle. The case of senator and former astronaut Glenn is an especially poignant reminder of how politics and its dealings can besmudge the edges of a national hero's reputation.

Among many youths today there is a sense of apocalypse. The general attitude is that the world may not endure much longer either because of war, pollution and population problems, earth changes, general disintegration of the social infrastructure or, more likely, because of a combination of all of these things. Bereft of a strong and functioning traditional value system to fall back upon, they have either abandoned social constraints altogether or, in many cases, attempted to devise their own value system(s). These attempts at a system(s) (e.g. "situational morality"), however meager in formulation, have been applauded by some sociologists. We cannot help but wonder why, for most of them are intrinsically self-interested and selfish and doomed to failure.

There is, undoubtedly, a kind of existentialism involved in this behavior. What is in some ways peculiar about it is that young people, and some who are not so young, in their desire to fill the moral void about them and within them have attached themselves with such passion to the worship of symbols of fleeting prominence (our "fame" theme again) which perhaps typifies their own feelings about the temporary nature of all things (and values). It is not, in essence, a philosophic recognition that all material things and human attachments are for naught, a "vanity of vanities" kind of position. Youth today is not philosophic and rejects overt thinking and analyzing anything. Rather, what we see is an attitude closer to "eat, and to drink, and to be merry" for tomorrow death may come. It is the gut reaction of animal man, earthbound-oriented man, asserting itself. The things themselves, however, in this view, strangely remain as if a neutron bomb has exploded leaving the material world intact — but the individual in his mind's eye sees himself as imminently perishable and his contact with these "things" unfortunately severed. The idea is to enjoy them while you can even unto frenzy in a kind of bacchanal which has forgotten Bacchus but remembers how to debauch itself. Perhaps this kind of display is the true tragedy of our time. Man's unique spirit and mind, everything within him that makes him different from other creatures, everything about him which is cause for hope, his mind-growth and his potential perfectibility, is minimized and often completely rejected. *Homo sapiens* becomes *Homo rejectus* by an act of anti-will.

There is a discernibly desperate quality to youth's celebration of the fame-symbols of popular culture, especially in its adoration of rock stars. Youth insists rather perversely, or with closed eyes, that these symbols are individually and societally positive influences, either the art itself or the individual "heroes" themselves, in spite of much evidence to the contrary. There has been a steady and traceable progression of degradation in the quality of the influence of these "heroes" since the end of World War II. Who would care to argue that Heavy Metal rock personalties, 2 Live Crew or Sid Vicious have had the same kind of influence on youth that Frank Sinatra, Louis Armstrong, Billy Holliday or Helen O'Connel had on a generation ago?

It is fascinating how many people today, the great majority now middle-aged, still worship the memory of Elvis Presley, his fame, his power, his money — Graceland, the many automobiles et cetera. Many absolutely refuse to acknowledge that this hero's life came apart piece by piece and that drugs and alcohol had much to do with it. They close their eyes to the evidence that he died from a drug overdose or, more accurately perhaps, from a failure of life style. How can they be willing to see the greater truth? They worship the life style their hero led. If they opened their eyes and kick-started their brains into thinking objectively and critically, they would, many of them, have to disavow their own life styles patterned in great measure after "the king" to whom they gave their allegiance. They are themselves just as attached to the idea of the importance of money, power and fame as he was. To admit that the quest for these attachments can lead to such an end, and often does, is totally unacceptable to them. It negates their reason(s) for being. Death is the price you pay for fame, many of them say. By thinking no further, they deny that their idol had a problem. If he did have a problem, some of the deeper thinkers assert, it was not of great importance. It is this kind of thinking or non-thinking which has filled the appointment books of psychotherapists and psychoanalysts and caused a glazed look of bewilderment to pass over the face of many new students of psychology and sociology who wish to understand the perplexing and often self-contradictory actions of humankind.

Adulation of this kind raises several questions. Is such a short, if glitzy, ride on the fast track worth depression and early death? As the song goes, "Is that all there is?" Is that what life is really about? The public has been led to believe so. We can, if we wish, pity them, the poor public so grossly deluded. And then, after all the pity, after all the platitudes are said and done, we are going to have to recognize, first, that part of the solution to public moral blindness lies in education and, secondly, that each individual must learn to take personal responsibility, must learn to make an effort to see through the false shadow show that is being performed all around us. Each individual must find for himself the eternal values and verities that are a real, meaningful part of existence and, once rediscovered, are not only life sustaining but life dignifying. These are the values of love, honor, faith, hope, inquisitiveness, respect for all life, belief in growth and the gradual perfectibility of human nature—the old values which reflect in one way or another cosmic law, order and harmony. To neglect them, forget them or disavow them is to forego our true cosmic evolutionary heritage—to return to bestiality and numb stupefaction. Not all the bacchanals in the world will ever succeed in thoroughly blotting from whatever is left of our human awareness, the dim suspicion that we could be, if only we tried, something far nobler and admirable than we have almost ever dared hope.

If I have seemed to rail repetitively against the dangers of becoming enamored with the false promises of power, money and fame, it is because the overwhelming evidence indicates to me, as it has to many others, that these values/goals are destructive to human development. They debase the inherent nobility of man. They are the way to debility, loss and death. And yet, packaged temptingly as they are, their virtues extolled everywhere by false teachers, advertisers and a vast array of charlatans, they have stirred the imaginations of men to delirious, pernicious dreams, like a subtle poison. Anyone who loves his fellow man and is aware of the truth is obligated, even if he is mistaken for some mad Jeremiah, to speak the truth and to repeat it over and over again until there is no longer a need. That time, that day now seems far distant, although it could be tomorrow — so quickly could man change (and the world) if he would only reorder several of his values and a certain few priorities.

When we read the long list of music and theatrical entertainers who have died of drug and alcohol abuse, or committed suicide, and study their lives at all objectively, we might wonder why followers and worshipers of these individuals cannot see where such life styles lead. A shortened list would include such names as Judy Garland, Marilyn Monroe, Jimi Hendrix, Jim Morrison, Janis Joplin, Sid Vicious.... Maybe we shouldn't be surprised at youth's refusal to look beneath the surface of these lives and read for itself the lesson of caution. To take an honest peak is too sobering, too graphic a demonstration to be ignored. It is easier to shut down the brain, close one's eyes, throw caution to the wind and admit the tinsel gods on our doorsteps who clamour so loudly for admittance to our lives and, once inside ourselves, promise us, at least vicariously, so much. When the discovery is finally made, if it is ever made, that these gods are frauds, it is often too late. A macabre progression has already begun: first anger, then depression, then life parting at the seams, then death. It is no doubt easier to accept these gods when one is convinced there is no alternative to them or if the only alternative is to believe in *nada*,

131

nothing. Thus have the tinsel gods fooled us, willing dupes of our own self-induced vacancy.

It should not surprise us in a world now apparently so destitute of positive values that people are more attracted than ever before to whatever is interpreted as success. But false gods are better than no gods at all only under one condition—that the worshiper, who has demonstrated a need to believe in something, is able through experience, perception and intuition to discover that what is offered him by popular culture, whether it be pseudoreligion, false social values or destructive entertainment, does not adequately reflect eternal verities and cosmic law. He must somehow discover that for himself. Then he will know how true it is that the purveyors of public pap are not truly interested in either his material well being or his soul life. The sooner he realizes this, the better he can protect himself and the more ready and able he will be to proceed with real growing. By finding and placing one spiritual stone at a time, a life is rebuilt, a world reconstructed and a New Age born.

It should be obvious to us by now that when we use the "love of" prefix, especially with combinations like money, power or fame, we are not speaking of real love at all. Like good Frenchmen, we should have formed that realization from the context—the context of our experience in the world. Attachment to material things or even certain abstract ideas—such as power—binds us as human beings and makes of us less than what we can be. We become slaves of our desires and can never have enough of them whether they are directed toward the accumulation of automobiles or votes. Slavery is slavery regardless of what euphemisms may be used to conceal the fact from us.

The state of being we have been exploring here is indeed a kind of slavery, perhaps the most insidious kind because many caught and bound by it have illusions that they are free. Such slavery has no discernible irons. It binds far more subtly. We are face to face again with a kind of Orwellian "doublespeak" or doublethink—the slave is told that the enervating habits

132

which bind him are not fetters at all but the badges of his freedom, for which he should be grateful. Such slavery is immeasurably demeaning to the soul-freedom with which we are born. In its most base form, it slowly smoothers the life out of people as they drag themselves to greater and greater physical effort, not just to feed and clothe and shelter themselves adequately, but to have the "best" and have it "now." This, of course, is another version of Thoreau's "lives of quiet desperation."* At its best, it may lead us to a long fat life of thoughtless hedonistic excess, unless, perchance, on a rainy day we should pause in our dotage, if we should be so lucky as to live so long, and have it all spoiled for us by having one last question irritably and repetitiously push its way, as the song goes, into our consciousness: "Is that all there is? Is that all?"

---

*A little bit more of Thoreau on such lives might be enlightening: "But men labor under a mistake. The better part of the man is soon ploughed into the soil for compost. By a seeming fate, commonly called necessity, they are employed, as it says in an old book, laying up treasures which moth and rust will corrupt and thieves break through and steal. It is a fool's life, as they will find when they get to the end of it, if not before." (*Walden*)

CHAPTER TEN

# The Way Home: The Release of Detachment

The Socratic injunction to "Know thyself" could just as well read "Love thyself." Without being able to love ourselves, a more comprehensive love and understanding of the world and the universe is impossible. To truly know ourselves, we must love ourselves but to love ourselves, we must know ourselves. Once again, we are faced with another of life's many paradoxes, in this case one with some of the maddening qualities of a conundrum. Which comes first, the chicken or the egg? How do we get to know *and* love ourselves?

Once we do learn to love ourselves, a rather miraculous thing occurs: we are able to love all creation, every least bit, every microbyte, and to understand the part we play and the place we hold in the greater scheme of things. We are at last able to love other men without questions and qualifications and to discard the false claims of external differences such as race, creed and color of skin which have been used to separate men. The existentialist feeling of being minimized by existence and trapped by circumstances disappears because we come to the realization that the part we play is in fact significant and meaningful to ourselves and others and only small in a relativistic sense. We sense, we know we are a vibrant note in the greater song.

As the cosmic quester-lover grows, he learns more and more about his particular note, and he becomes more and more eager to learn the rest of the song. Thus he finds himself propelled by his own energy more rapidly along in his journey which most probably began as an attempt at greater personal understanding but quite naturally, almost inevitably, metamorphosed into a journey toward a greater cosmic understanding, the immediate ends of which are forever receding before his eyes only to be replaced, most appropriately, by a larger vision, a promise of even greater understanding as he continues to explore the various and almost ineffable realms of creation. The understanding of the value of the journey never diminishes in the mind and heart of the cosmic quester after the first great moment of enlightenment. It continues to enlarge itself, much to his amazement and joy. He finds he is never beyond new revelations, that the marvels of unfoldment seem infinite as they may well be. He has got finally beyond the cocoon of his own skin, lost in good measure the heavy burden of the ever pressing narcissistic weight of his own ego. He is free of what has become today the neurotic concern for and awareness of "self." He is free to mount his spirit and fly.

Many of us want very much to become cosmic questers and to embark upon the journey described above. We want to truly know ourselves, we want to be able to love effortlessly and selflessly. The trouble is, it seems, the world keeps getting in the way. Other people seem to be plotting to make it difficult for us to accomplish any of these things. What is a man to do? Is there no hope? How can a man or a woman overcome the terrific feelings of loneliness caused in general by the way we have become accustomed to treating one another in the world today and overcome the dreadful despair which most often accompanies them?

We have already discussed many of the particular causes of this loneliness and despair but a brief summary of them does not seem out of place here. By putting them in a new perspective, we can perhaps work through to some answers to the preceding questions, especially to the greater problem of how we can get to know and love ourselves better, and therefore, become better able to love others.

Western culture is continually reminding us that we are

singular beings, each of us separate selves. Modern society, and particularly present-day industrialism, has reduced the individual to "cog" status. Having been made to feel expendable, the individual worker is made more controllable but less comfortable. He certainly has come to feel more fearful about his future prospects at work, at home and in the world generally. At the same time, commercial television and the movie industry bombard him with a steady fusillade of entertainment, much of which is extremely violent and is meant to demonstrate how dangerous life is but, nevertheless, how the successful individual takes advantage of opportunities and people to get what he wants. The suggestion, masked in a thin veneer of phony righteousness and justice, is that the ends desired, if desired enough, justify whatever means are needed to attain them.

On the other hand, commercial advertising pretends to patronize the consumer-worker, offers to assuage his pains, desires and loneliness. He is told that he is a unique individual, a valued person, a special customer. Why despair and miss out on the gusto of life? Why in the world, he is asked, would he ever want to be left behind? To palliate the consumer-worker's fears, remedies for his imagined inadequacies, for his feelings of unworthiness and fear, are generously offered -- particular products or services with the promise, stated or implied, that the consumer-worker will now be a happier being. Piecemeal substitutes for peace of mind are laid out in an almost endless line for inspection and purchase. The idea of buying happiness is nothing new to the American psyche.

To further palliate the consumer-worker, employer-manufacturers, who on the one hand have educated the worker to understand that he is expendable, tease him, on the other hand, with what, he is told, are generous vacations, insurance benefits, disability and retirement plans. The worker often becomes involved psychologically in a love-hate relationship with his job, his superiors and his fellow employees. He is pushed and pulled emotionally back and forth, not too unlike a Pavlovian dog who is continually reinforced with confusing signals and cannot, for the life of him, figure out what is really expected of him.

If the consumer-worker is confused about the inconsistencies of life about him, it is no wonder. If he turns for psychological support to the vestigial remains of what passes these days for Christianity, if he turns to modern-day churches, he is probably in for a rude awakening. Orthodox, conventional Christianity will try to convince him, if he is not convinced already, that he is a sinner and almost unworthy of God.* He soon finds himself at an impasse. He is unfit in the eyes of God and he is expendable on earth. How can he feel good about himself under the circumstances? How is he going to get to know and love himself? Where is he going to find such a program? Most of the old morality of his fathers is dead, rejected and broadcast to the winds. What is left of it is not sustaining enough to support civilized intercourse among men. The events of the day prove that. What is left of it no longer offers an adequate program. Indeed, there is a serious question whether it ever sufficiently met the challenge, even in the past when it was most effectively in force.

If we have learned anything in these materialistic times, it is that man does not live by bread alone. Neither by possession of mere things. The human spirit and heart demand a nurture beyond physical substance if they are to grow and thrive. They also need an atmosphere that is stable and peaceful. The world we have created for ourselves does not reflect stability; it is closer to Pieter (the Younger) Brueghel's painting of hell.

If we insist on trying to escape physically from the bedlam around us, we can "get thee to a nunnery" or carve out for ourselves some other kind of hermetic existence. But as a solution to our own personal problems, and the chaos of contemporary living, such a choice must be considered suspect. Turning our back to the world will in all likelihood neither alleviate our personal pain and loneliness nor contribute to a solution of the social problems with which society is beset. Few nuns remain cloistered today anyway, and for good reason. They have learn-

*Abigail Van Buren: "Churches are not for saints; they are for sinners."

ed better. The best way after all to serve creation, and to develop a larger capacity to love and to know ourselves better, is to immerse ourselves in creation, to study it to understand it better and to work for its improvement, no matter how repelling it sometimes seems. This is the path chosen by people like Albert Schweitzer; the way taken by every volunteer in the Salvation Army and all individuals everywhere who work at solving the world's great social problems and alleviating pain wherever it is found.

Change is natural to creation. Flux is normal. But the cruelty, crime and social unrest, as well as the despair and loneliness we see about us, does not have to exist. All of it exists by human choice. A more natural state for a species as intelligent as man is social harmony, which is in the interest of both the individual being and the body politic. Anything else is a perversion of reason and a caprice of the emotions.

When we learn to love our neighbors as ourselves—after we have learned to love ourselves—we come naturally to a love of the world and all its life; we come to see it as an extension of ourselves, just as we are an extension of it, and both it and ourselves as part of a greater unity. We are all corpuscles of one great cosmic body, vibrantly alive and sentient, all imbued with the same life-force in its many guises. This concept of the ultimate unity of being was Lao-tse's way, Gautama Buddha's way, the Great Nazarene's way. It is the final path toward which all others lead.

The Great Nazarene said, 'I am in this world but not of it.' The statement tells us of not only the possible extraterrestrial nature of Jesus but also is a warning about the dangers of becoming too attached to the things of this world. We are all in fact of this world and not of this world. Our heritage was from elsewhere; our future is elsewhere. But we do not make the future, our inheritance, real, it cannot be actualized, until we come to understand this paradox and begin to live it.

Most of humanity takes a shotgun approach with its attempts to overcome the illusion of aloneness, loneliness and fear. Our attachments become the lifelines we believe will save us. We try romantic, sentimental love—the old Doris Day, Fred McMurray, Rock Hudson style, the demise of which, as Mark Twain said of the news of his death, is greatly exaggerated. We indulge in the fiercest kinds of sexual love to blunt our pains and shade our desperation, many of us becoming addicted to it as to other pain killers like drugs and alcohol. We make our spouse or our family and friends our universe, minimizing the existence and importance of everything else. Or we become self-servingly pious, pretending we serve only an abstract God but how exactly we are never certain. At work, our professional ambition becomes the center of our life. Or we are dominated by the more material attachments to big money, prestigious objects and power, attachments which we have already explored at length in this work. Many of us obsequiously follow, even worship, those who possess much materially. After all, we tell ourselves, doesn't everyone have their price? We attach to this and that, often cynically, because we have been taught that these attachments are what life is all about; they will somehow make us happy, secure, comforted and even theologically saved. But they never suffice. The void within us remains. The pain stays. The loneliness lingers on. What often seems so solid and materially promising turns to water and drips through our fingers no matter how tightly we hold to it. Few of us realize that these attachments are a form of escapism. Even fewer that there is no place to run or hide.

Our attempts at physical, sexual love are not, considered by any objective standard, greatly successful at filling our lives with peace and contentment. We attempt all too often to possess and control our loved ones, change him or her into what our idealization demands, steer them in directions that please us. Physical love tends to be for many a palliative to life's daily drubbing, a release of tension or a pleasant momentary hedonistic indulgence. As such it is usually a self-centered exercise, not a true sharing. Over time it can easily become a habitual act and, as the partners become more familiar with each other (some would say "bored" with each other), the thrill of possession and the excitement generated by the act of love itself is not as great as it was in the past. The love-object then is perceived as less desirable. The attachment has lost some of its hold on the attached. Unless the attached has other attachments to compensate for the loss, he or she may go looking for a replacement. We all know this story, It is heralded in the press, in the cinemas, on television soap operas and passed by rumor in many of the kitchens and bedrooms of America every day. Most of us have learned by experience, each of us individually in our own way, that marriages and relationships which are based only on physical attraction, or primarily on youth's biological drive to procreate, sooner or later fail. In case we have missed the obvious, Ann Landers, Ruth Westheimer and Joyce Brothers, among others, have been telling us about it for years.

Few individuals understand themselves well enough, are in harmony with life and cosmic law well enough, to love gratefully and selflessly, to approach the act of physical coition as a thoroughly natural sharing of natural human bodily impulses, without any other expectations. Few, for that matter, have learned to share intimacy, whether physical, mental or spiritual, without dragging along as company their negative mental or psychological impediments. In fact, as long as that impedimenta exists with both partners or with either partner, and to the degree it exists, the possibility for true selfless loving, whether physical, mental or spiritual, is seriously compromised and may be impossible. We all have good reason, if we stop to think about it, to relieve ourselves of this impedimenta as soon as possible. There are no greater impedimenta to human growth than the impediments to selfless loving.

It would appear from the statistics available that approximately three to four percent of the population have no urge at all to perform the physical act of loving.* Most of us do, however. We should not normally deny our natural impulses, especially when they are aroused by legitimate affection. We should not try to pretend to be what we are not. In spite of

---

*Another 15 percent, according to a poll by James Patterson and Peter Kim, had rather watch television. ("The Moral Minority," *Newsweek*, May 6, 1991).

much nonsense to the contrary which has been broadcast about, despite the misunderstanding of much Eastern philosophy, physical loving and spiritual growth are not mutually exclusive.* They can exist together, even in concert, and are not necessarily antonyms for one another.

Mahatma Gandhi admitted that he quit having sexual relations with his wife when he was in his forties. The Great Nazarene, as far as we know, was celibate as was the more contemporary teacher of men, Paramahansa Yogananda. Many human beings less illustrious than these have chosen to be so. In each case, an individual choice was made to remain celibate, or to become so, for motives of which we can only speculate. It is, nevertheless, true that for most people sexual love tends to be, in one way or another, binding and often complicates emotionally a relationship that already is troubled. This fact is a reflection of the peculiar nature of sexual love itself and of the individual inadequacies of the partners in the relationship. To avoid such risks of entanglement, some individuals, who are by nature, experience or training more inclined to non-physical interests, choose to forego the possible complications of sexual love. That is their choice to which they have every right. What is right for one, however, it not necessarily good for another. It is always necessary to keep that idea in mind. There is nothing per se that is spiritually inhibiting about demonstrating one's feelings (and thoughts) physically if it is done in a thoroughly selfless manner. Nothing. The reality, unfortunately, is that such loving is a rare event.

Romantic love, either in its physical or more platonic forms, shows us, like a Janus coin, its other face sooner or later. Then we come to see our state as less blissful and our partner(s) as less charming, beautiful and desirable than the rush of our passion first supposed. Predictably, the result of our desperate seeking, whether pursued noisily or quietly, is disappointment, even frustration and great despair. The meek, such as T.S. Eliot's J. Alfred Prufrock, may be heard to observe, "I've measured my life out in coffee spoons," in scat-

*Originated by both authors and readers and assorted "thinkers."

tered attempts at "winning" (a very American word) happiness. A less meek man, such as the American actor George Sanders, might be heard to say, "People are unbelievably cruel," as he did shortly before his suicide. Few people, after indulging in a life of one physical relationship after another, are willing to sum up their experience as blithely as did a friend of the novelist Somerset Maugham who, on being asked his opinion of a life given to the pursuit of his passions, replied that he had no regrets.

Prufrock, we had best remember, had not "dared" to face life squarely. His was a failure to immerse himself fully in the potential of it. Few Westerners believe they are guilty of such omission. They have plunged headlong into the pool, dove repeatedly after pearls which when found have most often proved uneven, flawed and, if not worthless, in the main disappointing. What these divers have not done is taken the time to swim the extent of the pool, pausing thoughtfully now and then to inspect and admire the amazing variety of life, and all the possibilities inherent in that life, to be found there. They have not searched diligently enough for the myriad associations and affinities within this creation, have missed the telltale signs of the great interlinkage of this wondrous total ecology where the rhythms of life and being and even death interpenetrate and are so interdependent. Since Aristotle, we have been taught to look for differences rather than similarities, to categorize rather than assimilate, to pigeonhole rather than correlate. We have missed a great epiphany, a celebration of the concordance of all being.

In his autobiographical musings, Albert Schweitzer observed, "We are all so much together, but we are all dying of loneliness." Similarly, psychoanalyst Erich Fromm noted in his much celebrated work, *The Art of Loving*, "The deepest need of man, then, is the need to overcome his separateness, to leave the prison of his aloneness." He is well aware that most neurotic and psychotic states can be traced originally to feelings of "aloneness." He is also convinced of man's historical need to overcome his feelings of separateness and to achieve "union," to find an "at-one-ment" within the world.

The solutions that have been offered for this dilemma of aloneness, the answers to this great need, have varied from man to man and culture to culture. They run a limited gamut, everything from animal worship, human sacrifice, military conquest, hedonism, ascetic renunciation, obsessional work habits, artistic creation, to other forms of God-loving and innumerable ways and methods of loving man. "The history of religion and philosophy," Fromm concludes, "is the history of these answers, of their diversity, as well as of their limitation in number."

It seems all too evident that the solutions have been only partial ones. Men remain divided against themselves. However sound some of these solutions may have been theoretically, they have failed. And the reasons for this failure are many. Even sound advice is of little use if men refuse to implement it. Misinterpretation and misapplication of much good philosophy has, surely, contributed to man's dilemma. Most panaceas have their limitations. None has had the magical power to breakdown completely the barriers that separate men from one another and foster a general recognition of their commonalty. Men's philosophies have proved to be no better than the will power that sustains them. Men's souls have been frozen out of a realization of the warm intimate interrelatedness of all things because of man's stubborn resistance to seeing the truth. The problem is, as much as anything, a failure of will power. Humanity has demonstrated in a number of ways that it is capable of achieving almost anything, even putting men on the moon's surface. The day humanity realizes it is in its best interest in every way to embrace brotherhood, the antithesis of social and individual "aloneness," will be a great day, the real beginning of a New Age for everyone.

What, then, beyond an embracing of the idea of brotherhood, is the cure for this "aloneness" disease, for it appears to be such, infectious, insidious, often deadly and logically not at all the natural state of the species? The answer would seem to be education, education which leads to a seminal understanding of "self," a kind of education which may have had some currency and support at certain times in the earth's remote past but which has been lost to modern man for some time. Before the Copernican revolution man had a more confident idea of his significance as a created being and of the part he played in creation's drama. It is true that this confidence was based upon some spurious reasoning; for instance, that man was the only intelligent universal creature, God's chosen, and that earth was the center of God's creation. We need to recapture that confidence but for different, more accurate reasons. We are undoubtedly not the only intelligent life forms in creation. Many of our hard-nosed, relativistic, mechanistic, reductionist scientists have reversed themselves in the last thirty years and admitted to that likelihood.* We also know, or should know, that our physical bodies are certainly not immortal and that cryogenics or anything else is not going to bring them back when they play out and give up the ghost. Instead of "ghost," however, let us make a substitution. When our bodies give up their "vital energy" and "spirit," equally old-fashioned ways of talking about related, but dissimilar, aspects of the complex called man. If, finally, we are going to recapture confidence in our beingness, we are going to have to come to understand that we are here on earth briefly so that our consciousness, and especially that spirit within us, can learn and grow.

We need to discover now, as never before—having been stripped of our belief in the old governing morality that made us feel good and confident—that we are here for the definite purpose of learning and growing. Nothing must be allowed, once we realize this fact, to cloud our perception of reality and truth. Nothing must be allowed to subvert our newfound confidence in our newfound purpose. We are involved in (as we have said elsewhere in these pages) the Ultimate Game. There is no particular time limit to this game. It can be pursued at a leisurely pace or full out and fast. Whatever our choice may be. It can be played on earth or elsewhere, in body or out. But it

*Carl Sagan and the science writer, Walter Sullivan, are two examples from the 60s.

145

must be played.

We have either been placed here or made the choice to be here. It makes no real difference which. Wherever we find ourselves, whatever plane, whatever dimension, we will find the Game. All play, willingly or not. We are not cosmic biological accidents. All intelligent cosmic life forms are involved in the Game. It is cosmic law. If we listen to the still small voice within us we will come to understand the Game, and the purpose of the Game, much sooner. Resistance to it disappears with time and level of intelligence, even among the most intractable. Interestingly, once a soul or entity understands something of what the Game is all about, what it promises, this soul or entity is filled with an overwhelming desire to pursue it, to master it as well as possible. The entity is rearing to go, almost impossible to hold in check because the promise of the Game is so great. What is that promise? Simply this, an ever increasingly clearer vision of the ineffable primordial visage of creation and an everincreasing enlightenment for the quester as to the meaning of his intimate relationship with it. This is the Ultimate Quest. The quest beyond all quests. There is no other that matters. Adventures of fact and fiction, quests such as Jason's and the Argonauts' and the Sumerian king Gilgamesh's and the Arthurian grail search, or the medieval Crusades, are but addenda. The real thing overwhelms the soul with hope while quickly healing the wounds of the long suffering and long lost quester.

The Game is played, then, everywhere intelligence is found. It is, however, the hope of the living questers on earth today that mankind does not destroy itself and the planet in the process of the present learning experience. There are lessons to be learned here that are best learned here and nowhere else. What are some of those lessons? And if we learn them, will they make us feel less alone, take away some of the pain and loneliness and fear until that day, however distant or close, when we will understand with all our being the Game and its Director?

Almost all evidence indicates that the answer to the latter

question is "yes." It would appear that if we can bring ourselves to recognize a few crucial associations, to see several important affinities, much of our aloneness, loneliness, fear and despair will disappear like hoarfrost beneath a warm sun.

On the physical plane, we must recognize that everything inanimate as well as animate is intensely alive and vibrating. At an atomic and subatomic level there is no real difference, other than degrees of spirit, intelligence and consciousness, between a chair, a fish and a human being. The electrons, protons and neutrons (and subatomic particles) of every atom in all three, in all matter, in everything "alive" or "dead," are spinning at tens of thousands of miles an hour, each in its own peculiar way. We have these microsolar systems by the billions spinning within us. We must learn to see the affinity, and the interrelationship, between these little worlds and our solar system, our galaxy, which is similar to the preceding systems though on a much vaster scale, and the cosmos itself, centered with its own satellite galaxies moving about it.

In our own physical world, we must look more sharply about us and see how intertwined all life really is. The growing ecology movement is now contributing to our greater awareness of this intertwining although it is still difficult for the man on the street to comprehend fully, for instance, why the health of sea plankton is so important to his own health: that plankton feed protozoa which are, in turn, eaten by small fish which, in succession, are eaten by larger fish upon which he himself dines. It is largely a question of education and understanding, the former of which until lately has been scarce and the latter, consequently, lacking.

Gradually, but as soon as possible, for the sake of the planet's physical health and our own general health, and to guarantee humanity's physical survival in this nuclear age, we must learn to see our fellow human beings as composed of the same atomic stuff and the same spirit stuff as ourselves. We must see that we are all essentially alike. What one man is capable of doing (whether of positive or negative consequences) all of us are inherently capable of doing. We are all potential Einsteins and Schweitzers. We are also, unfortunately, prospective Jack the Rippers if we do not socialize out of ourselves our madness and baser instincts. Civilized law incorporates this bleak possibility within its parameters, but since the breakdown of traditional morality, it can barely contain the new lawlessness which is now raging.

When we are able to look in the mirror and see not only our neighbor but our professed enemy as ourselves, *we will no longer be lonely*. With diligent study, it soon becomes obvious that physical and mental as well as cultural differences among men are superficial. The Fuji Islander loves and also hates (unfortunately) just as does the Russian and American, and in very similar fashion. The Arab has just as strong a desire to understand the mysteries of God as does the Christian and Jew and the Zoroastrian. The problems of subsistence, living, loving and dying are much the same everywhere, as are human emotions, passions and desires. As we learn to love ourselves better and cast out unfounded guilts and personally contrived demons, we will be able to love all those about us without fear. We will be well along, then, on our way to enlightenment, learning the lessons that an environment such as earth can teach.

The idea hardly needs repeating that earth is a spectacularly beautiful place filled with a wondrous assortment of mineral, plant and animal life—a veritable Garden of Eden.* A wonderful thing happens when a man comes to understand the interconnectedness of these domains. His heart fills with love. He is brimful of it. He loves not only himself but all about him. He is able to offer his love freely, unafraid and unashamed, from a vast store which never is depleted and is ever replenished. He learns, if he has not already done so, that the more love he offers, the more is returned; that love when given away, unlike material attachments, does not diminish one's stock. He learns he can love all he wants and he will never find himself or the amount of love in his heart diminished. He also finds the more he loves, the easier it becomes to love. He becomes to those about him an object of wonder. They are, he finds, at-

*Yes, rocks are live.

tracted to the unfearing person, the confident individual who has his life thoroughly under control and who seems to have reached a peaceful understanding with existence, an existence that puzzles them and a peaceful understanding for which they themselves yearn. They wish to share in this largesse of fine living, in the warm energy radiated by this universal lover.

He soon learns just how greatly people are attracted to a loving soul. It is as if they hope his fearlessness, his confidence and, most of all, his lovingness will somehow rub off on them; that they by their proximity to him will also become like him. He learns what British theologian and philosopher C. S. Lewis observed long ago, that the only real gift he can give to his Creator is his love; and the only real gift he can give to his fellow mortals is the same love. He observes the give and take of love around him and concludes, quite rightly, that love is like a universal magnetic attractor, a permeating omipresent energy that binds all positive creation together.

He also understands that he has much yet to learn. He is aware, in Leo Buscaglia's words, that "The perfect love would be one that gives all and expects nothing." He knows he is not perfect and neither is his love. But he is not about to quit his efforts to learn more and love better because experience has taught him, and intuition has told him, that detached, selfless loving is the most sure way to a greater perfection.

When the individual human being has reached this point in his development, he has become a cosmic quester. He has by now recognized the futility and frustration of attaching his hopes and desires for fulfillment to the accumulation of material wealth or to less tangible but equally debilitating campaigns for power or fame. He has keenly registered the destructive results of such acquisitiveness and possessiveness (including the possessiveness of most human-love relationships) in his own life and in the lives of others and rejected the temptation of attachments completely or as much as he is at that time able to do. He now knows the folly and the pain and isolation to which they lead. He is looking by now for inspiration and understanding in far different quarters. He has powerful impulses to press to the source of things, as close to the eternal verities as he can get, and nothing now, he knows, can stop him. He will not let anything stop him. He is looking for root meanings. His destination is the live center of things. He wishes as best he can to penetrate primal essences and eternal realities. No one has described the desire, that unquenchable thirst to know them and to share in them better than the 14th century German mystic Meister Eckhart:

> Even so the mind, unsatisfied with infernal light, will press through the firmament and press though the heavens to find the breath that spins them. Yet this does not satisfy it. It must press farther into the vortex, into the primal region where the breath has its source. Such a mind knows no time or number: number does not exist apart from the malady of time. Other root, the mind has none save in eternity. It must surpass all number and break through multiplicity. Then it will be itself broken through by God, but just as God breaks through me, so I again break through Him. God leads this spirit into the wilderness and into the oneness of its own self....

It is true that many paths lead to this primal root, to oneness, to God. Each of us must find his own. It is not for us to judge another man or the path he chooses to follow. Who are we to know where he is really headed and what he must find? All we can do is wish him well, and, if he by chance asks for directions or assistance along the way, we can offer our best counsel and aid. No teacher, no guru, can do better or more for anyone.

Now I will intrude, if I may, a personal account which is relevant, at least in my own case, to much of what has been discussed here.

All my life I have had a particular passion. I love to fish. I fish as often as I am able. Many a friend, I imagine, has shaken his head over what he believed was this waste of time. But I must tell them, if that is what they believe, that I have not been wasting time. Quite the contrary. The hours I have spent trudging the banks of many splendid rivers or of shaking myself awake at dawn on some quiet, misty lake have been well spent. They have been an education, perhaps one that could have been got elsewhere but never in such a peaceful, repetitive and enjoyable manner.

The act of fishing has taught me many great lessons — of the year's seasons, of life's cycles and mysteries. I have learned it does not matter what ground or place the soul is taken to, it is ceaselessly active, eternally vigilant, always at work, joyously or painfully or in some intermediate state, in its effort to make sense of all things and their interconnectedness, whether these interconnections are simple and obvious or more submarine and hidden from the eye, "And you O my soul where you stand/Surrounded, detached, in measureless oceans of space/Ceaselessly musing, venturing, throwing, seeking the spheres to connect them/Till the bridge you will need be form'd, till the ductile anchor hold/Till the gossamer thread you fling catch somewhere, O my soul."*

Fishing, then, you might say, was one of the paths I chose. No matter that I chose it in the beginning for pure pleasure. Where it led me is what is important. What it taught me is what is of value. What I received from my experiences went far beyond pleasure.

Salmon were my great lesson. I saw in their primeval urge to reach the source of their beginning man's urge to discover the cosmic sources of his own beginnings. The salmon strove mightily, beating their way upstream, without really understanding why. But man's great brain, of which he uses so small a part, is continually urging him onward to make some sense of his begottenness and his being. There is a something in man that will not rest until he, too, has traced back his path to its source waters, to his creator. It is the ultimate coming home. The great return. And interestingly enough, he intuits, although sometimes dimly, that without this understanding of

*Walt Whitman, "A Noiseless Patient Spider."

his primal origins for which he is always searching, there can be no real understanding of his present or future. He is caught in the present between past and future, striving, sometimes almost madly, to make sense of the former so that the moment and the future moment will not overwhelm him.

But we need not pity mortal man. The riddles of existence which face him and so often perplex him are in the main the sources of inspiration which drive him toward becoming all that he can be. The players of the Ultimate Game are forged and tempered over time, like good steel by the heat of the fire and the blows of the hammer. The process can be described as a great paradox: Man, who is god but not God, is in the process of discovering himself to be God, which he, of course, always was. This discovery is (will be) the great unfolding after the original unfolding, after all the fearful wending through the woods of creation.

The grand cosmic sequence of growth has multiple variables in store for each of us, and yet wondrously, it would seem, we all learn the same lessons. Man loses himself to find himself. He is, by constitutional necessity, the sorter-outer of the threads of existence. He has chosen to be his own scout, his own explorer for good or ill. He has learned to play the Ultimate Game fiercely but has often underestimated the efficacy, the sheer joy of selfless loving. As he learns to love himself better, it is a sure bet he will learn to love others more gracefully, in fact all of creation warmly but selflessly. The man, the initiate, the Master; the loved, the lover, the Maker — all, finally interpenetrated, One.

CHAPTER ELEVEN

# The Education of the Cosmic Quester
# Amid National Educational Failure

In an ideal world, the main objective of the earnest cosmic quester—to uncover the true nature of things whether of an energetic, material or spiritual nature wherever found—and the objective of our national policy on education should be the same. Today, however, seldom do the twain meet. Regrettably, they are about as far apart as they can be without being complete polar opposites. This is an unfortunate state of affairs in many ways, not only for our quester, who in spite of poor conditions nevertheless propels himself along by an act of individual will power, but it is especially unfortunate for the average citizen who is left in confusion, minimally literate and almost totally uneducated as to his real potential.

It is obvious this is not yet an ideal world. It is also obvious, from a down-to-earth realist's point of view, that we are not graduating from our primary and secondary schools, and not in many cases from our colleges, children and young adults who have basic competence in reading, writing and computation much less an ability to reason well logically with consistency. Before we look at some statistics indicating a woeful illiteracy in our nation among young and not so young alike, we had best ask ourselves just what the professed objective of our national policy on education is. When a group of citizens, including primary and secondary educators, is asked that question, the answer they offer is a consensus-generalization, most often something like "Teaching our youth to be literate adults so that they will be prepared to enter the adult working world."

If the same question is put to academia, the professional (and professorial) reply is likely to be something such as, "Every student needs to know a little about everything and a lot about something so that he/she can make headway after leaving these ivied halls." The need for basic literacy is taken for granted, as it was with our group made up of citizens and primary and secondary educators. There is here, however, in addition to a recognition of the need for a general store of knowledge, a special stress given to the obtaining of a relative amount of specialized knowledge. I suspect "headway" with most of these people does not mean the kind of self-discovery that could be called developing a cosmic consciousness or exploring inner and outer states of consciousness. It means a good living.

I have no doubt these answers are offered as practical replies to the problems of realistic living (a.k.a. survival). I also have little doubt that this kind of nearsighted, misdirected thinking is usually offered in good faith with good intentions. I am also totally without doubt that these answers, when formalized into national educational policy, as they have been, are inevitably delimiting and debilitating to the human soul and eventually lead to a closure of the mind, unless the individual student/citizen is exceptionally strong willed and perspicacious, if in fact this mind was ever opened in the first place to the immense possibilities that surround us. People are being choked to death by misconceived and misapplied educational theories and practice. They drown in the laving lukewarm waters of a public education that is supposed to buoy them until they learn how to swim in "the real world."

Has the nation succeeded in its desire to make everyone, well, almost everyone, literate enough to survive effectively and with a modicum of happiness in the workaday world? Statistics, which are a kind of evidence Americans love and believe, suggest otherwise. In fact, what they indicate is appalling and saddening. They tell us that a great minority, approximately 60 million adult Americans, are either totally illiterate or functionally illiterate. How happy, I wonder, can the lives of these people be? If basic literacy is a starting point, a necessity, for the education of a human being who wishes to explore and understand as much about creation as is possible, what chance do the functionally illiterate have to make much "headway" in such a direction if one or more of them were to become convinced that it were desirable? What, you say? Our man/child doesn't necessarily want, or need, to become a philosopher. The world can only abide so many philosophers. All our citizen wants is a job and a little bit of happiness, a pretty wife or handsome husband, a nice house, some nondelinquent children, a decent car, a VCR maybe. You know what I mean.

I do know what you mean. And I have a reply. Your response is common enough and seems, on its surface, imminently realistic, although it is far more beguiling than even you may realize. First of all, the world needs all the philosophers it can get. It is likely that the wiser we become, the more loving and peaceful and, consequently, happy we will be. You, on the other hand, wish to put the majority of humanity in a box and throw it a few subsistence crumbs. But, truth to tell, now as always, man really does not live by bread alone. He cannot. It alone will not sustain him. What you are doing is encouraging not the growth of minds but the anesthetizing of potential before it has ever discovered itself. If national educational policy can not effectively insure basic literacy for almost everyone, as it long ago promised to do, then these undeveloped minds become political and economic pawns, actually prisoners in their boxes to be manipulated like marionettes by unscrupulous politicians, theologians and economic wheeler-dealers who are controlled by their simple lust for power and money. As Indian philosopher J. Krishnamurti explained, "Our many problems can be understood and resolved only when we are aware of ourselves as a total process...and no religious or political leader can give us the key to that understanding." And, it might be added, that understanding usually comes immeasurably easier and much quicker to a literate rather than nonliterate human being.

The manipulators that would use us, and particularly abuse the uneducated and the illiterate, are materially-grounded humans who come in many guises but have one outstanding characteristic in common: they think only of themselves. They are the opposite of the cosmic questers whom they perceive as their enemy, threatening to instill, so they believe, rebellion among the ranks of those they control, if word of true human potential should ever reach the inadequately educated masses. This fear is their special paranoia, a demon of their own making. For truth to tell, the cosmic quester is not at all interested in fermenting physical rebellion of any kind. He is interested, however, in seeing his fellow men freed from the delusions to which ignorance and illiteracy are heir. And he is willing to do anything in his power peacefully to accomplish that end.

Many writers have pointed out the inadequacy of the present system of American education. Jonathan Kozol, in *Illiterate America*, offers us a summary of some of the more devastating statistics which limn a vivid picture of America's fall from greater literacy to a much lesser literacy in the past 27 years. Here are some of his figures compiled from a variety of standard sources. Twenty-five million adults cannot read product labels, letters or daily newspapers. Another 35 million read at levels which make them functionally illiterate. "Nobody's updated figures for the 'functional' or 'marginal' together is less than 60 million," he says.

The disturbing truth has more to it. In total numbers, white native-born Americans make up the largest group. However, in proportion to population, blacks and Hispanics have higher percentages of illiteracy. Forty-four percent of blacks and 56 percent of Hispanics are functionally illiterate. Among young blacks, 47 percent of all 17 year-olds are functionally illiterate. What hope is there for long term stability in urban areas with figures like that? What chance for a marginally happy life do people have who are burdened with such a handicap?

156

National reading rate scores are discouraging. It would be quite fair to call them a national disgrace. Among recent graduates of urban high schools, 15 percent read at less than sixth grade level. This figure hardly surprises me. I taught for some time at a suburban junior college on the outskirts of Chicago. Our entering freshmen, according to test scores, read at an average sixth grade level. Many of them, rather surprisingly, thought they read fairly well because they could read better than their parents. And these students, we should be careful to remember, are the motivated. They, after all, had come back to school. But what of all these that had not?

According to Kozol's figures, 85 percent of the juveniles who end up in the courtroom are functionally illiterate. Among mothers receiving welfare, over a third are functionally illiterate. If the federal poverty-line standard is invoked and applied to heads of households who fall below it, over half of those heads cannot read at the eighth grade level. But then approximately one million teenagers between 12 and 17 do not read above the third grade norm.

What happened to bring us to such a state? The answer is, like so many of today's problems, complicated by many factors. After reviewing the accelerating slide in national literacy that began in 1963, Paul Copperman (*The Literacy Hoax*) had some pertinent observations to offer. Students, he noted, are not taking as many academic courses as they did prior to the early 60s. Electives, which often provide an escape from sterner fare, have increased. Work demands in traditional courses have decreased. For instance, teachers estimate that the average student is assigned 50 percent less reading and writing in comparison to the early 60s. There has been a corresponding lowering of standards for the reduced amount of written work assigned. Publishers in the 60s and afterward wrote new, and rewrote old, textbooks at an alarmingly reduced reading level, on the average of one or more years lower than the grade level for which they were intended. Add to these problems innovations which did not work out, such as the New Math and a liberal Open Classroom style of education in the lower grades, led often by teachers who (ironically) wanted to be considered the equals of their students, friends really rather than leaders, and the problems soon compound.

The problems were additionally multiplied at all levels of education by an inflation of grades, which caused the grade averages of high school and college students to soar amazingly faster than their academic skills, which were, in fact, plummeting. I can remember sitting in a department meeting during the Vietnam War. We were encouraged, although not specifically ordered, to avoid flunking troubled students — to find for them a different niche, another program within the college. This would be, we were led to believe, a program where he or she could find success. Failure was a last resort. The reason for this course of action was not primarily teacherly doggedness coupled with a commendable human resolve not to accept the idea of failure. It was something much more practical — the realities of government reimbursement.

After reviewing the breakdown in the traditional structure of American education in the early 60s, and the results of what followed after the early 60s, Copperman observed, "With skills down, assignments down, standards down, and grades up, the American educational system perpetrates a hoax on its students and their parents...I call it the literacy hoax."

Factors other than purely academic ones have definitely influenced American culture, and educational results specifically, since the early 60s. I doubt if anyone feels like denying the impact that the breakdown of the traditional family unit, an increasing number of illegal immigrants, drugs, street violence and a host of other causes have had on American literacy levels. These additional factors weigh heavy, how heavy it is almost impossible to calculate. An observer who had visited America at the turn of the century and had now arrived for a return visit might well conclude that our culture was undergoing a breakdown of its moral infrastructure (see Chapter Four, "Revolt of the Masses"). If this visitor happened to be a Westerner, a European, for instance, he might well conclude that what he was witnessing here was the same movie-like footage being played at a speed more or less faster in his own homeland. Such is the galloping progression both here and abroad of this great social disease, the moral malaise which infects Western culture generally at a rate almost proportionate to the rate at which it has abandoned its believe in the old, established morality, mores and customs of the past. The greatest tragedy is that the old moral underpinnings, flawed as they were, have been abandoned before a new morality could be found to take their place. I am convinced that a new morality exists, can be defined and can be voiced, but too many people with vested interests in the manipulation of their fellow men have no intention of trying to define it or support it when it is offered by others.

Such considerations aside, what in particular can be done today within the schools themselves to improve overall literacy, to facilitate a greater ability to reason effectively, to inculcate within the average student at least a minimum of basic knowledge which he or she needs to function generally as a citizen and, more specifically, as a happy, productive employer or employee, as a head of a household or family, as a successful, functional human being?

Many critics of contemporary formal educational practices have offered suggestions and, in some cases, whole programs of reform in the past several decades, people such as John Holt, A.A. Neill, James Herndon, Edgar Z. Friedenberg, Herbert Kohl, George Denison, Ivan Illich, Harry S. Broudy, Neil Postman, Charles Weingartner, Alvin C. Eurich, Myron Lieberman, David Melton and Charles Silberman as well as Kozol and Copperman. The list could be extended almost interminably as could any list recapitulating the various reforms advocated by such critics. Whether they are supporters of greater liberalization, such as the Open Classroom advocates, or more conservatively bent individuals, such as those calling for a "return to basics," they are all in agreement on one score. They see the American educational system as in critical condition. Some see the patient as almost comatose.

Of all the proposed reforms, the one that seems to offer

the most hope and have the greatest chance of success, and the one which would potentially most benefit the young, future, cosmic quester, as well as society at large, is the Paideia Program as outlined by Mortimer Adler and the Paideia Associates in conjunction with the Institute for Philosophical Research and the University of North Carolina at Chapel Hill. The word *paideia* is Greek for general, unspecialized, human learning. The Latin synonym, with which most people are much more familiar, is *humanitas*.

Before constructing a proposal for the Paideia Program, Adler explored five prevalent errors in American education. Briefly they are as follows: (1) the thought that only some children are truly educable; (2) the thought that education ends after high school or, at the latest, after the college years; (3) the thought that teachers alone are the principle cause of student learning (i.e. the failure to recognize the activity of the student's mind as primary); (4) the thought that a didactic approach — an active programming teacher and a passive absorbing student — is the only really effective kind of teaching; (5) the error that schooling, whether basic or more advanced, is primarily intended as job preparation.

Adler is concerned about basic literacy and the accumulation of a relative amount of knowledge as such in the student's mind — but he is more interested in teaching familiarity with the great ideas in Western culture and especially in teaching the student the ability to manipulate those ideas, along with his own ideas, critically and comparatively in his head. He realizes the rich intertwining nature of all these areas of education. Simply put, however, his first priority is the encouragement, the teaching as far as possible, of methods of logical thought.

Adler's initial Paideia Proposal, and the Paideia Program which followed, lays out a three part structure which is intended to teach basic literacy, the accumulation of some necessary knowledge and the acquisition of thinking skills which the student can carry with him for the rest of his life, *continually* honing them and improving their cutting edge, as he/she *continues* the process of learning from cradle to the end of all flesh. It is an ambitious program but not terribly complicated. The greatest problem probably will be training (or retraining) teachers to be Socratic seminar leaders, gracious but demanding inquisitors capable of opening students' minds to pertinent questions which, it is finally hoped, will arise from their own thought processes rather than from the teacher's.

Another potential problem is initial implementation of the Program, once teachers have been adequately trained. This, as Adler points out, need not be done all at once. One solution is to begin the Program as a one-day-a-week exercise (the so-called Wednesday Revolution, although any day will do), until familiarity and the comfort quotient of all participants, students and teachers alike, rises to the level where the Program can become the daily norm.

Here in skeletonized form is how the Paideia Program would work when fully implemented:

The Paideia Program recognizes three kinds of teaching, and there is an inevitable overlapping which is necessary and desirable. These three kinds of teaching are (1) didactic instruction (e.g. lectures and responses, textbook instruction), (2) coaching (such as with exercises and supervised practice), and (3) maieutic or Socratic questioning (both teacher to student—directed and student to teacher and fellow student-directed).

The didactic instruction is usually appropriate to the lower grades. Its purpose is the acquisition of organized knowledge (including basic literacy). Its special areas, operations and activities would also include subject matter in Language Arts, Literature and the Fine arts; Mathematics and Natural Science; History, Geography and Social Studies.

The purpose of coaching as an active technique of teaching is to develop the intellectual skills, the skills of how to learn. It is a movement away from, a step or two beyond, the more didactic approach, though the latter, as we have seen, has its place. Coaching's areas, operations and activities would include reading, writing, speaking, listening, calculating, problem-solving, observing, measuring, estimating and, finally, exercising general critical judgment. There is an appreciable overlapping with the subject matter of the more didactic approach which is intentional. Now, however, the student is being asked progressively to think and do more and more for himself.

The purpose of the Socratic questioning-type of instruction is to progressively and increasingly enlarge the student's understanding of ideas and values. It prepares the student to be an effective thinker and questioner for the balance of his/her life, all the while having a basic understanding of Western (and worldwide) values and ideas to refer to when necessary. The areas, operations and activities it concerns itself with are all knowledge and areas generally and, specficically, with the discussion of books (but not textbooks) and works of art and involvement in artistic activities such as music, theater and the visual arts.

How long does such a program continue? "Each of the three...designates a kind of learning that must continue, in ascending difficulty, for the full thirteen years, that is, from kindergarten through grade twelve," says Adler. It is made clear that, although all three kinds of instruction accompany the student during the full 13 year period, the coaching and Socratic techniques begin to dominate instruction soon after the earliest school years. Adler also specifies, beyond this three-fold approach to teaching, twelve years of physical education, six years of manual training (but not vocational training) and two years of a very gradual introduction to the working world.

I have given, admittedly, a bare bones description of the Paideia Program and its objectives. One of the things which is so remarkable about it is that it is neither a rigid return to 19th century rote methods of instilling basic literacy nor is it a capitulation of the responsibilities of teaching which seems inherent in some of the wilder proposals for evermore "open" classrooms. If the door is opened far enough, there will be no educational institutions, no teachers, no students, which is what, it would appear, some of the deschoolers want. But that is asking for, at best, anarchy, at the worse, utter chaos, in addition to the great illiteracy problem which already threatens our culture. Just how far we are now from social anarchy is a disturbing question. What is most remarkable about Adler's program is that it offers the hope that we can recapture the lost literacy levels of an earlier time while recognizing that the most important contribution to society a teacher can make is to help young students learn better how to think. In a similar vein, the most important contribution a student can make to the welfare of society and to himself, in his formal education years and beyond, is learning how to think more logically, consistently and compassionately first, perhaps, with the help of instructors and later on his own.

I have only two suggestions in regard to the overall Program. I see no reason to limit the Socratic seminar discussions to ideas found only in, or stimulated by, the great books of the Western world, which is Adler's first inclination. Why not be more cosmopolitan in an age that demands an international kind of understanding. Good ideas are good ideas no matter where found or where from. Intercultural understanding has many potential benefits, not the least of which is a promise of a more peaceful world. We might have, for example, avoided the late Gulf War and even the Israeli-Palestinian situation, which has lingered like a deadly cloud over the Middle East for so long, if men could be persuaded by good logical thinking that more can be accomplished talking earnestly over a conference table than apart and at odds in all the various ways that men have contrived to separate themselves, and their interests, from others.

What of the question of the perpetually unruly student? The one who causes day by day disturbances that upset the learning process of others. One solution would be a special school in each school district where such students could be sent. They would be given the very same kinds of instruction from a curricula identical to the one at the school from which they had been removed. The only difference would be that the teachers at this kind of school would be a specially trained, superhardy lot who knew what to anticipate in such a situation, knew how to cope with the expected and the unexpected. This obviously requires a very special type of person with unique talents.

The kind of education the Paideia Program promises to deliver would seem to guarantee young children and teenagers their best chance at literacy and rudimentary training in effective thinking. Both these skills are a must in a culture such as ours in a world such as it is. Without the acquisition of each by all the nation's citizens, the movement toward a "kinder, gentler" America will be much more difficult. Likewise, until almost all people everywhere are afforded the opportunity to gain literacy and better thinking skills, and are willing to avail themselves of the opportunity, the movement toward an effective world government sensitive to the needs and aspirations of people everywhere on the face of the planet will be impeded. And it almost goes without saying that the successful march toward a New World Order, a New Age which is responsive to true cosmic laws, is dependent on the experience, including the formal educational experience, of the marchers. Ignorance breeds separation, misunderstanding, selfishness and incapacity, all of which the old world order, with which we are so familiar, has in abundance.

The cosmic quester, who is not satisfied with only basic literacy and who wishes to plumb the heights and depths of understanding and knowledge, whether it be planetary, solar or cosmic, wherever he or she may find it, soon realizes that formal education, as it is now available, falls far short of what is desired. This kind of individual soon discerns that most of what is taught today as gospel in the sciences and humanities will be considered rather quaint or downright false a century or less from now. The quester realizes this despite the remonstrances of teachers, professors, scientists and acquaintances who adamantly believe that they, or their colleagues, have discovered final truths good for all time. The quester soon observes that there is always present in all educational fields, including the sciences, a modishness, an acceptable dogma, that tends to sweep the day, not unlike the public fads for hoola hoops, fashions or popular songs. The quester must learn as quickly as possible to look beyond such limited and often prejudiced mental programming. He (she) must learn to question everything and to keep questioning until thoroughly satisfied that inquiry has adequately searched the heights and plumbed the depths before reaching final conclusions about anything. He (she) will probably find that becoming thoroughly satisfied about anything is difficult and that drawing final conclusions is dangerous, if for no other reason than that life, and further study, will often indicate that the "final conclusion" wasn't so final after all. Most likely the quester will learn, as a wise friend once warned me, that 80 percent or more of what he (she) has been taught by others, whether in a classroom or without, is inaccurate. He (she) may well find that much of what he has taught himself in the past, including his personal prejudices, is also inaccurate or fatally flawed. He will perceive that the main reason for this inaccuracy, a majority of the time, is inadequate inquiry.

It takes courage to begin the journey of the cosmic quester. It takes even more courage, once the journey has begun, to continue it. In the beginning the way seems excruciatingly lonely. After all, what kind of fool, he is tempted to ask himself, would cut himself away from so much which seems to solid and is so comforting? Why not just accept the acceptable, the politically correct, the scientifically admissible, the socially praiseworthy and let life go as it may? Maybe life would then be simpler, more pleasurable, less painful.

It doesn't take the true cosmic quester long, however, to cast off such temptation. All he (she) needs to do is look carefully about him. Life for those who are unawakened, for those who have, for various reasons, accepted the status quo in all things, is not simple, full of pleasure and painless. Accepting the acceptable has not led the world to a "kinder, gentler" state. In fact, as we all know, it has led us to the brink of the abyss, and it is just a question of which intermediate agent, most of which we have created with our own hands, will push us over the edge. Will it be worldwide pollution, world over-population, world war...?

The cosmic quester's mind is too active, his spirit too alive, to accept easy answers to difficult questions. His mind, growing ever wiser, will not let him so utterly fool himself. His heart, growing ever more tender, is too full of affection for his fellow human beings to allow him to adopt courses of action, be they personal or public, which are intrinsically based on false assumptions or false information. When he is convinced of the need for action — for example, recognizing the urgency of the need to begin a global clean up of our polluted air, land and seas — he is willing to take that action. He does not, nor should he, retreat into an ivory-towered mental and physical withdrawal from the real world and its problems.

As time goes by, the cosmic quester usually becomes less lonely. He learns how possible it is to love all men because he can foresee, if only dimly, what they will someday become in their greater perfection. He learns to sympathize with their problems. He learns true empathy. He comes gradually to a better understanding of human aspirations, even while recognizing that many of them are misplaced and self-defeating. He has become adept at loving mankind in the abstract, as he well knows, but strangely, almost marvelously, he finds, at the same time, that he is able to love individual beings with a non-passive intensity that he was not capable of before. As he walks, as he learns, he comes into contact gradually with others like himself. Some of his loneliness begins to dissipate, like an unwanted fever breaking and retreating from an unwilling patient. In such a troubled world, meeting like hearts along the way is always cause for health and joy.

CHAPTER TWELVE

# The Catastrophic Return of Biblical Wormwood and Evidence of Other Cyclical Earth Changes

The surface of the world to come is likely to be vastly changed if we are to believe Judeo-Christian prophecy as well as the prophecies of many other ancient and modern cultures. To the list of the foretellers of catastrophic change must be added the voice of many contemporary psychic men and women who are also convinced the world is due shortly for great geologic and meteorological events. There is also, as a matter of fact, some compelling hard scientific evidence that this world of ours may well have recently undergone a cycle of catastrophic geological change that nearly wiped out the civilizations of man at periodic internals for the last several (and probably longer) tens of thousands of years. It is only lately, because of new and improved methods of searching the earth's geologic past, that some of the more convincing evidence of this kind (such as ice core samples) has begun to be revealed.

There is, as one might suspect, a judicious need to consider this evidence impartially to establish whether or not it supports the proposition of a recent periodic cycle of earth changes. There is, what is more, an equally great or greater need, once this cycle is accepted as a reality, as I believe it will be one day soon, to consider this evidence in relation to the prophetic warnings of earth changes to come, such as, for example, the catastrophic appearance of Wormwood described in the book of Revelation. We all are interested in human destiny and the odds of human physical survival centuries into the future. Therefore, it is in our best interest to investigate whether or not there is a correlation between potential cyclical geologic changes in the earth's past and the appearance, or possible reappearance, of this cosmic body or, for that matter, any future force or body which might greatly alter earth's ecology.

This kind of investigation and the attendant speculation that goes with it, no matter how much it is needed, no matter how much the evidence warrants its pursuit, is, nevertheless, filled with problems. Academic and professional geologists, glaciologists, geophysicists, paleontologists, oceanographers, astronomers, astrophysicists, and a host of individuals who are members of related disciplines, do not take kindly to intrusions into their respective bailiwicks. As a rule, they tow the line of conventional interpretation as has been established as acceptable protocol within their field. This is safe. It protects careers. He who dares to contradict accepted dogma, or crosses over momentarily from his own bailiwick into another to make a pertinent observation, is often shunned or ostracized. A good example of this kind of treatment is offered in astronomer-astronaut-philosopher Brian O'Leary's recent work, *Inner and Outer Space*. O'Leary gives a revealing description of how painful peer pressure can be when an individual, such as himself, diverges from what is considered proper research and acceptable inquiry.

Scientists as a rule, having narrowly defined scientific methodology so that it excludes much phenomenology, seek refuge in that very methodology. As a group, they appear to be uninterested in expanding in any way its parameters. Each discipline has become highly specialized, as we all know. Glaciologists do not keep up much with astrophysics. Geologists are not much interested in astronomy. And so down the line. The right hand does not know what the left hand is doing. Or what it may have found. Comparative science, much like comparative literature, hardly exists. This is especially true in the United States.

The lack of comparative science brings our problem of earth cycles and their possible relationship to a potentially reappearing cosmic body, such as Wormwood, clearly into focus. Not only are the separate scientific disciplines often unaware of developments in other scientific fields, but the members of such disciplines would consider it scientific blasphemy — and there definitely is such a thing — to mention such a phenomenon as prophecy or the evidence of ancient literature in the same breath with the data from their own field, which may or may not, for that matter, be accurate. Or, to rephrase the problem in terms used by Brian O'Leary, the "outer space" experimenters, that is, the physical scientists, are not much interested in the exploration of "inner space." And this is true today even though we have increasing evidence that inner and outer space, like all things, are intimately related. An example would be the quantum physicist's realization that the experimenter, simply by his presence, acts upon and influences the results of some, if not all, subatomic particle experiments.

The proposition that the earth has undergone periodic cyclical catastrophic changes within the past several tens of thousands of years can be demonstrated, I believe, with some rather compelling evidence. The proposition that these cycles may have been caused by a cosmic object with a very long but relatively consistent orbital period, an object variously referred to as *Nibiru* ("planet of the crossing," by the Sumerians), Marduk (by the Babylonians), Wormwood (by John in Revelation) and Planet X (by some of our present-day astronomers), deserves some close attention. The Russians, it may be noted, theorized as long ago as the 60s that there may be not one but three planetary bodies existing in our solar system beyond Pluto. Aberrations in the orbital motion of Neptune and Uranus have convinced many of our own scientists that there is a strong likelihood that some kind of large body (possibly another planet or planets or even a brown or twin star) exists in solar space beyond Pluto and exerts strong gravitational attraction on the outermost known planets.

Therefore, we can say that if in fact the cycle we have spoken of exists, we may find that one of the most logical explanations for it is to deduce that it is caused by a foreign planetary-like body making regular, predictable appearances.

Why, then, haven't our men of science found the evidence for this cycle? Where is it hiding?

In *Extraterrestrials In Biblical Prophecy and the New Age Great Experiment*, I wrote a long chapter titled "Prophecies of Earth Changes During 'End time'" In that chapter I explored some of the ancient literary, folkloric and contemporary scientific evidence for a cyclical change last occurring in ca 1,600 B.C. and having occurred as well in ca 5,200 B.C., ca 8,800 B.C., ca 12,400 B.C., ca 16,000 B.C., ca 19,600 B.C. and, by logical extension, approximately every 3,600 years previously for a period of unknown time. My impetus for originally formulating such a hypothesis came from three directions. First, there was the often maligned work of Immanuel Velikovsky which demonstrated rather convincingly that there was massive evidence of both a literary and scientific nature that great catastrophic earth changes had wrecked the world sometime during the middle centuries of the second millennium B.C.* He had in fact settled more or less on the date 1,450 B.C. which I have, for evidential reasons, extended to 1,600 B.C.

The hypothesis itself that a 3,600 year cycle might be involved actually began to form after I familiarized myself with Sumerian and Babylonian traditions relating to a "planet of the crossing" (*Nibiru* or Marduk) while researching ancient texts (such as the *Enuma Elish*) and Judeo-Christian scriptures in a search for evidence of extraterrestrial involvement with early man and the possible influence of that involvement on the scriptures themselves. At the same time I became acquainted with the extraordinary Sumerian-Babylonian research of Zecharia Sitchin. Sitchin's premise, which seems to me a very

*Velikovsky's critics almost invariably attack out of total context lesser pieces of his overall theory, refusing to acknowledge the logic and evidence supporting the greater theory itself or the possibility of the validity of a very similar theory. Nit picking never addresses adequately the existence of the whole ball of cotton.

strong one backed by good logic as well as literary and natural evidence, is that the planetary body *Nibiru*/Marduk makes approximately a 3,600 year orbit of our sun. He speculates that it has made this orbit many times, and supports his speculation by referring to the abundant evidence hidden in Sumerian and Babylonian texts. He has not tried, however, to track these appearances to any great extent, to set likely dates for them, or to marshal geological evidence to support his contention that these appearances have, most probably, been going on for eons.

I then put together mentally Velikovsky's observation (based on evidence) that a great catastrophe had struck the world ca 1,450 B.C. (his date) and Sitchin's observations (also based on evidence) and my own hypothesis about the recurring passages of *Nibiru*/Marduk. What physical evidence, I reasoned, counting backward at intervals of 3,600 years, could be found for a periodic upheaval of the earth caused quite possibly by such influences as gravitational attraction and electromagnetic interplay between the earth and *Nibiru*, both of which we might expect if such large bodies came periodically into close contact?

The evidence I found was appreciable. But there is one appropriate qualification to make. The natural evidence is somewhat stronger for some dates when compared to others; strong for ca 8,800 B.C., ca 12,400 B.C., ca 16,000 B.C. and ca 19,600 B.C. and less strong but still impressive for ca 1,600 B.C. and ca 5,200 B.C. The evidence which is most impressive comes from recent ice core research done in Greenland and Antarctica, which I will address presently. But before proceding in that direction, it is necessary to clarify several issues.

Why is the evidence stronger for some dates than others? There are several reasons that immediately present themselves. One is related to our present scientific capacity to register (or fail to register) the evidence that is available and to correlate accurately what has been registered. Ice core sampling and testing is a new science. Its practitioners are working mightily to correlate the large amount of new information now being gathered from the cores about soluble and insoluble particles and from studying isotopic indications, such as $^{18}O$. They are also endeavoring as quickly as possible to develop an accurate time-scale suggested by the data being studied. All is not perfect and there are many miles to go. A few years ago much of the raw data now available did not exist, which partially explains why the cycle which I have proposed was not more easily spotted.

Another compelling explanation for why some dates appear to have more natural evidence associated with them than others is simply because there is more natural evidence in existence for these dates. This is most likely due to the fact that planet Earth's position relative to the sun's position and *Nibiru's* position on *Nibiru's* periodic approach is a crucial consideration. Sometimes the Earth, because of its position, has been more protected than at other times. Consequently, the effects caused by *Nibiru*, either immediate or longer term, have varied from passage to passage. Less severe effects cause less natural evidence. When the Earth is on the same side of the sun as *Nibiru*, as it passes by in its orbit, the changes are great; when the Earth is on the opposite side of the sun relative to *Nibiru* during *Nibiru's* orbital passage, the changes are probably somewhat feathered or lessened primarily, we might assume, because of less gravitational and electromagnetic influence. There are, obviously, passages when Earth and *Nibiru* will be in an intermediate state, somewhere between the two extremes as described above. In fact, most passages to one degree or another would fall into this category. During these times, the earth changes would probably not be as great as when Earth and *Nibiru* are head to head on the same side of the sun or as feathered as they would be when the body of the sun separates them.

Before proceeding to a detailed exposition of the ice core evidence for an approximate 3,600 year catastrophic earth cycle, it would seem that here is as good a place as any, and more appropriate than most, to address the criticism that has been directed against the possibility of a *Nibiru's* existence; also

172

against the possibility of *Nibiru* having a retrograde (clockwise) orbit (as originally suggested by Sitchin).* Some astronomers and astrophysicists don't like the idea of a *Nibiru*-like body at all. It muddies the waters of too much traditional thinking. John White summed up their objections in *Pole Shift* a few years ago. White is in agreement with the anti-*Nibiru* thinkers, and his opinions seem strongly influenced by those of C. Leroy Ellenberger. Ellenberger has made part of a career out of attacking the arch villain Velikovsky and anything he preceives as being remotely Velikovskian.* Some of his statements, however, are patently false, such as his assertion that Sitchin has claimed that the last passage of *Nibiru* was around 200 B.C. Ellenberger reasons that since there is no evidence of an earth calamity at that time, Sitchin's theory is false. But Sitchin has claimed no such thing. White, Ellenberger and other critics of the extraterrestrial body hypothesis are too quick and too willing to discard the concept of *Nibiru's* existence. Such bodies, they argue, do not jive with orthodox Newtonian physics and our present understanding of celestial mechanics. Or so they think.

Actually, many astronomers, astrophysicists and scientists of related disciplines aren't at all convinced that a 10th planet (which would be the 12th planet for the Sumerians and Babylonians because, it appears, they also counted the sun and Earth's moon as planets) may not exist.** They refer to the possibility as Planet X. Robert S. Harrington of the Naval Observatory, Thomas Van Flandern, also of the Naval Observatory, astronomer Gerald Hawkins and Tom Chester of the Jet Propulsion Laboratory are just a few of the many scientists who do not rule out the possibility of such an object. Van Flan-

---

*The orbits of all planets in our solar system that we know of are counterclockwise. Some planetary moons, however, as well as some comets move in a retrograde orbit.

**Ironically, he was once a staunch Velikovsky supporter.
***The Sumerians and Babylonians seem to have known for a fact, perhaps through extraterrestrial visitor sources, that there were, counting the sun and moon as planets, four more planets beyond Saturn, making a total (by their accounting method) of 12. The 12th was *Nibiru*, "planet of the crossing."

dern has headed a theoretical study of just such a possibility.

Many of these same scientists are not at all convinced that such a planet as *Nibiru* violates Newtonian physics and our present understanding of celestial mechanics, however imperfect that may be, even though that same traditional physics has an impossible time explaining, for instance, why the light of our sun does not shine in the darkness of space and does not give off heat until the sun's rays, or its radiation, reaches our atmosphere. It now appears, it almost goes without saying, that the "new" physics, particularly quantum physics, is going to radically change our ideas about the physical relationships between cosmic bodies. How much of the old Newtonian physics will survive is questionable.

That *Nibiru*/Marduk quite likely orbits in a clockwise direction, unlike the other planets we know about, does not, in spite of Ellenberger's misgivings, contradict Newtonian physics and contemporary celestial mechanics. A clockwise orbit would explain why certain comets also follow clockwise or retrograde orbits—especially if we understand that it was *Nibiru's* close passage to ancient Tiamat, and *Nibiru's* satellites striking Tiamat during one of those close passages, which destroyed Tiamat itself while creating from its debris the asteroid belt between Mars and Jupiter and, at the same time, sending some chunks flying off into space, because of impact, which became the retrograde comets.* Also we must recall that there exist moons in our solar system which have retrograde orbits similar to that proposed for *Nibiru*/Marduk. Recent space probes have discovered several. Ellenberger is not impressed by the possible effects such a body (his estimate being the size of 5 earth bodies) might have on the earth's stability. He maintains that at best the tidal effect of Marduk on Earth would be "about one millionth the mean tidal effect of the Moon on Earth." There is, however, no particular reason to ascribe a 5 x size to *Nibiru*/Marduk. It may, if it exists, be much

---

*Tiamat is the Babylonian name for the erstwhile body that, upon being shattered, left us with the asteroid belt between Mars and Jupiter and, quite possibly, some retrograde comets.

larger — or smaller. He also does not consider the effects of possible electromagnetic exchanges between Earth and the intruder, something our science still knows very little about. Most importantly, he does not consider what effects might occur to the system of balance that exists at any given moment between the inner planets and the sun. *Nibiru*/Marduk, if we are to believe ancient sources and natural geologic evidence, is a supreme destabilizer, particularly as it draws close to the inner planets. Having a wild card, and a large one at that, introduced into our present understanding of celestial mechanics can precipitate unforeseen consequences — just the sort of thing that so upsets traditionalists. This celestial wild card would seem to play itself so infrequently that human civilization, or the survivors of it after a passage, may have only a dim memory of what befell it. This is unfortunate for both man and his science. Such a calamity may seem to these same survivors to have been an extraordinary, but singular, occurrence seemingly unrelated to former events which, if they happened, happened so long ago that they, too, have been forgotten or almost forgotten and remembered only dimly as terrifying, unrelated catastrophes.

What is, specifically, the evidence supporting a cyclical return of *Nibiru*/Marduk to which I have previously alluded and to which I promised earlier to return?

In *Extraterrestrials in Biblical Prophecy and the New Age Great Experiment*, I began to explore the evidence which indicates such a cycle. I am presently continuing that exploration and plan to present all of it soon, including evidence from ocean sediments, ocean level studies, studies of foraminifera die offs, tree ring samples, varves and, as best I can, the "record of the rocks" of traditional geology, in a work titled *The Catastrophic Return of Biblical Wormwood: An Ancient Cycle of Destruction.* Here now I will present some of the most compelling evidence I have found. It comes, as I previously indicated, from the relatively new science of glaciology. Some of the techniques recently invented by glaciologists to evaluate and date deep ice cores, which contain a readable record dating back at least 100,000 years, promise a revolution in our understanding of earth's geologic history. They also promise quietly, as a dividend of unequaled value, to give us a much greater understanding of *Homo sapiens'* development, including a look at some of the catastrophes which befell him.

Only three ice cores have been drilled since 1966 which completely penetrate to bedrock the Greenland and Antarctic ice sheets. These are the Camp Century (1480m) and Dye 3 (2037m) ice cores from the Greenland cap and the core drilled at Byrd Station, Antarctica. The Camp Century core reaches back more than 100,000 years. Other cores have been taken from intermediate depths (less than 10 of them) and from shallow depths (about 2 dozen), including the Dome C (1000m), Vostok (2083m) and the Mizuho Station (700m) cores from Antarctica. All these cores offer us a window to the past because the soluble and insoluble particles found among the ice crystals, as well as the presence in varying quantities of the stable isotope $^{18}0$, now allow glaciologists to date, albeit somewhat imperfectly, the layers and to discover in large measure what was probably happening on the surface of the earth.

What do the Greenland cores indicate as to a possible cyclical reappearance of a *Nibiru*-like disruptive phenomenon? It would seem a great deal. Why haven't scientists recognized the cycle? It would appear they have not been looking for it.

A cycle so short has not, up to now, been seriously considered as a real possibility. Although there is natural evidence supporting such a hypothesis, it can and has been explained in the past as having been caused by various long-term uniformitarian natural processes and by at times localized one-time-only geologically traumatic events (earthquakes, volcanicity, etc.). These explanations have satisfied almost everyone. Nothing as startling in nature as a *Nibiru* passage has been seriously considered for the Holocene period (roughly the last 10,000 years) or for a longer period encompassing, let us say, the last 100,000 years. Velikovsky and his supporters, like Donald W. Patten, although recognizing that a serious worldwide natural catastrophe occurred ca 1,450 B.C. or thereabouts (and that several somewhat less severe ones, possibly associated with an errant Mars, had occurred in the 8th and the 7th centuries B.C.), failed to recognize this catastrophe as part of a long-term cycle and ascribed the cause of it to a symptom (a Venus out of orbit) rather than to the real cause — a passage of *Nibiru*. Such thinking, even though closer to the truth than almost anyone else had heretofore supposed, so outraged orthodox science that it refused to do any serious follow-up thinking.

And now we have the ice core data. It will, as time passes, wrench and wrack many time-honored earth-science theories. It will force many conservative, orthodox astronomers to reconsider what is possible and what is probable. And there is likely to be much cursing and much pain and a great deal of ill will, as is usually the case when the pseudo-sacred, which has been held in high esteem for so long, is dethroned and replaced with a truth which is a more legitimate contender.

If we take ca 1,600 B.C. as the last appearance of the *Nibiru*/Marduk cosmic object, we find corroborating evidence in the Dye 3 Greenland ice core that a major geologic event(s), seemingly of volcanic origin or having volcanicity associated with it, occurred on earth in ca 1,645 B.C. The evidence appears in the ice core as acid fallout $(H+)$.* This concentration of acid fallout strongly correlates with the variation in $^{18}O$ seen for that year in comparison to the years immediately preceding and succeeding it. It is a pronounced signal hard to miss.

In an article titled "The Minoan eruption of Santorini in Greece dated to 1645 B.C." which appeared in *Nature*, August, 1987, C.U. Hammer and H.B. Clausen, both of the Geophysical

*High levels of $H^+$ indicate elevated levels of acid fallout, as do high levels of $SO_4^-$(sulfuric acid). High levels of $SO_4^-$ and $H^+$ ions suggest earth changes of magnitude are taking place either regionally or worldwide, especially volcanicity which could be triggered by the passage of a *Nibiru*-like body. Under certain circumstances, elevated levels of Cl- (chlorides) and Cl-/Na+$_m$ (chloride salts) can accompany volcanicity. Large, rapid changes in the $^{18}O$ isotope readings also indicate earth changes of magnitude. These also could be triggered by a *Nibiru*-like passage.

Institute, University of Copenhagen, along with W.L. Friedrich, Geological Institute, Aarhus University and H. Tauber, Radiocarbon Dating Laboratory, National Museum (Copenhagen), speculate that a 1,645 B.C. event may have been the cause for the destruction of Santorini (Thera) and other Bronze Age Minoan settlements. It is Hammer who developed the ECM (electrical conductivity method) for determining the acidity of solid ice. And it is Hammer, Clausen, Dansgaard and other members of the Geophysical Institute and its Isotope Laboratory at the University of Copenhagen who have perfected the method of $^{18}O$ analysis of ice cores.

There is no question that the Santorini event happened. The acid signal is very strong. The $^{18}O$ signal likewise. The only question is exact dating, because as of yet, neither the ECM or $^{18}O$ analysis used separately or in conjunction are infallible, incontestable dating procedures. They can tell you what is there, in what quantity, but not infallibly when it got there. These techniques are, however, several among many, such as $C^{14}$ dating and tree ring analysis, which are making it possible for scientists to zero in closer and closer to accurate dating of geological-geophysical events of the more recent past. The margin of error factor, nevertheless, that is inherent with $C^{14}$ dating has been a stumbling block in a ratio almost proportionate to the increasing age of the carbon-based specimens under consideration. Carbon based results from very ancient samples are too flawed to be relied upon to date the very distant past. Also, $C^{14}$ dating is not at all possible with noncarbon-based ice cores. Using other radioactive isotopes, when practicable, offers the best future hope for accurate dating of very ancient geologic specimens. At present, acidity measurement and $^{18}O$ profiles of core samples offer the best possibilities for dating Antarctic ice, and $^{18}O$ profiles for dating ice cores of the Arctic region, because Arctic ice older than the Holocene (i.e. 10,000 years old or older) is alcalic.

In an earlier article ["Greenland ice sheet evidence of post-glacial volcanism and its climatic impact," *Nature* 288 (November, 1980), pp. 230-235] Hammer and Clausen, along with Dansgaard, presented evidence from the Camp Century ice core indicating a pronounced geologic event that in fact correlates with the Dye 3 Santorini evidence. They note the "Unambiguous volcanic signals in the Camp Century core increments spanning...1300-1500 B.C." produced by acid fallout. The more recent article of 1987 reconsiders, as can be seen, the 1300-1500 B.C. date for the Santorini/Thera event and adjusts it to 1,645 B.C., not only because of the new Dye 3 data but because of cross-correlation with 14 artifact samples that were found at Akrotiri on Santorini and $C^{14}$ dated.

Several considerations now become very important. Was the ice core data registering, as Hammer and his colleagues have implied, only a large regional event? The ice core data tell us it was a rather large event. Might not it have been much greater than supposed by some? Claude Shaeffer's lifelong archaeological investigations in many parts of the Mediteranean and Middle East led him to conclude that the natural catastrophe which occurred at the end of the Middle Kingdom in Egypt, causing it to fall, devastated by earthquake and fire almost every populated place in Crete, Cyprus, the Caucasus, Persia, Syria, Palestine and Asia Minor generally.* That's some "local" event. Logic, and the evidence available, should tell us that the Santorini event and the event spoken of by Shaeffer are one and the same. We might add that the old accepted date for the fall of the Middle Kingdom was approximately 1,580 B.C. — very close to the 1,645 B.C. date offered by Hammer and colleagues for the Santorini event. This may also have been the time, as I have indicated in previous work, when the Greater Exodus of the Hebrews out of Egypt occurred and also the time of the Hyksos invasion of Egypt.

Another consideration we need to become aware of is the tendency of some scientists, especially the anti-Velikovskian critics, to try to explain away all evidence of great earth changes having occurred about his time. Velikovsky's date for

---

*See Claude Shaeffer, *Stratigraphic Comparée et Chronologie de l'Asie Occidentale* (London, Oxford UP), 1948.

these changes was, as I have indicated, the middle of the 15th century B.C. The ice core samples now indicate that the changes happened closer to 1,600 B.C., which I have suggested in *Extraterrestrials in Biblical Prophecy*...as the approximate date for the last *Nibiru* fly-by. The ice core data in no way rules out a larger scenario than has been written for the Santorini/Thera vicinity alone. It does establish that earth changes of some force *did occur* around 1,600 B.C. Velikovsky was correct about the reality of the phenomena happening. And, considering the difficulty of precise dating of both phenomena and artifacts that are several thousand years old, an error of one or two hundred years is not great. Until we have more precise dating techniques, we will have to live with such errors.

Relatively accurate data can't be washed away or hid in a closet because it makes some critics foam at the mouth. This applies to Velikovsky's date or anyone else's. Velikovsky's sin was offering nonconventional ideas during a very conventional period of American history.* Whatever Velikovsky's final contribution to science will be, will depend greatly on how accurate time demonstrates his ideas and data to be. It may turn out, as I suggest, that his primary contribution will be his recognition that extraterrestrial objects have in the past played havoc with earth's geology. It may also turn out, as I also suspect, that the main player in this solar drama is *Nibiru*, of which he had no suspicion, and not an errant and misbehaving Venus and Mars as he had come to believe. That Venus and Mars have been destabilized by some cosmic force(s) in the past, probably *Nibiru*, seems now more and more likely.

The Dye 3 and Camp Century data is supported by core samples taken from the drilling at Mizuho Station Antarctica. Yoshiyuki Fujii and Okitsugu Watanabe, in "Microparticle Concentration And Electrical Conductivity Of A 700 m Ice Core from Mizuho Station Antarctica" [*Annals of Glaciology* (10,1988), pp. 38-42], demonstrate that "large-scale environmental changes possibly occurred in the Southern Hemisphere

*The cynic would say all periods are conventional. I would tend to agree. Some periods, however, are more conventionally inclined than others.

180

in the middle of the Holocene," that is, within the last 10,000 years. Their depth profiles of "microparticle concentration, electrical conductivity and $^{18}0$ with age, according to Nye's time-scale" indicate a spike in readings for microparticles, electrical conductivity and $^{18}0$ at ca 1,600 B.C. Forces on the earth's surface were, for some reason, propelling unusually high concentrations of microparticles and acid fallout into the annual snowfall layers. The $^{18}0$ reading would suggest a period of colder climate.

What is particularly interesting is that this disturbance, with varying degrees of intensity, may have been going on for some time but reaches a peak, as if given a large shove, ca 1,600 B.C.

If we now move backward in time another 3,600 years, or approximately the theoretical time of *the last appearance of Nibiru preceding ca 1,600 B.C.*, and consult Fujii's and Watanabe's depth profile for evidence of a passage at ca 5,200 B.C., we will not be disappointed. The evidence appears but it is not as startling as that for ca 1,600 B.C., not as strong. As I have said before, not all passages of *Nibiru* are likely to cause the same magnitude of earth changes. Those changes, whatever they may be during a particular passage, will depend on the position of earth relative to the sun and *Nibiru* as *Nibiru* approaches closer and closer to the sun and passes through the asteroid belt. The effects of the ca 5,200 B.C. passage, because they were not as great as the effects of some passages, have gone somewhat unnoticed. You might say it is the partial exception which proves the rule-cycle. You might also say that, unfortunately, the lesser evidence for the ca 5,200 B.C. passage has made the cycle harder to recognize, especially since almost no one was busying themselves looking for such a short-term cycle in the first place.

But the effects of the ca 5,200 B.C. passage did register. The microparticle concentration and electrical conductivity profile are both raised in the Mizuho Station data when dated to ca 5,200 B.C., although the $^{18}0$ profile is about normal. There is even a "visible volcanic dirt band" at 500.7 meters. This may represent the same event(s) that deposited an ash band at the Byrd Station core at 799 meters in depth. What is fascinating, and what drew Fujii's and Wanatabe's attention, is that the time internal represented by core samples taken between 400 meters and 240 meters, which is dated by them at approximately 4000 to 1000 B.C., appears to have been a time of relatively high microparticle and acid fallout, a time period when the $^{18}$0 profile suggests that the climate was getting colder and may have stayed colder, at least in the Antarctic area, until A.D. times. A careful glance at these profiles reveals that Fujii and Wanatabe could just as well extend their prediction/conclusion to the 500.7 meter level, where the "volcanic dirt band" exists, which happens to be the ca 5,200 B.C. date—which is where the extended period of elevated readings really appears to have started. If this is, indeed, the case, we have potentially a good example of delayed effects caused by a *Nibiru* passage. The immediate effects, though observable, do not always compare in total magnitude to the long-term aftereffects caused by the stress of a passage. Here is another reason why the cycle has gone unnoticed. The long-term aftereffects in some cases partially veil the primary event by the volume of their delayed evidence—which is much greater, for instance, than the volume or amount of evidence available for the time *immediately* following the ca 5,200 B.C. event—and sometimes by the spectacular violence of some of these delayed effects, which cause profiles to register spikes of evidence greater than those registered for the primary event itself.

We might sum up the Mizuho Station ice core data by saying that *Nibiru* is capable of setting off prolonged periods of earth changes that would, many of them, be above the levels of ordinary uniformitarian geologic change. These changes, which are usually immediate and vast and glaringly noticeable during and immediately after a given passage, sometimes show up, such as those after the ca 5,200 B.C., more gradually. The ca 5,200 B.C. passage, if it had had more effects which had been more immediately noticeable, might have led to the discovery of an approximate 3,600 year cycle—if, and it is a big if, anyone had been looking for a recent periodic cycle of this nature.

According to the *Nature* article of 20 November, 1980, and demonstrated there by a table and graph, there is conclusive evidence of high acidity signals ($H^+$) in the Camp Century ice core which has been tentatively dated by Hammer, Clausen and Dansgaard at 5,470 $\pm$ 120 B.C. This, as noted, by them, may agree with the proposed Hekla eruption H5, radiocarbon dated to 5,450 $\pm$ 190 B.C. (Tauber, 1960) and also possibly with the largest Thjorsa lava flow, which has been dated by Thorarinsson to approximately 5,500 B.C. All this may be relatively accurate, although it is wrong to assume, I believe, that other earth changes, including volcanicity in other parts of the world, might not have been taking place at about the same time and contributed appreciably to the high $H^+$ level at the Camp Century site. What is established by this particular acidity record is that activity was taking place and, acknowledging the problems of accurate dating, fits the parameters for a ca 5,200 B.C. *Nibiru* passage. The extant geological evidence is of the kind we should expect to exist and to show up someplace in the geologic (here the glacial) record if such a passage did occur.

Further evidence of a ca 5,200 B.C. event or series of events comes once again from the opposite hemisphere. Michel R. Legrand and Robert J. Delmas, both of the *Laboratoire de Glaciologie et Geophysique de l'Environment*, offer some provacative and startling support for a *Nibiru* cycle of ca 3,600 years. In the article "Soluble Impurities In Four Antarctic Ice Cores Over The Last 30,000 Years" [*Annals of Glaciology* (10, 1988, pp. 116-120] they graph the $^{18}O$ variations and the ionic componets ($Na^+$, $NH_4^+$, $Ca^{2+}$, $H^+$, $Cl^-$, $NO_3^-$ and $SO_4^-$) found in ice from the Dome C core, Antarctica. The time-scale for each ionic component level as well as the $^{18}O$ reading stretches beyond 30,000 years B.P. If we convert B.P. to B.C. and look for a cycle of approximately 3,600 years amid their data, especially a cycle that correlates closely to passages of our theoretical *Nibiru* which might have occurred in ca 5,200 B.C., ca 8,800

B.C., ca 12,400 B.C., ca 16,000 B.C., ca 19,600 B.C. and so forth, *we find almost unmistakable confirmation that such a cycle exists.*

The Legrand and Delmas graph speaks for itself. If we superimpose solid vertical lines upon the original, it can clearly be seen that these vertical lines will intersect the tips, or very close to the tips, of the spikes made by many of the ion constituents of the core ice during the periods ca 5,200 B.C. and ca 8,800 B.C. It is not surprising that the vertical dashed lines given by the authors to define (in two instances) the LGM (Last Glacial Maximum) stages and also (in one instance) to define the beginning of the Holocene period are very close to my solid vertical lines for three proposed dates for *Nibiru* passages. These were times of great geologic stress. But why? The 3,600 year cycle hypothesis/theory becomes very logically compelling. The data seem to support it, although I believe my solid demarcating lines may be a little closer in time to the inciting event(s) than Legrand's and Delmas' dashed lines when it comes to demarcating transition-moments/passage-events. Whatever the case, we are in essential agreement as to these transition-moments.

It would appear from the Legrand/Delmas data that cyclic periods of ca 3,600 years can be extended onward, as one might expect if the periodic cycle does in fact exist. The chronology used by the authors was after Lorius and others (1979) and suffers slightly from the dating inaccuracies of all attempts so far to date the geologic past. My dates (after conversion from B.P. to B.C.) differ by several hundred years from the authors'; for example, approximately 300 years at the line representing the ca 5,200 B.C. date; approximately 600-700 years at the ca 12,400 B.C. marker. *These are not great differences*, given our chronological knowledge, or lack of such, of the earth at this time. Other time-scales in use, if applied to the ice core data generally, would vary in proportion to their own peculiar nature.

The proposed ca 1,600 B.C. event(s) is noted by slight rises in the ions $Na^+$, $Cl^-$, $Cl^-/Na_m^+$, $NO_3^-$ and $NH_4^+$. There does not appear to have been much volcanicity registered at this time in the Southern Hemisphere, otherwise we would expect more sulfuric acid indications which would show up as $SO_4^-$ and $H^+$ indications. The Santorini/Thera event does not seem to have had the effect here that it did in the ice core samples from Greenland.

The evidence for a proposed ca 5,200 B.C. event(s) is strong in the Dome C core. There is an elevation in $Na^+$ (sea salt sodium), $SO_4^-$, $H^+$ and what appears as a delayed deposit of $Cl^-$, and $Cl^-/Na_m^+$. The $SO_4^-$ and $H^+$ ions suggest volcanicity, as would the $Cl^-$ and $Cl^-/Na_m^+$ under certain conditions.

The proposed ca 8,800 B.C. event(s) is well marked, the best so far. I have indicated in previous work that if there was universal flooding (a Deluge), it quite likely occurred at about this time. The $^{18}O$ isotope variation is noticeable, as is the rise in sea-salt sodium ($Na^+$), elevated levels of $Cl^-$ and $Cl^-/Na_m^+$. The extreme spike in the $SO_4^-$ and $H^+$ readings suggests widespread volcanicity, including the high $NO_3^-$ count and the slight rise in $NH_4^+$. It is appropriate to conjecture that great earth changes are happening at this time.

If ca 8,800 B.C. is well marked, the proposed event(s) for ca 12,400 B.C. is even more so. This is the time generally accepted for the end of the Wisconsin Ice Age. The data suggests that is a fair evaluation. But what caused such a change? The authors' graph demonstrates how relatively quick and vast the change was — and a passage of *Nibiru* would explain so well the trigger mechanism. The great isotope $^{18}O$ variation is evident. We have a peaking in $Na^+$ deposits as well as very pronounced spikes in $Ca^{++}$ (calcium), $SO_4^-$, and $H^+$ in addition to a slightly delayed deposit of $NO_3^-$. The $SO_4^-$ and $H^+$ readings again suggest a possible period of increased volcanicity which would be one predictable effect of a close passage of a *Nibiru*-like object precipitating stresses on the earth's crust and core.

Evidence for a passage of *Nibiru* is also very strongly indicated at ca 16,000 B.C. There are elevated levels of the ions $Na^+$, $Cl^-$, Aluminum, $Ca^{++}$, $SO_4^-$, and $H^+$, $NO_3^-$ and $NH_4^+$. The $^{18}O$ variance stands out, as we might expect.

Evidence indicating a passage at ca 19,600 B.C. is likewise impressive. We find elevated levels of $Na^+$, $Cl^-$, Aluminum, $Ca^{++}$, $SO_4^{--}$ and $H^+$. It is sometimes said that the land surface turmoil of the Ice Age is responsible for these elevated readings. But what caused the turmoil? To ascribe it to cold temperatures and their effects is not convincing. What caused the cold temperatures? And why especially the spikes in the deposit levels of these ions *at predictable intervals*? These are questions to which earth scientists must now address themselves anew — particularly to the most latter question. If predictability is indicated, it deserves immediate attention.

The date of Fujii and Watanabe from the Mizuho Station core, which we have already mentioned, also confirms the Legrand and Delmas data as to an event(s) ca 8,800 B.C. At approximately 675 meters, the Mizuho Station core records elevated particle readings and raised electrical conductivity. A direct correlation between the time-scale used by Fujii and Watanabe (Nye's scale) and my proposed time-scale is missed by approximately 500 years — not, under the circumstances, a very appreciable difference.

The earth changes which are recorded at intervals in the Antarctic ice cores, and which correspond to the proposed 3,600 year cycle, are also found extending backward in time in the data from the Greenland ice cores. We have already presented some of it correlating to events ca 1,600 B.C. and ca 5,200 B.C. The problem as of now with dating the Greenland material is that the cores from there become increasingly alcalic as we move backward in time from the beginning of the Holocene period. It might be wise to let the data itself lead us and conclude that the last glacial age, the Wisconsin, more or less ended with the startling earth changes represented at ca 12,400 B.C. which, as we have indicated, corresponds to a *Nibiru* passage. Be it as it may, the alcalic character of the ice cores before ca 8,800 B.C. neutralizes the acid content present making the cores, unlike the Antarctic ones, which have maintained their acidity, unresponsive to electrical conductivity methods of analysis. The Holocene Greenland cores are not, however, alcalic in nature. This makes it possible to compare $^{18}O$ variances during this period with acidity readings, thereby gaining the advantage of two diagnostic tools instead of one in the search for more accurate dating and understanding. This comparison method works quite well, as we noted earlier, with all the Antarctic cores.

The members of the Geophysical Isotope Laboratory of the University of Copenhagen, who have been in the forefront of dating the Greenland cores, have had to rely to a great extent upon $^{18}O$ readings to date the pre-Holocene Greenland cores, using when possible other cross-referencing aids such as comparisons with deep-sea core time-scales which in themselves reflect foraminifera variations called Emiliani stages. These stages are, in turn, caused by changing earth and ocean conditions. The $^{18}O$ variations found in the Dye 3 and Camp Century cores have been graphed, in the Dye 3 case to bedrock. The Camp Century readings have been graphed to just above bedrock. The overall time-scale represented by these readings covers the present moment to over 100,000 years B.C. The existence of such a continuum of samples would suggest that there has been *no major pole shift* within that period of time, although there may have been considerable minor shifting. In other words, nothing during that rather long interval of time has caused the Greenland ice cap to melt substantially. The area has remained a rather chilly world unto itself.

In "A New Greenland Deep Ice Core" [*Science* 218 (December, 1982), pp. 1273-1277], W. Dansgaard, H.B. Clausen, N. Undestrup, C.U. Hammer and colleagues provided a vivid graph of the $^{18}O$ variations found from the present to + 100,000 B.C. in both the Dye 3 and Camp Century cores. They have also attempted to cross-date the cores with each other, which is possible because the signals given off in one core reflect generally quite similar signals given off in the other.

What do the $^{18}O$ readings of Dye 3 ice and Camp Century ice reveal about the existence of a 3,600 year cycle? A great deal. They seem to confirm it. Major $^{18}O$ variations are found at the approximate depths we would expect them to be found if the theory of such a cycle is to be reflected in reality. There is usually a dramatic shift in readings, lasting until the next major shift. The shift is either to substantially higher or lower reading, signifying large changes in the earth's weather and the deposit, or lack of deposit, of fresh water by various means, most likely snowfall. Whether the shift is upward — which might signify a period of slightly warmer temperatures worldwide, or downward — which might suggest a period of colder global tempratures — is really not the crucial question here. What is important is that the shifts occurred. And they occurred at what would appear to be rather regular intervals approximating an interstitial period between major shifts of 3,600 years duration. The scientific time-scales constructed so far are not perfect, as we have already indicated. In fact, they are far from being totally acceptable or close to what is desirable. This is recognized by almost everyone. The present errors that exist in the time-scales due to interpretation of the $^{18}O$ readings and the errors which exist in non-ice core time-scales, which have been compared and sometimes correlated with the $^{18}O$ ice time-scales, have caused the researchers who have made them, including glaciologists, to fail to recognize up to this point the cycle with which they have been dealing. Their intentions have been good. Their science has been good science. When it becomes a little better, which will probably be very soon, the skewing in the time-scales will be corrected and the cycle will then probably become all the more evident.

What specifically do the Dye 3 and Camp Century $^{18}O$ readings tell us? Dye 3 indicates appreciable earth changes at a depth of 1227.5 meters. This has been dated by Hammer, Clausen et al at 1,645 B.C. and corresponds with a similar signal in the Camp Century core. The Dye 3 core indicates a revealing $^{18}O$ variation at approximately 270 meters from bedrock level. (Measurements will now be given as meters from bedrock, as indicated by the authors.) This variation correlates with the Camp Century core and registers the *Nibiru* passage ca 5,200 B.C. The Dye 3 core reflects a large variation at approximately the 250 meter level. This also is reflected in the Camp Century core and indicates a destabilization at ca 8,800 B.C. There is also a large $^{18}O$ variance beginning at approximately the 225 meter level in the Dye 3 core matched by a similar variance in the Camp Century core at the same corresponding level. This indicates a passage ca 12,400 B.C. Another large variance in $^{18}O$ appears at approximately the 215 meter level with a correspondence found in the Camp Century record which equates with a ca 16,000 B.C. passage; yet another large variance in Dye 3 readings at approximately the 205 meter level, with correspondence in the Camp Century core, which equates with a ca 19,600 B.C. *Nibiru* passage. The correspondence in $^{18}O$ variations, as well as the eye-opening cyclicality of many of the major variations or variances, continues onward and downward in the ice core record of the Wisconsin Ice Age. Just how long the pattern is discernible is conjectual, as we might expect. We will, however, stop our inquiry at this point.

Why is it that others haven't spotted this cycle, including the isotope ice core researchers whose evidence for such a cycle is the strongest in the sciences? We have already suggested some of the reasons. It isn't that they are blind—or that researchers in other disciplines are incompetent. Primarily it is a problem of mind-set. We simply have not been educated to believe that such a rapidly recurring cycle could exist. Out of belief, out of mind. It is also a question of adjusting time-scales so that they more accurately reflect data and true time-progression. When that is accomplished, more will become evident more quickly. And, finally, there is a peculiar psychological problem involved in such researching. If earth has been to one degree or another periodically bent, busted and bruised by a series of cyclical catastrophes, it is not a pleasant thought. The mind often avoids such thinking. What is not pleasant, what no one suspects as true, what has had (seemingly) little evidence (up to now) to support it—is easily put out of mind, dismissed. Out of mind, out of sight.

But here is a stunner of which we had all better take cognizance. If *Nibiru* exists, if *Nibiru*'s recurring passages are a fact, if the last passage occurred in ca 1,600 B.C. as would seem to be indicated by geologic evidence, especially ice core data—then we are due for a passage sometime soon. Very shortly. It would be much preferable to be forewarned and at least partially prepared, than to be caught unsuspecting and off guard, as mankind has been, it would appear from ancient literary evidence, untold times before.

# CHAPTER THIRTEEN

# Apocalypse Now?

People have been prophesying the end of the world for at least as long as historical man has been walking the earth, and probably a lot longer than that. The idea that a doomsday is at hand, or has recently passed, leaving a small band of human survivors to struggle for subsistence, is understandable, especially after we have studied the geologic record and come to realize just how often the earth has undergone localized and even global catastrophes. Most cultures have predictions, stories or tales telling of the end of the world, the end of the last human cycle, the end of the cosmos.... They are almost as common as creation tales. Does this mean, then, that we should discount them? Or relegate them to the mere fancy of heretofore savage peoples? Specifically, what are we today to think of the prophecies of doom and "end time" found in the Old Testament, in the books of Jeremiah, Isaiah, Daniel, Ezekiel and Zechariah and in the New Testament gospels, including the Book of Revelation?

It has been observed by some rather wise men that prophecy and the prophet serve a great societal function, whether or not a particular prophecy or a specific prophet turns out in the course of time to be accurate. In this I would agree wholeheartedly. The rationale for such thinking goes as follows. The prophet is a critic of his time. He listens to his inner voice or to the "gods," observes the human course of events and the greater natural course of events. He recognizes a disharmony.

191

Perhaps men are not living according to cultural tradition or proper religious tenets of behavior. He, as seer and messenger, is more in tune with cosmic law and cosmic harmony. He feels compelled to publicize what he knows in his heart is the truth, perhaps what he has been told by otherworldly godly agencies is the truth. He foresees (or is made to foresee) the consequences that will follow if his people (or all humankind) persist in pursuing the path they have chosen. He predicts doom, calamity, destruction *unless* the populace withdraws from the negative course it has set for itself. *Unless* it reverses itself. In other words, the prophecy need not come true, need not have to come true if the cause and effect sequence which set it in motion is broken.

In the particular case of prophecies of natural disasters (including those caused by man's interference with natural law), the gods (or God), intuition, astrology, astronomy and natural signs may all contribute to the prophet's (whether he is ancient or modern) prediction of violent earth changes to come. If his (her) prediction(s) comes to pass, he will probably be honored if he is so lucky as to survive the event. If his prediction(s) fails to materialize, he may be persecuted (a la Jeremiah) or, at the very least, publicly discredited. The wag might observe that if you must prophesy, make the prophecy for the distant future, thus relieving yourself of the burden of being found inaccurate in your own time. Or, at worst, an out and out fraud.

The Judeo-Christian prophecies almost invariably rest on the premise that the prophet has spoken directly with "God" or his messengers, the "angels." The Old Testament prophets (and John in Revelation) have been bidden, after the appearance of an entity which appears humanoid but otherworldly or the appearance of a group of entities with a humanoid looking spokesman, to carry certain messages to their people. These messages, as I have said before, offer moral instruction (particularly in the case of Moses), general information and very often apocalyptic warnings. This is especially the case in all the predictions of the Great Nazarene who affirmed that he was perpetually in contact with the Overlord of creation.

I have analyzed the problem of extraterrestrial entities and their influence on biblical, and worldwide, prophecy at great length in *Extraterrestrials in Biblical Prophecy and the New Age Great Experiment.* I think, however, a brief summary of that analysis would be helpful here, particularly if we are to come to any satisfactory conclusions about the viability and potential accuracy of biblical apocalyptic prophecy as it applies to the world today. And as it may affect us, you and me, now or very soon. As it may well affect everybody everywhere on the planet. If the Old Testament and New Testament prophets were accurate, and if their prophecies (at least some of them) apply to this age of man, then, as we all are pretty much aware, we are in a very troubling time. And things are likely to get much worse for us before they get much better.

Who were these "gods" (or this "God"), these messengers who contacted various Hebrew males, making them into prophets?

The Old Testament gives us graphic descriptions of angel-astronauts interacting with man. Angels are mentioned well over 200 times in the Old Testament alone, most often in situations which suggest extraterrestrial interaction with man. Orthodox theological research has been tardy in its recognition of the true nature and significance of these encounters for a number of reasons. In the first place, theological scholarship moves at a snail's pace.* Standard translations and exegeses of texts — with few exceptions — have remained virtually unaltered for centuries. Space-age awareness is only now gradually having its affect on established and well entrenched ways of viewing scripture. Greater understanding of past mistranslations of certain key words such as the Semitic word *shem*, found for example in the crucial Genesis 6:4 and Genesis

---

*For instance, it is outrageous that more than half of the translations of the Dead Sea Scrolls discovered at Kirbat Qumran more than four decades ago have not been released to the public. The reasons: ego, theological elitism and politics.

11:4 passages, and the radical change in interpretation of scripture *and our total view of Judaism and Christianity* which would take place if we substituted the early root meaning of that term (*shem* = "spacecraft" or "rocket ship") in place of the much later definition of "name" or "renown," has just begun to dawn on orthodox scholars, who have generally up to the present moment accepted the errors of their predecessors. Accepted them in many cases because they did not know better. The woeful truth is that the public is two generations behind in their awareness and understanding of new developments in scriptural research. And it is not all their fault. Most everyday clergymen are a generation behind.

The second main reason for the tardy reaction to new scholarship is that theologians and theological scholars are generally very conservative people. They are unwilling to accept a radical reinterpretation of the scriptures that recognizes the contribution of extraterrestrial messengers (*angelos* is Greek for "messengers") to our religious thought. It is too upsetting to the apple cart, to bruising to business as usual which has been very profitable. To admit that they have errored in translation and interpretation is to admit their fallibility and to loose, in their minds, some credibility and control of their flock.

What is more, the Old Testament, the New Testament and certain apocryphal and pseudepigraphal texts give us a plethora of evidence that the *Elohim, Nephilim* and Watchers were of extraterrestrial origin, were nothing short of cosmonauts visiting earth for reasons we cannot be completely sure of but visiting nonetheless. The evidence tells us that whatever their motives for dropping in, they brought us much wisdom in the process. They have presented it to us on numerous occasions and at various places on the planet's surface. That much is certain.

Our cosmic visitors most often seem to be speaking for a Greater God, a greater authority than themselves, although some of their actions and words may have been self-serving as well. We should not discount the idea that they were some-

194

times mixing business with pleasure and the wisdom of a Greater God with their own less perfect thinking. We should realize that it is man in most cases who insisted on interpreting these cosmonauts as God Supreme — and taking everything that came out of their mouths as the word of God Supreme. It is also man, in his confusion and ignorance, who often insisted upon interpreting even the machines of these visitors as God. We see compelling evidence of this in the Book of Enoch, in the Book of Ezekiel, in Daniel and in the Book of Revelation, to name only several of the most outstanding examples.

It seems to have been the attitude of our extraterrestrial visitors that if man, in his rather primitive mind, insisted on interpreting their substantial bodies and their craft as God(s), so let it be. There was no great harm done and the message(s), after all, which was the most important consideration, was getting through. First things first, in other words. Our visitors did on occasion warn earthlings *not to worship them*, but to worship God. Man, however, remained confused as to whether the cosmic "lords" standing before him were or were not *the* Cosmic Lord of Lords. We see an outstanding example of this in the Book of Revelation, actually the last page of the New Testament, a salient spot from which to drive home an idea, "I John am he who heard and saw these things. And when I heard and saw them, I fell down to worship at the feet of the angel who showed them to me; but he said to me, 'You must not do that! I am a fellow servant with you and your brethren the prophets, and with those who keep the words of this book. Worship God.'"

Any individual who is interested in discovering the connection between our biblical extraterrestrial visitors and the information imparted to the Old and New Testament prophets, as well as the connection between them and the teachings of the Great Nazarene, must as a minimum study closely chapters 1-14, and especially chapters 14 and 86, of the Ethiopic version (called 1 Enoch) of the Book of Enoch, a work which was held in the highest regard by the Hebrews until Gnostic times* as well

*The Gnostics also prized it.

as chapters 1-3, chapters 8-11, chapter 38 and chapters 40-44 of the Book of Ezekiel, chapters 3-5 and especially chapters 7-12 of the Book of Daniel and chapters 1 and 4 of the Book of Revelation. He will discover, if he does his research diligently, such things as the *Merkabah*, the "flying throne of God," which is described so well in Ezekiel and some of the other books mentioned here. He will learn revealing facts, such as that all speculation about and discussion of the *Merkabah* in Ezekiel was forbidden by the rabbis for centuries. We see here early on in Judeo-Christian tradition the tendency to suppress thinking when it threatens orthodoxy, a tendency which became stronger and stronger as the orthodoxy became more solidified. It is in such ways that the free play of men's minds is braked and the motion of his growth is impeded and slowed.

Once the quester after greater truth has satisfied himself about the connection between biblical extraterrestrials and the apocalyptic scriptures, he faces an even larger task. He is drawn invariably to forming several other questions. Are the biblical extraterrestrials and today's extraterrestrial activity interrelated? And is apocalyptic scripture that credible, and if so, is it relevant to, is it perhaps describing what is happening in the world today? Have we really, in plain English, approached the "time of the end" described by Daniel, Ezekiel and John in Revelation? Is the end of the world upon us?

Anyone approaching these questions is faced, first of all, with one large fact among many others. UFO activity, from the time of the Hiroshima and Nagasaki atomic holocausts, has been staggering in its growth and diversity of operations. There has been a massive monitoring of civilian life and military installations. Even if we discount all the contactee statements that our visitors are here because man has almost perversely put himself up against a wall and is threatening to pollute and irradiate himself into extinction while degrading at the same time the planet's surface and near space—even if we discount these warnings, and I do not believe we should, we are still left with the twin realities of a massive UFO presence and a world which is in the shadow of death and perpetually on the brink of committing global suicide. If ever there was a time in the world when conditions fit so perfectly an "end time" scenario, it is now.

There is within man a unique set of mind that encourages him to think in a positive fashion, to be optimistic and look always for a brighter day. This attitudinal bent is life-giving, life-supporting and should be praised. There is also, however, within human nature a tendency to ignore the reality at hand, especially when it is an unpleasing one, to think light of it, to minimize it, to rationalize it away. This latter attitudinal bent is now an extremely dangerous one to hold. It is not life-giving or life-supporting. Unless it is overcome, the graves may have been dug and the bodies interred before the last band of human survivors admits to a miscalculation of the severity of the problems confronting the human race.

Although there is some disagreement among professional theological scholars as to what biblical prophecy applies to what time and what people, and the congruent feeling that much prophecy has already been fulfilled, the consensus among theologians is that the "end time" prophecies have not yet been fulfilled. In this I concur. We are assuming here, as do the professional theologians, that any question about the over-all credibility of biblical apocalyptic prophecy is pretty much a moot point. There is, after all, enough historical evidence so far accumulated to substantiate the validity of much of that prophecy, if not all. Whether the balance of it will (has to?) run its course, with the gory climax to human irresponsibility and lack of compassion described by Daniel, Ezekiel and John, is a disturbing thought. But it may be the main reality of our day. The kind of reality human nature likes to discount and minimize because it is not pleasing.

If we accept the idea that man is primarily on this earth the master of his own fate, then we can embrace the idea that prophecy, if accurate, is only the foretelling at the moment of what is mathematically probable in the future. We assume here that the major prophets spoken of were reading that probability correctly, *as it was registered at their moment of history.* If this is the case, man can alter his future by altering his thinking and actions. Let us hope so. Then perhaps we can, through finding the keys of understanding and unlocking a greater compassion which lies latent and yearning within our hearts, deflect from us the horrors of an Armageddon-like situation which we seem to have created. Then world war becomes avoidable. Greater brotherhood among men becomes a surer possibility.

It may well be that certain natural cycles, earthly, solar and cosmic, must come to pass. This would mean that there is little, if anything, we can do about certain prophesied earth changes such as the large asteroid impact described in Revelation (Rev 8:8) along with the catastrophic destruction of the planet's surface caused immediately afterward by the effects of a close passage of Wormwood (probably *Nibiru*/Marduk) described in the same chapter (Rev 8:10). But what we can control is ourselves. We can control our perverse impulse to treat strangers and even loved ones differently from the way we would prefer to be treated. We can, if we like, assure ourselves of an advent to a future, a New Age without the prelude of a senseless bloodbath, if we will only change our attitudes and actions a little. So say the Sunday preachers (and our wisest philosophers) as the congregations of men and women sit stolidly by only half listening, dreaming their self-contained dreams of a better future for themselves which can never become a reality unless they break down the walls of their self-containment and embrace their fellow beings with the same enthusiasm as they embrace themselves and their fantasies.

The choice is ours. One would think the sensible side of human nature would have no trouble choosing what is in its best interest, what promotes its welfare and the future well being of its progeny. The jury is still out on the question of man's durability as a life form. Human history is filled with all too many pivotal examples to date in which mental sensibility did not predominate. The signs at present are as dark as they are hopeful. Will we choose the pit or paradise on earth?

The most recent crises in the Middle East, including the

Gulf War, have many of the characteristics which would seem to further fulfill the prophecies of the "end time" scenario. If we wish to be cynical, we might conclude that man has an irrational compulsion to realize his worst dreams or his worst prophecies.

In previous work, I have offered an interpretation of the apocalyptic prophecies as they pertain to the "end time" scenario, especially the sequence of events described in the Book of Daniel. At that time I offered a disclaimer of infallibility of judgment. It was not offered out of a sense of modesty. I believe any mortal has the responsibility to be continually aware of his limitations of interpretation and foresight. I have now, as I did then, no pretense of omniscience or clairvoyance. Some critics, I'm sure, will sneer, call such words false modesty, and say that is "so good of him." To such criticism I can only answer that we all have a responsibility to ourselves and others to try to understand our lives and the conditions under which we live them. This responsibility includes addressing ourselves to the challenges of prophecy. To the best of my ability, I have tried to understand the probable sequence of events related in the apocalyptic scriptures, making mental compensations when I felt they were needed for changes in the mathematical probability of some events occurring in the future. Needless to say it is an inexact business, far from a "scientific" methodology. One begins and ends by relying on what one has learned, on his guiding spirit, on intuition, on the "still small voice" within. All of these influences are synonyms, when properly understood, for the spirit of the Supreme Creative Force which dwells within us all, an idea and a term which is anathema to some men of "science" who pride themselves on knowing so much and yet can explain so little. One can only hope finally that one has studied hard enough, listened well and heard correctly.

Because the Middle East drama continues to ebb and flow with larger events conjoined to subevents and a large cast of shifting characters, some active one day, others the next—the interested observer, attempting to correlate the present play of events with recorded prophecy, is faced with a formidable task. Shifting events, like shifting sand under a hot sun, often give momentarily the appearance of a mirage-like central reality. We blink, nevertheless, and the next second the true picture seems to be something else altogether.

I have suggested earlier that the "king of the north" spoken of in Daniel is the "beast," and that this beast is related to a resurrected Roman Empire centered in the European Community and led by, presumably, a European leader (also called the "beast") who is yet to be recognized and yet to make his dark mark. This still seems to be a most probable scenario. How large a part the United States will take in such historical (and prophetical) developments seems problematic, but if we are to draw any conclusions from present evidence at this very hour, we would most likely have to agree that it will be a large part.* And it is not an impossible thought that the true leader of this resurrected dark empire might eventually turn out to be an American, even a Russian.

There are further possibilities at the moment worth consideration. It is quite possible that the "king of the north" spoken of in Daniel refers to more than one king and to several "norths." For instance, in Daniel 11:20-21 we are distinctly told of two despots, one replacing the other, the latter being the final one, the true "beast." Previous to them have existed still other historical kings of the north.

It is possible, even likely, that Saddam Hussein qualifies as one of these kings of the north. Iraq is northeast of the Holy Land. This being the reality, then Saddam Hussein may be the king spoken of in Daniel 11:14-19. If this is indeed the case, then the fulfillment of the remaining prophecies of Daniel are imminently close at hand.

The present entente between President George Bush, Mikhail Gorbachev, Prime Minister John Major, the European Community and even the United Nations, which has developed into a united front opposing (or pretending to oppose) destabili-

---

*In earlier work, I stated it might not be a large part.

zing developments now happening in the Middle East, would seem in some ways, under the wrong scenario, to augur badly for the future and to support the thesis that this is the "beast" in process of formation. The bellicose prewar noises made by Bush and Margaret Thatcher, and the primitive *machismo* of Saddam Hussein and his Arab supporters even in defeat, bodes ill for a long-term peaceful solution to either the Iraqi situation specifically or the larger Palestinian-Israeli question. Sadly, regrettably, almost infuriatingly, we are no closer to a Mideast solution than we were 40 years ago. In some ways, since the '67 and '73 wars, the situation has deteriorated.

The intransigent attitude of many present-day Israeli to the Palestinian question, and specifically to Palestinian demands for resettlement and a homeland, does nothing to cool off the perpetually overheated present moment. Such acts as the massacre of 19 Palestinians at the Temple Mount in Jerusalem during Palestinian rioting in October of 1990, and the earlier inexcusable bloodletting at the Sabra and Shatila refugee camps, should serve as a warning to all Israeli. It is easier than one thinks to become what one professes to loathe if one is not exceptionally watchful. There is always the danger that we will consciously or unconsciously begin to imitate our persecutors or former persecutors. Those who personally experienced, or have a thorough education about, Nazi atrocities must resist with all their heart becoming the mirror image of the beast which terrorizes. It would be foolish for any Israeli, simply because he is an Israeli, to assume that he is God's chosen and therefore above the cosmic law of individual responsibility for one's actions.*

Palestinians, who seem to have abandoned at times almost any reasonable willingness for discourse and compromise, who seem to have so thoroughly committed themselves to wholesale emotionalism, are making any solution to the Mideast problems increasingly difficult. Terrorism, which is as mindless and heartless in its motives as it is nondiscriminating in its victims, is not the mark of a civilized society. It springs from the

*Call it "karma" if you like.

dark side of human nature and is a throwback to the most savage impulses of earthbound-oriented man. As a political and social (actually antisocial) tactic, it is ultimately a one-way ticket in this day and age to biological extinction.

Until Jew and Arab, and all men, subjugate their baser emotions, many of which are extremely destructive, to higher mind and durable spiritual precepts, which are above any tinge of race, nationality and secularized religion, we will be living on the brink, forced by the baser part of our natures to be less than we can be.

Prophecy does not have to be fulfilled. There is no cosmic law that says that because something is likely to happen, it must happen. Man, through the exercise of his free will (and will power), can easily change the course of history and the fulfillment of apocalyptic prophecies. He can make great changes or changes of smaller measure. The power is his. It is as simple as that. Regrettably, he seems most often unaware of the great power he has within him to influence events and remake probabilities. Those who would control him, and they are many, would prefer that he does not discover this power.

Several decades ago V. Gordon Childe wrote a book called *Man Makes Himself.* It became a revered standard text among many anthropologists and archeologists and students of those disciplines. Yet not even Childe understood just how true it is that man, once bioengineered into his present form, becomes the "maker" of himself, whatever he chooses to become. His pride in his more recent development is understandable if not always defensible. He fancies he has progressed from an Age of Enlightenment through an Age of Reason into the technological discoveries of the Industrial and Atomic Ages. This rapid evolvement, which seems so great to him, but which has been repeated innumerable times in the earth's ancient past (a fact of which he is generally ignorant), has caused of late a virulent strain of smugness to wrinkle his brow which does not at all become him. He now believes his technology alone will solve all his pressing social problems and even conquer outer space without destroying him in the process. He sees little necessity to improve himself spiritually to accomplish his dreams. He refuses to see just how limited, how small his present dreams are. Or that cosmic forces greater than himself may insist that he develop himself further before they will assist him and allow some of those presently reckless dreams of his to be realized.* Earthbound-oriented humanity acts like an intractable, willful child whose myopic vision of reality makes it forego all proffered good advice and instruction which might save it from many bruises. It can be a dangerous little cuss, armed with lethal weapons of mass destruction, with egocentric fantasies of greatness and too often little concern for the havoc it wrecks in pursuit of its short-term desires.

Today's earthbound-oriented human being has yet to learn the "song of the red ruby," the way of true self-knowledge, and the release of the "diamond way," the way of nonattached loving; or the truth of the idea that through will power, the mastery of both or either is possible; that finally it is necessary to master both if the greater potential of man is to be fulfilled and he is to become worthy to take his place as a respected, enlightened member of the greater society of intelligent life forms among the stars. Then apocalypse becomes epiphany. Man finally discovers the godliness within himself that has always been there. At last he recognizes himself for what he truly and essentially is. All thought of conflict among brothers, earthly or otherwise, becomes unacceptable.

*Such as some of our present-day extraterrestrial visitors *and those entities in the hierarchy above them that advise and guide them.*

# CHAPTER FOURTEEN

## The Reversed Image Parable

The extraterrestrial visitor saw the man and mused, "I am more refined than he. There, but for the grace of God, go I."

The man looked at the extraterrestrial visitor and thought, "He is more developed than me. Someday, by the grace of God, like so will I go."

At that moment, a professional photographer happened by. Observing the scene before him, he thought, "What marvelous reversed images."

CHAPTER FIFTEEN

# UFOs and the New Age

It has become gradually evident to the perceptive observer that many of the vast changes, both physical and spiritual, that we see occurring on earth today are in many ways associated with UFO activity. This activity, like the changes themselves, has been growing successively (though sporadically) more intense since the end of World War II in spite of the many official attempts to stifle inquiry. A correlation between New Age events and New Age thinking and UFO activity was noted years ago by a small group of pioneer UFO investigators, most of whom worked separately and were obligated to no one but themselves. Among this group were Helen and Bryant Reeve, George Van Tassel, Meade Layne, Mark Probert and like thinkers, all vitally interested in the UFO phenomena which was then so perplexing to the public at large.

In fact, the Reeves noted in *Flying Saucer Pilgrimage* (1957) that, "The flying saucer fraternity is alive with enthusiasm for new age concepts." It was a while, however, before most of the early New Agers became convinced that UFOs were significantly involved in the ushering in of the New Age itself and that the majority of ufologists were not kooks or sensation-mongers. What is most significant and intriguing is the depth of this change in attitude which has been going on for forty or more years and has accelerated greatly the past few years. How and why, we might wonder, did this change come about?

We need to keep in mind several very relevant facts as we approach this question. First, we must remember that the public ninety years ago never thought men would fly. The general consensus was that Orville and Wilbur Wright were off on a lark and would do better flying kites rather than themselves. Secondly, science at the time considered earth man to be a unique species, the only intelligent one in the cosmos. Man was still central to creation, even if the earth was not the center of the universe. Thirdly, theologians interpreted and taught scriptures as the scriptures had been taught to them and their theological forefathers. There wasn't, in other words, much new under the sun in biblical revelation.

By 1946, when a spate of strange rocket-like objects first made an appearance in Scandinavian skies, men had become quite accustomed to the idea of aircraft manned by *Homo sapiens*. Scientists, particularly astronomers, were much more aware of the magnitude of the cosmos than formerly but were generally still maintaining, with a few relatively quiet exceptions, that man as an intelligent life form was *probably* alone in the galaxy, if not all of creation. Theologians were still holding the line, although the discovery of the Dead Sea Scrolls at Qumran and, to a lesser extent, the Gnostic scrolls at Nag Hamadi, had some clerics worried that a revision of certain texts might be necessary after the newly discovered material had been analyzed and carefully translated. This worry (fear?) may explain, for instance, why, as I have noted previously, more than 45 years after their discovery, half or less of the material has been made available to the public.*

Then several significant changes in attitude occurred within a relatively few years. By 1959, exobiologists (extraterrestrial biologists), astronomers and mathematicians such as Joshua Lederberg, JBS Haldane, Howard Shapley, Frank B. Salisbury, Freeman J. Dyson, Iosif Shklovsky and

*What is really going on? Is the wolf at the door? Are the scholars afraid of a public reaction, such as some revision of hallowed interpretation? Whose afraid of what here? The situation is disgraceful.

Carl Sagan had begun to speculate seriously (partially prompted, one suspects, although they have never admitted it, by massive worldwide UFO activity) on the probability of life forms existing in outer space and concluded gradually that such a probability (they would say "mathematical probability") was likely.* Hence we have such statements as Salisbury's written for a *Science* article in 1962, "And from there [the existence of plant life] it is but one more step (granted, a big one) to intelligent beings," and Sagan's statement to the American Rocket Society on November 15, 1962, "...Other civilizations, aeons more advanced than ours, most be plying the spaces between the stars."** In 1964 Walter Sullivan, science editor for *The New York Times*, summed up recent developments in his book, *We Are Not Alone*, and, not surprisingly, was able to say, speaking as well for many exobiologists, "Yet the conclusion that life exists across this vastness seems inescapable. We cannot yet be sure whether or not it lies within reach, but in any case we are a part of it all; we are not alone!"

These changes in attitude, as can be clearly seen, are large changes indeed. We must remember that all the while, from the mid-40s throughout the 60s, UFO sightings were numerous, were in fact increasing, with a great wave of sightings in 1956-67, and have continued unabated, with certain peak periods, until the present time.*** During all this time an increasing number of people claimed to have seen extraterrestrials disembark from their craft. Many claimed to have made contact. Some claimed to have been abducted. The Air Force and allied federal agencies involved in UFO surveillance and

*This was an about-face. Previously, the consensus was that the "mathematical probability" was otherwise. It would appear the science of mathematical probability has changed rather rapidly.

**Sagan, however, has adamantly refused to consider the terrestrial evidence that UFOs are visiting earth at this time. Does he know more than he pretends, has he been blinded by a false scientific bias or is he a career opportunist?

***And yet today the national news media, except rarely, maintains a strange silence, as if the long-term government pressure to avoid such reportage has worn them down and made them skittish. Most reported UFO sightings and encounters appear now in the local presses, if at all. The number of these sightings today, however, remain considerable.

investigation have made over time many contradictory remarks. In the late 40s and early 50s they even vouched for the legitimacy of certain evidence pointing to the reality of extraterrestrial craft, such as radar sightings and pilot reports. Then they began to back off.

From approximately 1953 onward, about the time the CIA orchestrated Robertson Report was compiled, the federal government became increasingly closed-mouth about UFO phenomena. Then in 1969 the Condon Report was published, a thinly veiled government-sponsored wash-job.* Its preformed conclusions were used as justification to abandon Project Blue Book, which ostensibly was the last major effort of the Air Force and allied federal bureaucracies to publicly investigate unidentified flying objects. Anyone who has closely studied Project Blue Book material is likely to come away with the disturbed feeling that only a minimum of effort was ever expended to investigate anything and that the conclusions closely followed a special formula—when in doubt, minimize.

Much of the history of the federal government's involvement in various UFO projects can be gleaned from the seminal books written by former NICAP (National Investigations Committee on Aerial Phenomena) director Major Donald Keyoe written in the 50s and 60s and the many books of APRO (Aerial Phenomena Research Organization) founders Coral and Jim Lorenzen. The federal government's attempts at camouflaging its interest in UFO activity, and the subsequent lengths it went to mislead the public about its very large true interest, have been well documented in Lawrence Fawcett's and Barry Greenwood's work, *Clear Intent*. The authors relied as heavily as possible on the Freedom of Information Act to chip away revealing documents from the ice block of official secrecy and elusive behavior kept in the cooler of official disdain. It is a matter of conjecture how large that block of information really is, but common sense should tell us that what Fawcett and Greenwood came up with, as revealing as it is, is only chips and

*Also called the "Colorado Project."

210

splinters compared to the much larger cache from which it came.

All this is now history—although history of which few Americans are adequately aware. That a great cover-up has existed, is obvious to almost all conscientious investigators who have been willing to dig out pieces of the appalling story.* What is most interesting, however, is the reaction of the majority of today's exobiologists and scientists in general, men and women almost invariably either directly or indirectly government-funded or dependent on government largesse of one kind and another for their research and reputations. They have, with few exceptions, consistently refused to consider the evidence of extraterrestrial visitations to earth in the ancient past or in the present moment, while many of them still maintain the likelihood of the existence of extraterrestrial intelligent life and the equal probability that intelligent extraterrestrial life would quite likely, when able, extend itself outward into space by exploration. A curious situation, this. As if exploration were likely but not here. The lack of logic is disturbing.

The question must be asked, How do you know earth has not been visited and is not being visited now if you refuse, for whatever reason (and none is good enough), to consider the evidence? Does the human ego fear so much the existence of life forms which might find human intelligence and human science woefully underdeveloped? Has fear of peer group disapproval, a disapproval which can destroy professional and public reputation, suppressed a bonafide interest? Has governmental pressure muffled dissent of governmental policy in the name of some kind of warped idea of what is in the best interest of national security? We are faced with a number of questions which would make a person of ordinary conscience lose sleep at night, especially once that person has become aware of the overall situation, which the public has not.

*Two of these early investigators, authors Timothy Green Beckley and Brad Steiger, also deserve credit lately for their special effort to demonstrate the interconnectedness of New Age ideas and events with UFO phenomena.

If only a few of the accusations being made today by former naval intelligence officer William Cooper (*Behold A Pale Horse*) are accurate, such as the charge that our government may possibly have made a secret agreement with a certain group of opportunistic ETs allowing them to abduct numbers of young Americans for biological experimentation in exchange for a sharing of some advanced technologies, then the public has been more than hoodwinked. It has been betrayed. If any of the accusations about the existence of underground UFO bases in the far West, manned by either extraterrestrials alone or a combination of American military personnel and extraterrestrials, are true, as William Hamilton, John Lear and Robert Lazar propose, then we have all been foully deceived. Even if our government has by chance captured one or more crashed UFOs and somehow learned to make it (them) operable, we have been boldly lied to, as if we were children undeserving of the real truth. This, quite obviously, is not how a republic, a democracy with elected officials, who are the servants of the people, is supposed to work. The idea that a wildcat clique within the government might get control of such technology and use it for their own personal interest, and possibly even use it to take control of the country, is a thought that should make us all shudder.

As scientists in the past were reassessing the probability of extraterrestrial life, and as increasing evidence of present-day extraterrestrial visitations to earth was building, a few brave souls were beginning to wonder what evidence might be found in the Judeo-Christian scriptures of past extraterrestrial involvement with man. They began to look rather tentatively into the matter. Predictably, these people were not, with several noteworthy exceptions, professional theologians. Massive resistance to any evidence of extraterrestrial involvement in biblical affairs could be expected from both Jewish and Christian professional clerics and exegetes. It was, not surprisingly, quickly forthcoming, as witness, for example, the angry (and very illogical) rebuttal to Erich von Daniken's early evidence of ancient astronauts by Clifford Wilson (*Crash Go the Chariots* and *The Chariots Still Crash).* The threat to conventional, orthodox interpretation of the scriptures, if such evidence was found to exist, was just too great to ignore. And, as might be expected, most priests, ministers and rabbis to this day are unwilling to touch such a hot potato—although many of them are not remiss, when given the chance, to damn the very idea of the potato. They refuse adamantly to consider the large amount of evidence in the scriptures which points to extraterrestrial involvement and influence. As a corollary to that unwillingness, they have refused to face the even greater issue of what the evidence implies about our understanding of how many of the scriptures came to be and what effect they were intended to have and why. Any revision to pat answers to these questions upsets them. Better to hide new light under the old bushel basket—even when the times, more than ever, cry out for all the light, all the truth, possible.

In order of appearance, the most notable of the early works which explored the connection between ancient extra-terrestrial visitors and the Judeo-Christian scriptures were: Morris K. Jessup's *The UFO and the Bible* (1956), Brinsley Le Poer Trench's *The Sky People* (1960), P. Thomas' (a pseudonym for P. Misraki) *Les Extraterrestres* (1962), which also had an English version, Barry H. Downing's *The Bible and Flying Saucers* (1969), which has been recently reissued, and two notable works by W. Raymond Drake, *Gods and Spacemen of the Ancient East* (1973) and *Gods and Spacemen in Ancient Israel* (1976). Finally, Virginia Brasington published an enlightening small work called *Flying Saucers in the Bible*, the last edition appearing in 1982.

These works all laid the foundation for serious investigation but, unfortunately for the serious student (our cosmic quester) interested in searching out essential truth wherever it may be found, with the exception of Downing's republished work, the other materials, to the best of my knowledge, are now out of print and hard to find. It is doubtful today, even with these pioneering works, that the public is very aware of the evidence of extraterrestrial involvement in the scriptures and especially of the quantity and quality of the evidence to be found.

Von Daniken's remark that much more investigation of the scriptures was needed piqued my interest. I read Josef Blumrich, the NASA engineer, half expecting to disagree with his conclusion that there was a great deal of evidnece in the Book of Ezekiel of extraterrestrial involvement with man. I was surprised how much I agreed with him after a close textual analysis of the prophet's book. In short order, I was scanning the other books of the Old Testament, particularly the books of the prophets and some of the pseudepigrapha and apocrypha. What I found startled me—incident after incident that, read with 20th century space-age eyes, seemed to prove almost incontrovertibly that extraterrestrial visitors (real, substantial beings, not wispy, ethereal "modern angels") had not only been around in ancient times but that they were on a mission to program certain candidates (who became "prophets" after the fact) so that these men could pass on to their people, and mankind in general, moral instruction, practical advice (sometimes quite political) and warnings about future apocalyptic events, such as wars and earth changes, which were likely to happen if the tribes of Israel and Judah and, by extension, the human family did not get the affairs of their house in order. If they did not, war—including what sounds like nuclear war in the books of Ezekiel, Daniel and Revelation—seemed almost inevitable. The concomitant earth changes mentioned in some of these prophecies may well be inevitable, being the effects of natural cosmic processes outside of man's influence or control but devastating to him and the planet nonetheless.

After marshaling the evidence, I wrote *Extraterrestrials in Biblical Prophecy and the New Age Great Experiment*. It is the first work that attempts a thorough biblical analysis of the evidence for extraterrestrial visitations and influence in the Old and New Testaments, including pseudepigraha and apocrypha. Its conclusions are based on textual analyses with the thought always in mind that the early Hebrews did not possess

214

a language rich in technological terminology. They used the only language they had, and it is always necessary to project into their minds and try to see with their eyes the extraordinary phenomena sometimes taking place about them. It is not necessary to stretch our imagination and read things into texts which are not there. Evidence aplenty can be found in them. But it is described with the limited metaphor, idiom and basic language of the day. Each individual prophet had his own style and his own limitations of expression.

As one proceeds in such investigations, he soon discovers that long before Moses, the Sumerians, Akkadians and Babylonians of the Tigris and Euphrates fertile crescent were having their own experiences with visitors from the heavens. A look at the root meaning of various Sumerian pictographs proves almost beyond any doubt that they had terms for spacecraft, various stages of rocket ships, even spacesuits. Even more astonishing is the large amount of literary evidence originating from the same cultures indicating that these "gods" from space were involved in bioengineering experiments, eugenic experiments, which aimed at modifying *Homo erectus* into *Homo sapiens*, making us physically and mentally what we are today.*

Not only need we conclude, as organizations such as the Ancient Astronaut Society have done, that UFOs visited earth in the past, we must go a step or two further. We must recognize not only the scriptural evidence in the Judeo-Christian archives, but all the other evidence in other religions, literatures and folklores around the world—for example, Hindu texts, Mayan literature-folklore, Incan literature-folklore, Chippewa literature-folklore, Hopi literature-folklore—and realize the extent of the effort our extraterrestrial visitors have made in the past to influence, not only one "chosen people," but peoples throughout the world.

*Neanderthal man (*Homo sapiens neanderthalensis*), which some people might be tempted to place between *Homo erectus* and *Homo sapiens* on a natural continuum as an intermediate form, is really a distinct species, as are, for that matter, *Homo erectus* and *Homo sapiens*. Neanderthal man and *Homo sapiens* appear to be laboratory-improved. The leap in brain size from *Homo erectus* to Neanderthal man and modern man, which was accomplished within the space of no more than several hundred thousand years, is quite remarkable.

How good was their advice? If we believe from the evidence that the sacred Vedas of India were passed on to the Indus Valley civilization by our visitors, thereby virtually establishing a culture and its laws, then we must be impressed with its effect. If, after a study of Sumerian, Akkadian, Babylonian, Hurrian, Assyrian, Hittite, Canaanite and other Middle Eastern cultures, we come away with the idea that there was at times massive involvement between extraterrestrials and these civilizations, we must be somewhat awed by its depth and breadth. But how *good* was it? It certainly seems to have been essential. With the Sumerians, for instance, who began the first notable sequence of civilization in the Middle East, it was *the essential impetus* to civilization. The same can be said for many of the other cultures mentioned here. Either they were contacted directly by the visitors or they inherited the "advice" from an older culture. Law and order and general morality in all of these cultures, we must conclude, was either created or much influenced by the visitors.

The early Hebrews are the direct descendants of these Sumerians and Babylonians. Recall for a moment that Abraham was from Ur and resided for awhile in Haran. If the Hebrew prophets were programmed by our visitors as the evidence seems to suggest, who wishes to argue that the Ten Commandments are bad advice for any group of semi-savages — which is what the Hebrews were in Moses' time — wishing, or needing, to civilize themselves? The Ten Commandments, and other Mosaic precepts, we might further conclude, are good advice for any culture at any time, no matter how civilized it fancies itself to be or how uncivilized it may in fact be.

If the Great Nazarene was intimately associated with our visitors, or was one of them, as so much evidence indicates, who wants to play the devil's advocate for very long and argue that his advice is anything less than quintessential good sense as well as cosmic law? What could be more basic to true civilization than the First Commandment, to honor one's Creator above all else, and the Golden Rule, to treat one's fellow man as one would like to be treated? It could be argued, rather convincingly I think, that no enduring civilization is really possible without following the latter advice, and that it would be foolish, once we understand our cosmic roots, to avoid the former.

As I have already made clear, the Hebrews were not the only people brought "the word." The *Midrashim*, the Jewish commentaries on the scriptures, make it quite plain that cosmic law, as interpreted by our visitors, was given to all peoples everywhere. Each great culture in its time has been contacted and apprised of the truth. Each has added over time its distinctive interpretation to those laws, often, as with orthodox Christianity, with unfortunate obfuscation of the original message. It is the height of foolishness for any culture to feel they, and only they, are the sole carriers of the divine message of cosmic law. And yet that is pretty much the state of affairs we find extant in the world today. The effect of such cultural and theological ethnocentrism divides men and creates artificial barriers to universal brotherhood and harmonious world government. All we have to do is look around us now to see confirmation of that fact.

Once we have become aware of the reality of the presence today of large numbers of UFOs in our skies (and on land), we need to follow through, if we have not already done so—and most people have not—in our thinking. It is necessary, if we are to come to any meaningful final conclusions about their significance, to familiarize ourselves with as much evidence as possible. This greatly increases our chances of approaching more closely the greater truth. We need to study the evidence for the contemporary presence of our visitors and the evidence of their influence on ancient cultures, especially the Sumerian, Babylonian, Egyptian, Indian, Mayan, Incan, Hopi and other American Indian cultures where evidence is available and ascertainable. We need particularly to study the evidence that suggests our visitors "programmed" certain Hebrew individuals with cosmic law, moral instruction and apocalyptic warnings. These individuals became, of course, the prophets of the Old and New Testaments. They, and what they passed on to us, have immensely affected us and made us in large measure what we are today.

Furthermore, we need to look meticulously at the evidence that indicates that the Great Nazarene, such figures as the Aztec and Mayan Quetzalcoatl, the Incan Viracocha and the Hopi Pahana were intimately involved with these visitors, were in fact their spokesmen, if not visitors themselves. In addition, we need to follow the tracks through historical time which suggest that at various periods of world history our visitors have continued to monitor us, their Great Experiment, in what seems like a continuing Great Overseership. One of those periods is now. It may well be the most crucial time in the history of man.

This educational program, if we carry it out, is a good beginning but we are hardly at the end of our observations and need for study and thought. If we are to make the most sense out of all this accumulating evidence, we must go even a few steps further. We have got to make the logical connection between our building pool of historical evidence and our own time, today. Even if we distrust the probity or intentions of some of the contactees and abductees, we need to listen carefully to them. It is difficult to believe that all of them, even the majority of them (who number in the thousands) are suffering from the same or similar delusions. Many of them have been quite vocal in their insistence that our visitors are here now because mankind has reached a crossroads in its development and its physical survival, as well as its psychic well being, is threatened. Many are firm in their belief that this planet is in grave peril. We may find ourselves coming to the same conclusion(s) because of the large amount of evidence we ourselves have accumulated.

If we follow the logic and make the appropriate connections, we might very well conclude the following:

(1) Extraterrestrial entities are manifesting themselves in our skies (and sometimes on land) in great numbers.

(2) They appear to be monitoring us—our actions and the

products of our minds and hands (including military hardware and installations).

(3) Most of these entities—and there are several groups—have demonstrated that they are basically friendly.

(4) They appear to be in a holding action, gathering information but not overtly involving themselves in human affairs to any great extent.

(5) It is possible, even logical, to associate their presence and activity with the course of events described in the biblical Book of Revelation (and the Books of Ezekiel and Daniel), because the signs of the times suggest we are close to an "end time" scenario.

(6) It may well be, as various contactees and psychics have maintained, that our visitors do not intend to interfere directly with human affairs, no matter how terrible a calamity humanity visits upon itself or no matter how destructive natural earth changes may become, *unless they are ordered to.*

If these are some of the tentative conclusions we might come to, there are a few others, more final and perhaps more compelling, that we should consider. It is difficult, for instance, with the evidence now available not to conclude that our present-day visitors are not intimately connected with the beginnings of a potential millennial New Age on earth. In biblical terms, this, wonderful as it sounds, is only a prelude for the growing spirit. The vista, the hope and the promise, stretches far out beyond the New Age, to "new heavens" and "new earths," to planes and dimensions where the spirit that was once earthbound and limited by its physicality can continue to grow indefinitely in its spiritual journey homeward to its Source, its greater enlightenment and its glorification.

Our visitors may well be, in biblical terms (although it is possible to use others), the "armies of heaven" spoken of in scripture who are to appear with a great new world leader at a moment when mankind has contrived to self-destruct itself.* If

*Of course, man must be cautious not to confuse in his mind a demagogic "beast" with a true new world leader. How difficult it is in these times to distinguish between wolves and sheep much less between good shepherds and potential butchers.

our extraterrestrial visitors are in fact the scriptural "armies of heaven," they have made so far one thing certain by their actions. They will not interfere or offer their good advice and counsel to worldly governments so long as those governments, interested only in pursuing their selfish ends even to the detriment of those they are supposed to represent, ignore them and pretend they do not exist. The tragedy of our time, perhaps, is that a few selfish men on earth control the physical destiny of the mass of uneducated humanity. A more encouraging note today is the realization by more and more people that no one, no government, no agency earthly or otherwise, can destroy a spirit; that the spirit will continue to grow in love and knowledge and truth so long as it wills to do so, in body and out, on planet Earth or elsewhere.

## CHAPTER SIXTEEN

# The Early UFO Contactees Reconsidered

The men and women of the 50s and 60s who claimed physical contact with extraterrestrial entities were considered an embarrassment by many of the more professional, "serious" UFO investigators. They seemed too much like simple opportunists, grandstanders, hustlers and egomaniacs. It was whispered about that some of them, like George Adamski, made a huge "killing in the market" with their books and frequent public appearances. Almost forty years after the alleged first modern contacts, hindsight coupled with new evidence plus a dose of clearer logic has softened the resistance of many of these investigators still living. It would appear that the time is ripe for a reevaluation of many of these contactees and their stories. Time for a new look and new attitudes.

There is today among many of the younger new investigators an acknowledgement of the likelihood — if for no other reason than the sheer bulk of evidence which has accumulated over the years — that contact between some extraterrestrials and some humans has taken place in the past and is probably taking place now. Rather startlingly, the majority of the present physical contacts in this country appear to be forced abductions, a far cry from the peaceful, friendly tête-à-têtes many early contactees claimed to have experienced.

There is, of course, more than one way to make contact. There is physical contact, such as Truman Bethurum, Howard Menger, George Adamski, Orfeo Angelucci, Buck Nelson,

Cedric Allingham, Daniel Fry and a host of others claimed to have had. And there is mental contact such as Mark Probert, George Van Tassel, George Hunt Williamson and many others claimed to have experienced. Some claimed to have had it both ways which, if one accepts the premise that physical contact isn't unreasonable, then, evidence considered, why should it be unreasonable that mental contact might not have occurred in some cases as well? Sometimes along with physical contact, sometimes without. If we need precedents for such goings-on, how about referring ourselves to the Old Testament books of Ezekiel, Daniel and Zechariah and reading carefully?

Many of the well publicized early contactee stories dealing with physical contact seem today to be without even a modicum of convincing, hard-core data buried within them. They may well be true accounts but still fail to convince for several—some would say innumerable—reasons. Many do have details, but these details seem to contradict a large base of rather consistent, recurring data which has built up over the years. Thus they are immediately suspect. We have to remember that swirling around this consistent, recurring data, and some would say polluting it in the intervening 40 years plus since the earliest accounts began to surface, are hundreds, actually thousands, of people worldwide who have claimed physical contact with all manner and kind of extraterrestrial beings. You name the possibility, somebody somewhere has claimed within those decades to have seen it, talked to it, been loved by it or been abused by it. Once this fact is understood, it is not so difficult to understand the skepticism residing in the heart of many a UFO investigator when he confronts a new tale of interworldly adventure.

Let's take a look at several of the above-mentioned alleged encounters which made waves of sensation at the time of their occurrence or shortly thereafter.

There is a romantic halo surrounding several of these tales which does not wear well in an age which professes itself to be hard-nosed and ultra realistic, an age which likes its entertainment with magnum-force violence. Howard Menger's account, originally titled *From Outer Space to You*, and Truman Berthurum's experiences, related in Gavin Gibbon's *On Board The Flying Saucers*, are both susceptible to charges of mawkish romanticism primarily because each of these men becomes emotionally enthralled with the beautiful physiognomy and fetching personality of their respective female extraterrestrial contact, and neither makes any attempt to conceal his rather sophomoric crush. In *Son of the Sun*, Orfeo Angelucci also indulges in a romantic infatuation with the enlightened space beauties who guide him on a Venusian excursion. If you have already guessed that it was quite common for many of these early male contactees to fall for their extraterrestrial female hosts, you're quite right. Many did. A comparison of these relationships with, say, Whitley Strieber's more recent relationship with his female "gray" abductor is a revealing turnabout, to say the least. But that's another story.

Actually, Menger's story starts much earlier than most. He first meets his beautiful space visitor sitting "on the rock" one day in 1932. The prose becomes, if not purple, some shade of mauve, "an overwhelming wonderment froze me to the spot...a tremendous surge of love and physical attraction...emanated from her to me."* It is, however, this kind of writing wedded to sophomoric attitudes of mind which undercut the potential credibility of the material as a whole and make it seem foolish and totally unbelievable for some people.

Menger is told that he will one day meet and marry Marla, a sister of the space visitor but an earthling nevertheless, and that Howard himself will have many future meetings and conversations with extraterrestrial visitors. All these predictions, by the way, come true.

Menger also describes a trip to the moon, moon space potatoes, and electromagnetic experiments he believes he was encouraged to perform. He also offers the reader an interesting array of photographs of flying discs photographed earthside and on the moon, including one shot of a space visitor

*Like most contactees, he is not a Proust or even a Hemingway. And, in all fairness, he has never claimed to be.

standing in front of his vimana. The photographs are worthy even today of further research. They were given scant serious attention by early UFO investigators as were those of George Adamski, which also deserve a second look. But more about Adamski shortly.

One of the problems with Menger's work today is that in the past few years he has hedged about the authenticity of some of his material. He has adumbrated that long ago government agents encouraged him to add new wrinkles to his original material. Remarks such as these have tended to compromise whatever is true in his account. Now Menger seems to be saying that he did observe spacecraft landings and did have conversations with the occupants on several separate occasions, but that the government, at the time his book was being written, encouraged him to add certain details to see what the public reaction would be. If Howard Menger's story is basically true, if he did agree to add material to the story because of official pressure to do so, it is indeed unfortunate for us all. Not only is this a further indication of government having its finger in the pie, which it so stoutly maintains it does not and never has, it is a good example of how difficult it often is in UFO matters to decide where fact ends and fiction begins. Until Menger is willing to go line for line through his text and show us what is genuine and what is spurious, we will have to reserve any final judgment on the value of the whole or any of its parts. It is worth noting that 32 years after the publication of his book, Howard Menger still maintains in public talks that the core of *From Outer Space to You*, like the core of a good apple, is still sound.

Almost all of the well known early contactee cases deal with extraterrestrial humanoids that look much like you and me, what have been called "blonds," "Swedes," "Caucasians" or "Eurasians." Did the early days of UFO phenomena have a "wasp" inclination? Was there some kind of psychological projection going on? Were people seeing what they wanted to see, preferred to see? Or could it be that the majority of protagonists on the stage, i.e. UFO occupants disembarking on *terra firma*, have changed considerably, at least as far as the unfoldment of the drama in the United States is concerned? It is, after all, not an illogical possibility that the "grays" have superseded in quantity the "blonds" and "Eurasians." From the number of abduction cases involving "grays" that have surfaced lately, it is fair to conclude that the "grays" have now taken center stage with a vengeance. And they appear much less interested in chatting with bystanders.

At any rate, no extraterrestrial space maiden seems to have been more alluring, more captivating (without being an abductoress) than Aura Rhanes, captain of a space "scow," who inadvertently, accidentally meets Truman Bethurum, a man who just happens to be at the right place at the right time. She deeply impresses him with her dark beauty and quick wit, so much so in fact that his marriage is threatened, just as Menger's had been altered by his meeting with the lady "on the rock." She would seem to fit the description of the Eurasian-type extraterrestrial, a type infrequently reported, although Charles Silva had his head turned by one, in the person of Rama (Ramatis), on whom he elaborated greatly in *Date With The Gods*. And Mara, space officer-guide extraordinary in John Langdon Watts' little known work, *Visit Venus*, also fits the type. This latter book, however, appeared somewhat later than the other tales.

According to the captain, 'our only purpose in landing is for our education, and to relax a little and replenish our atmosphere tanks....' She dispenses wisdom hesitantly in answer to Berthurum's questions, 'Your people could co-operate and act in unison instead of constantly warring,' while rueing lost human opportunities, '...and then you'd find your Earth a beautiful place.' It is as if she, like so many other space visitors, is being extremely cautious as to what she divulges to earthlings, presumably to avoid interfering directly with planetary evolution, which is a theme or subtheme found in many accounts, 'governments only represent those they govern, so the change of outlook, if it is to be permanent, has to come from within your Earth and not be forced from outside.'

Captain Aura Rhanes does make many pertinent observations that echo similar statements made by other space visitors and which have been passed on by their contactees. She notes, for example, our interest in atomic power and comments on the likelihood that other space civilizations may be surveying us. 'If you blow up your own planet, it would cause considerable confusion in the space around you,' she tells him. This is a pertinent enough observation and one that is undoubtedly true if, as has been surmised, some of our visitors come from different dimensions and planes that overlap or interpenetrate our own, living perhaps on different vibrational frequencies (atomic frequencies) than ourselves but existing nevertheless within our own solar system or close by. These possibilities were not given much consideration in the 50s and 60s. Even today they are too frequently ignored by scientists, UFO investigator-theorists and layman alike.

On her 12th visit, Aura Rhanes explains to Truman Berthurum what he can do to facilitate man's development into a peaceful culture. The conclusion we seem to be led to, and not accidentally, is that, although the initial meeting with Berthurum was accidental, unlike the planned contacts with earthlings arranged by space visitors from places other than Clarion, this Clarionite commander has decided that Truman can make a large difference. He is encouraged to found a Sanctuary of Thought and to purchase the necessary acreage where such a project can become a reality. Here 'understanding' can be taught, the kind that makes war impossible. In time, then, war can become an anachronism. But first it is necessary to educate, to make the people themselves more tolerant, more universally aware of what life can be. Governments, she observes, are no better than those they govern. They are a reflection. It is necessary to convince the people to change interiorly and exteriorly their reflecting surfaces.

Ideas such as these can be found in much of the contactee literature. They have been called simplistic and banal. I cannot for the life of me understand why, unless we have become so spiritually and mentally blind, so used to hearing abstractions such as understanding, peace, love and tolerance *misused* and bandied about carelessly, even cynically, that we have forgotten that they in fact are intended as symbols of legitimate practices, states and mental and emotional operations that are essential to survival and do in fact exist in reality. And these abstractions do in fact refer to that reality. These words are tools we use to give us a handle on that reality, that help us manipulate and control that reality so that our lives can be more successfully lived.

How can anyone who is mentally stable refuse to agree that conditions in the world would be much better if there was more of each of these "abstractions" present is beyond my comprehension. It is plausible to conjecture that, given the ethnic and international tensions which now exist in the world, and the technological doomsday machines of one kind and another that man has invented, humankind has placed itself in a position, which it continually exacerbates, which makes its survival more and more precarious. Given such a state of affairs, a human being who does not support understanding, peace, love and tolerance toward all intelligent life (including extraterrestrial life forms) is either irresponsibly asleep, unacceptably unawakened or is homicidal, suicidal or both. Such people, and they are many, are contributing little or nothing to their own growth and even less to the welfare and enlightenment of those about them.

Anyone who cannot see the advantage to the human race of cultivating greater understanding, peace, love and tolerance is truly benighted and becomes a serious drag on the upward momentum of human development. Those who are cynical about such ideas are a danger to themselves and those about them. Cynical world leaders, politicians and other men and women of vast influence, who often disguise their true feelings, are selfish walking time-bombs. The fallout, literally and figuratively, from their actions can contaminate (has contaminated) all those around them.

The most controversial of the early contactees was George Adamski. His was the greatest noise. His alleged experiences, offered up to the public in *Flying Saucers Have Landed* (with Desmond Leslie), *Inside the Space Ships* and *Flying Saucers Farewell* created a great stir. In fact, his words set many critics boiling. His warnings, such as the one about the dangers of nuclear power, and his messages, like the one that our visitors wish us well and are willing to help us advance culturally, if we wish them to, are all pretty much consistent with what other contactees have said. Yet he rubbed many investigators the wrong way. There was something about this immigrant's personality, his somewhat nonprofessional, halting, laid-back, slightly seedy style — or his overwhelming success at drawing multitudes to hear him — that brought out the sarcasm and nastiness in many normally reserved people. Frank Edwards, then a well known news commentator, and ordinarily a gentlemanly advocate of the legitimacy of saucer phenomena, referred to him as a "former hamburger cook," which Adamski, by the way, denied. Even recently, in *Report On Communion*, Ed Conroy, probably yielding to the traditional consensus, referred to him as a "dink."

Edwards, anyway, wondered why interplanetary travelers would want to cross millions of miles of space to converse with a man of such lowly background. It might have occurred to him that these travelers may well be experienced enough in human affairs to realize how little is to be gained by contacting most political leaders, military authorities and powerful industrialists whose vested worldly interests *militate* against admitting extraterrestrial visitations and all that implies. This might have occurred to him, but if it did, he never indicated it.

It is time now, I believe, to carefully reconsider Adamski, not as a messiah, as some of the wilder fringe have done in the past, but as a man who may, after all, have been importantly involved in a great pivotal moment in history. A man who, by the way of his involvement, had some legitimate information to pass on to us. His discussion of electromagnetic and geomagnetic lines of force, that create potential roadways on earth, between planets, between stars and planets, and exist in what appears as a grid structure in and below the ionesphere on earth, needs to be studied. His seminal statements in this area predate some of Aimé Michel's ideas (*Flying Saucers and the Straight Line Mystery*) and those of Bruce L. Cathie (*Harmonic 33* and *Harmonic 695\**).

We can now, if we so choose, rise above parochial knee-jerk emotional responses of disbelieving anything out of the ordinarily acceptable. We can give him and his data a fairer hearing. It is not, after all, really important that his data is not couched in polished prose, that his descriptions are sometimes pedestrian, uninspired, vague and frustratingly generalized. What is important is to recognize that it is representative of a kind of experience that he, and many others since him, claim to have had (with variations), and to work at coming to a more accurate assessment of its validity, if that is possible. And I believe it is definitely possible.

Adamski's many photographs and his movie films also deserve much closer attention. It is true that some of this material is blurry (possibly because of electromagnetic radiation) and seems amateurish. But it is also true that the three-ball-landing-gear type of saucer that appears in some of his pictures as well as the cigar-shaped mother ships he photographed look very much like photos taken later by others. The shuttlecraft photos are very similar to those taken by Eduard ("Billy") Meier, the controversial Swiss farmer who has produced the clearest, best movie and still shots of saucer-type craft ever taken. They are also similar to some of the photos taken by Howard Menger around the same time. The mother ship photos, for instance, are almost identical to one snapped above New Jersey by Joseph L. Ferriere and those taken by aviator "Mel Noel" (Guy Kirkwood) and his fellow crew members at close range from the cockpit of a commercial airliner.

What the final consensus will be, if there ever is one, about Adamski's experiences remains to be seen. We must not

*The latter work was published in the United States with the title *UFOs and Antigravity* (1977).

ever assume, however, that "consensus" is a synonym for accuracy or truth. Adamski may be no prophet. He never claimed to be. But he certainly was not the bumbling ignoramus that self-appointed critics tried to make him out to be. Some of his statements are as bright and luminescent as anything we can expect out of the mouth of man, such as the following excerpt taken from a tape-recorded lecture, as it appeared in the Danish IGAP journal *UFO Contact* (February, 1987):

Jesus is a man, Christ is a principle. It was not Jesus that proclaimed himself the Christ. It was Peter proclaiming him. Jesus only acknowledged it. He also told you that he was not as high as we give him the credit to be now. For he said, if you do as I have taught you, greater things shall you do than I have done. Proving then, to us, that there was a growth even beyond his attainment. And he also called his disciples and said, 'I feed you with milk, and not with meat, for ye are babes in Christ.' And they were men, like you and I, that he was talking to.

Christ is a Universal thing. The word Christ is derived from the Cosmic Consciousness, that may be called, if we label it, the Supreme itself; and we are but a single ray of it, which blends the Cause and Effect into one being. We today in the religious field are living the Effects. I know of no institution today that has the slightest amount of spirituality in its makeup, for where there is division there cannot be unity, and they are all divided in one way or another.

In fact, I will say this. Unless the Effects are glorified equally, as the Cause is, which you call spiritual, there is no growth. For the Mother Earth is just as holy as the father you worship as the "father of your being." For it is the Mother Earth that gives you the body, without which you could not have a body. And it is the father which is the Cause, Earth is visible, and the Cause is invisible, which has given you the best of life; which even now no one can see, and without which no one can live and be a being, which you are. Unless you combine them both as a unit, which the space people have done, then your efforts are in vain in what you are doing.*

Orfeo Angelucci's experiences in the early 50s also deserve more examination, especially the accounting of them offered in his first book, *The Secret of the Saucers*. It would appear he was chosen for contact because of his lifelong interest in physics and science in general (he wrote an earlier unpublished work called "The Nature of Infinite Entities"), his open mind and his ability to serve as a sensitive transmitting body. He had very little, if anything, to gain personally from finally publicizing his experiences. In fact, the threat of ridicule from his fellow workers at Lockheed Aircraft Corporation and people in general would have discouraged most men from opening their mouth and going public, unless they were secretly harboring egomaniacal desires for fame and instant celebrity.

Orfeo Angelucci, however, does not seem to have been the kind of personality that craves attention. He made no great sum of money from publishing his experiences—a predictable result. The same can be said of almost all contactees, then and now. If we are to believe him, he felt compelled to pass on to the world information that had been given to him by extraterrestrial visitors; first, because he had been asked to do so and, secondly, because he understood the value to mankind inherent in what he had been told. As for the motives of these visitors (who looked pretty much like you and me**), we can let them speak for themselves, as related by their contactee: 'We will do everything in our power to aid the people of Earth, but we are definitely and greatly limited by cosmic law. It is because the life evolution in its present stage of material advancement upon Earth is endangered that we have made our re-appearance in the atmosphere of your planet.' Any human with an iota of perception would have to agree, I think, with

---

*IGAP information service: lb Laulund, Vinkilvej 15, Lunde, 6830 Nr. Nebel.
**That is, as Angelucci was told, when they are not in their more ordinary etherealized state.

this oft-repeated comment of our visitors, as passed on to us through innumerable contactees, that our present worldly civilization is threatened as never before, at least as never before in historic time.

Of all the early contactees, Daniel W. Fry's story is in some ways the most compelling. A technician at White Sands Proving Ground in New Mexico during the infancy of America's rocket program, he claimed initially to have been contacted by a remotely controlled shuttlecraft and to have been taken on a 4th of July evening flight to high above New York City and back. During this brief trip at approximately 8,000 miles per hour, he was instructed by "Alan" through an intercom hookup to the mother ship, which was hovering far above the earth's surface. Fry has maintained since this experience that he has met Alan face to face on earth a couple of times during the intervening years.

There are several things about Daniel Fry and his experiences which stand out. One is that as a governmental employee, a scientist, he had much to lose and nothing to gain professionally at the time by claiming to be a contactee. Contactee claims were being ridiculed by our government and the press then as they still are today, when they are not completely ignored, which is now more likely. Another thing to keep in mind when judging the character of this particular contactee is the fact that he has spent at least half his working life since his experiences, and a considerable amount of his own money, promoting the need for greater universal understanding among all men in personal relationships as well as in the various fields of human knowledge.* Years ago he formed Understanding Inc. to further this need. Many study groups supporting the program of Understanding Inc. were formed in the United States and other parts of the world to promote greater universal understanding which, in and of itself, as Fry well knows, generates love and world peace.

Fry has spent large sums of his own money publishing his

*Fry and Menger are the last of the early well known contactees who are still living.

232

own work, such as *The White Sands Incident* (1954 and many later editions), *To Men of Earth* (1973), *The Curve of Development* (1965), *Steps to the Stars* and *Atoms, Galaxies and Understanding*. Often he gives copies of his work away. At the most, he charges the minimum — whatever his publication cost per copy. He has also sponsored and paid the publication costs of several other contactee accounts — any work he felt gave additional insight into the reality of extraterrestrial visitations and the reason(s) for them.

If Daniel Fry's motives were selfish, if he were out to make a killing in the marketplace, it would be very hard to prove from the existing evidence. As he has pointed out, he was told early on by his extraterrestrial mentor that there would be nothing to gain personally from assisting the visitors in their work other than the satisfaction of knowing he had helped spread the greater truth. When asked if that were enough of an inducement to secure his help, he said simply "yes."

Fry is by far the most careful thinker and the most polished writer among the early contactees. His experience at White Sands and his later discussions with "Alan" drew his attention to the larger problems of human conduct and life which have weighed so heavily on the human race. "Why is it," he asks in his pamphlet *The Area of Mutual Agreement*, "that an intelligent species, which mankind has always prided itself on being, has not, and apparently cannot achieve true peace, even with the sincere and dedicated striving of thousands of persons in every country, and the longing for peace that is felt by all normal humans?"

In *To Men of Earth* he offers more insight in the same direction, "It is their leaders who seem to be the laggards. The disease of political or economic power seems to confuse and mislead them, although they usually manage to find logical sounding excuses for the things which they do."

The solution to the problem of gaining peace on earth, Fry is convinced, can only be found through a process of education. Not the kind of self-serving educational processes that we have

233

become accustomed to. What we need is radical surgery performed on our understanding of the social sciences, our understanding of our relationships to one another, to our loved ones, our friends and colleagues, our fellow countrymen, people from other countries and even other worlds, even those we call enemies. He is looking for a real, workable "genuine social science." What we have now is social arts. An effective social science would become a true science worthy of the name. There has never been a war, Fry reminds us, that resulted from a disagreement in the physical sciences because the rules and laws of the physical sciences are universally accepted.

Daniel Fry believes a worldwide congress needs to be convened to explore ways of making social science a true science. Areas of mutual agreement would be explored "since there are far more ways in which all men are alike, than ways in which they are different." These areas of agreement could then be specifically determined, defined and documented. "The congress shall have one purpose only; to determine, through mutual discussion, and to document, through the minutes of the meeting, all of those principles, postulates and rules or methods of procedure that are found by all of the delegates to be generally accepted as valid principles of the social relationship of mankind." This he believes would be a giant step forward for mankind, surpassing any human footprints on the moon, any endeavor man has carried to fruition. I heartily agree and wish a multitude of people of every kind and occupation, of every color and political persuasion, of every religious persuasion, would step forward and publicaly endorse an international congress of this kind with such an agenda. The "principles" once agreed upon would serve as a ready reference to which nations and individuals could turn when faced with questions of propriety and conduct. It is possible, quite likely in fact, although Fry does not address himself to the possibility, that one day a world government, a New World Order, will use just such mutually agreed upon principles to govern a culturally diverse but undivided planet.

The public attitude about the possibility of this planet being visited by extraterrestrial entities has changed greatly in the last 44 years—and this in spite of massive governmental efforts to convince the public that such things are impossible or highly unlikely.* Now over 80 percent of the American population believes UFOs are a reality and probably in many instances visitors from elsewhere in the cosmos. In the 50s and 60s those who claimed contact were often ridiculed. Perhaps the mental and emotional circuits of too many people were overloaded then with too much which seemed too new, too revolutionary, even frightening. During those two decades many professional investigators would rather have died, probably, than admit publicly that they were also frightened by the amazing things which seemed to be happening around them.

It is time once again to reconsider where we have been to better understand where we are going. No longer is the idea of human contact with landed entities considered unlikely or strange or particularly frightening. It is more or less taken for granted among most serious UFO investigators and by much of the public that such contact is likely, that in fact it has already taken place numerous times. The center of attention now is not on the question of whether contact has been made in the past—despite all the official malarkey from the Seti program to the contrary—but rather on the increasing evidence that human abductions have been taking place for what appears to be at least several decades.

These abductions, interestingly enough, if they are in fact taking place, and I think the evidence definitely warrants drawing that conclusion, are being performed by somewhat humanoid looking creatures,** called collectively the "grays," who have been part of the UFO story from almost the beginning—but, significantly, were not involved in the early contactee cases which gained so much attention in the past.***

*See especially Fawcett and Greenwood's *Clear Intent* referred to earlier in this work.
**Brad Steiger and others believe they may well be a biologically advanced reptilian form.
***I am excluding here the Betty and Barney Hill case, the Betty Andreasson case and similar cases, which came later than the accounts of the 50s.

The extraterrestrials of those early cases were also humanoid looking, much more so than the "grays" and, it would appear, their manners were much better.

The serious student studying the puzzle of what is man, his relationship to the cosmos, his destiny, would do well to pause and carefully consider the early contactee stories. He can, if he wishes, squeeze them of their juices, as if they were some exotic fruits capable of yielding up, if the choice of specimens has been judicious, all kinds of sweet insights. Not all may prove to be sweet and true accounts by any means. But in some cases, such as that of Daniel W. Fry, the evidence is teasingly compelling. The message he returned with, whatever the ultimate truth may be, is worthy of any sky god. To ignore it would be, it seems to me, human folly. To digest it and put it into practice would indeed be a giant step for mankind, much greater than anything else which I can conceive of the species now accomplishing at this stage of its development. It would indicate that man has conquered the greatest dangers of his inner space, which he must surely succeed in doing if he ever expects to go into physical space beyond earth and moon to the stars.

# CHAPTER SEVENTEEN

## Abductio Ad Absurdum?
## (Or: Why Are the "Grays" Abducting Us?)

A few years ago contactees were laughed at by the majority of serious UFO investigators. The idea of any kind of UFO craft other than substantial, materially-made ships operating only in our own dimensional time frame (the standard extraterrestrial hypothesis) was considered by the same investigators to be highly speculative and unworthy of much serious consideration. The acceptable canon, if indeed you were a "believer," was that the craft were material objects originating either from bases within our solar system or from the more nearby star systems. This view was held in spite of some evidence to the contrary. The idea that human beings were being abducted for whatever reasons was greeted early on with hoots of derision. This view also has predominated until quite recently in spite of some earlier evidence to the contrary.

What a difference a decade or so can make. In some ways professional UFO opinion and much of public opinion has come light years in understanding. Attitudes toward UFO phenomenology have changed greatly. We know a lot more than we did — and yet we don't know very much. Whether there has been real progress in thinking depends on one's perspective; a kind of glass half full or half empty psychological teaser. Certainly there is now more flexibility of judgment, which is usually a good sign.

There is now also general agreement among most investigators that extraterrestrial entities have most probably made contact with human beings during some of the reported cases of landings. This should encourage us, impelled by simple logic and a sense of justice, to reevaluate many of the early contactee claims, which were so summarily dismissed a generation ago, although there seems to be resistance, caused perhaps by false pride, to undertaking such an enterprise. There is also a growing agreement among many investigators that there is sufficient evidence to suspect that at least some UFO phenomenology reflects the possibility that we are being visited by life forms that are either primarily interdimensional or capable, at any rate, of crossing over from one dimension to another, which would be one explanation for the observed ability of some phenomena (read "craft" if you like) to be visible and trackable one moment and disappear the next, even from radar. This is the familiar blinking in and blinking out phenomenon, of which there was much earlier evidence which was either passed over gingerly by early investigators or ignored.

And now for the real shocker. The idea that humans have been in the past (Antonio Villas-Boas) and are now (the Hills, Betty Andreasson, Christa Tilton, Licia Davidson, "Kathie Davis," Whitley Strieber et cetera) being abducted by the extraterrestrial group known as the "grays" does not generally draw hoots of derision from the better informed. As the evidence mounts, the contemplation of such a reality is causing consternation and fear among many people, including some UFO investigators. We need answers to some very large questions concerning "gray" activity. If we cannot find final answers, draw final conclusions at the moment—and it appears we are a long way from being able to do so—we had best ask ourselves some serious questions and try as best we can to sort out possible motives and meanings for what appears to be transpiring.

As any good safari guide knows, sometimes it is necessary to backtrack first to understand better not only what has happened previously but in order to understand better how you got where you are at the moment and which direction in the future might be most profitable to explore (or, alternatively, where the beast has been and where it may now be lurking ahead). A brief, and sometimes historical, recapitulation of certain outstanding considerations might be helpful to us at this point, so that we may better understand how the "gray" phenomena has been able to come out of the bush, as the safari boys say, and take us by surprise the way it has.

Anyone attempting to understand what is happening in the large number of reported abduction cases, why it is happening, and why we now seem to be surprised by it all, must first consider the longstanding brick wall of official denial at all federal levels, a denial which has undoubtedly suppressed much vital information—including much earlier data from the 50s, 60s and 70s—about human-extraterrestrial contact just as it has kept on ice much technological knowledge which could help us all better understand UFO phenomenology. But then whoever said the federal government and its entrenched bureaucracy, supported by powerful leaders in the military-industrial complex that Dwight Eisenhower warned of long ago, wanted an informed public? If anyone did, he must have been a naive soul though perhaps a well meaning one. The rude reality is official government is very satisfied with a blind and deaf electorate, metaphorically speaking, of course—and this despite all constitutional considerations to the contrary and the generally recognized fact that no democracy can long endure without an informed, educated electorate.

If these last statements sound like a political polemic that has little to do with UFOs and abduction, I apologize. I ask you to defer judgment on that score for awhile. I also wish to assure you I am not a candidate for public office nor do I plan to be in the near future. The relevance of the above criticism will become obvious, I believe, as we precede. But first things first or, rather, let us look at the earlier picture before reviewing the whole montage and coming to any conclusions, even tentative ones.

Any attempt to understand what is happening must consider how gradually the evidence suggesting the existence of an abduction epidemic surfaced to the light of day. The case of the Brazilian, Antonio Villas-Boas, which has already been alluded to, seemed to most investigators at the time of his adventure (1957) as interesting, possibly significant but highly bizarre. After all, skeptics were quick to point out, men have been known to fantasize about being abducted by a woman and forced to perform sexually. Now, looking back, it seems the case may well have been a harbinger of things to come, a key to understanding a kind of case that was to be reported repeatedly, and increasingly frequently, in the future. More specifically, what kind of a case was that? Simply this. Little gray-skinned men abduct either a male or female human, sometimes both together, and take him/her to a waiting spacecraft where he/she is medically examined. This exam often includes inspection of the genitalia. Sometimes with male abductees it includes performing coitus with a hybrid-like female (both Villas-Boas and Strieber qualify here), one that is neither completely human nor solely "gray" in features. It may include the taking of sperm samples. Both male and female abductees often report incisions made in their flesh, including what many believe to be implants placed in various parts of the body, particularly up the nasal passage.

Some alleged female abductees are reporting repeated abductions during which, they believe, eggs and embryos have either been removed from their tubes and wombs or they have been artificially inseminated in advance of embryo removal at a later date. All this, of course, sounds very sinister. If it were not for the increasing number of such reports, and the great similarity of reports down to the finest details, we might be able to shrug it all off as preconditioning caused by an individual reading or hearing reports of such things and being subconsciously influenced, as collusion among hoaxers or mass hysteria or some other mental anomaly predictably to be found in a small number of people in any large population. But very similar cases are appearing in staggering numbers, first dozens, then hundreds, then thousands. It will be difficult for even the most dedicated myopic debunker, such as a Philip Klass, to write off this large caseload because of such a factor as preconditioning, especially when many of the subjects/victims have had no previous interest in UFO-related things, although you can bet he, and others like him, will try. We had better hold off shrugging for awhile or jumping to conclusions such as this one: Because everything doesn't smell scientific enough, or fit preconceived patterns, it is not happening. To relegate the idea of human abduction by extraterrestrial entities to the waste can of unbelievable absurdities, given the existing evidence, could be very unproductive to any search for truth. And it could also be, sooner than we might realize, very dangerous to our collective well being.

What are some of the observations and even tentative conclusions that a reasonably sane man, who has done his homework, might draw from ancient and modern abduction reports?

(1)   There are strong historical precedents to the contemporary abduction phenomena. The Old Testament Book of Ezekiel is a stellar example.

(2)   Generally speaking, contactee cases in the 50s, 60s and 70s did not involve the three-and-a-half to four foot "grays," the *Communion*-type extraterrestrials whose likeness adorned the cover of Whitley Strieber's first encounter work. We have the contactees' own words verifying this fact.

(3)   Increasing numbers of abduction accounts involving "grays" have been recorded in the last several decades by investigators such as David Webb, Leo Sprinkle, James Harder, Jerome Clark, David Jacobs and others.

(4)   Budd Hopkins' works, *Missing Time* and *Intruders*, seem to have unlocked a gate through which a multitude of people are now passing, willing at last and ready to disburden themselves of the abduction experiences that occurred to them in the 80s *and in*

*previous decades.* These individuals must first break through the brainwashing, that is, what appears to be posthypnotic suggestions to forget their encounters that have been placed in their minds by their "gray" abductors, before they are able to remember relatively clearly, usually under hypnosis, their experiences with the "grays."

(5) Strieber's "gray" works, *Communion* and *Transformation,* are less clinical in their presentation of ideas and experiences than Hopkins' though in some ways more broadly analytical and more willing to consider the possible benefits that mankind might receive through such contact. They have further opened the gate for cathartic recall of abduction experiences. In addition, his works, along with Hopkins', because of their commercial success, have made the subject of extraterrestrial abduction in many quarters a publically acceptable subject of discussion. This, in itself, is an important event.

Serious UFO investigators are well aware of the various recurring types of UFO entities reported by witnesses. Notable among these types are the "blonds" or "Pleiadians" who look Caucasian in features, the seven foot giants with small heads, the one-eyed cyclopeans, the Eurasian look-alikes, the three foot pumpkin-heads, the short, hairy men, even the winged flying "mothmen" among a host of others. Reports of latter creatures, by the way, were cataloged and ably studied in years past by John Keel in *The Mothmen Prophecies.*

Most of these types are infrequently reported. As to the fact that there seems to be so much variation in observed life forms, it might be prudent to keep at least two possible explanations for such diversity in mind. First, as theoreticians have pointed out in the past, we may well be hosting a rather large assemblage of cosmic visitors whose origins are diverse as to place and even dimension. Secondly, it might also be wise to keep in mind that alien intelligences, friendly or unfriendly, may have the ability to appear in our dimension in any material form they so desire. After all, because we know so little about the possibilities of the transubstantiation of matter, it would not be very intelligent of us at this stage to make final pronouncements about what is possible and what is not. Better, perhaps, to remain humble in spirit, and judgment, while keeping curious and open minds.

The "grays," however, unlike other extraterrestrial types, are frequently reported, at least in the United States. They are involved in 95 percent or more (my estimate) of the present-day reported cases of abduction. It is only in America that abduction now seems rampant. If it is happening in large numbers elsewhere—and it well may be—awareness of such has not reached professional investigators or the public.

If the abductions are in fact happening, and if the "grays" are primarily active as abductors only in the United States, as they seem to be, we had best ask ourselves why? Is it because we are more technologically advanced as a culture and have spurred their special interest? Actually, many Western cultures are as technological as we are. Could it be, then, they have bases on our soil, the possibility of which has been suggested by John Lear, William Cooper, Bill Hamilton and Robert Lazar, and we are conveniently available? Could it be that our government, unknown to most of us, has made secret deals with an alien culture, allowing a certain number of abductions to take place in exchange for alien technology? This is a possibility that John Lear and William Cooper have lately advocated.

Thoughts like these are disturbing. If Lear and Cooper are close to the truth in any way, it is definitely a truth which bares out the great bard's warning from Hamlet's mouth that there are, indeed, more things in heaven and earth than are dreamt of in the philosophy of Horatio or most folks living down the block. Thoughts like these tend to stretch our credulity, challenge our sanity, making us feel vulnerable. Like Sigmund Freud, however, too many people, including many UFO investigators, are afraid of slipping off into "the black muds of mysticism" and so, to protect themselves, refuse to consider the extraordinary alternative, to think the unthinkable and thereby become classified as unpredictable, unscientific and undependable. Before we hastily discount the possibility of underground "gray" bases, we had best carefully explore and consider the testimony of such alleged abductees as Licia Davidson and Christa Tilton, both of whom claim to have been forced to submit to physical probing and possibly artificial insemination. The line between truth and science fiction may be a narrow one, but we had better make sure we discover it as best we can without prejudgment of what is and is not possible, what may or may not be happening.

The possibility that Christa Tilton's alleged experiences could be true is taken seriously by many UFO investigators today. And that is interesting for several reasons. As we have previously noted, the general consensus in the 50s, though by no means shared by everyone, was that the contactee stories like Adamski's, Angelucci's and Bethurum's were frauds and hoaxes. Investigators were just beginning to learn how to stretch their minds. They were not being encouraged at all by conventional science or their government. They were having a hard enough time accepting the available circumstantial evidence which indicated that extraterrestrial visitors might in fact be here. But, at the time, it was too much for these same minds (most of them, anyway), under constant pressure to produce some hard evidence, to stretch so far as to accept the reports that aliens were actually in some cases making contact with humans. NICAP, for instance, under the direction of retired Major Donald Keyhoe, would have nothing to do with such reports. This curious rejection of the notion of contact coupled with an acceptance of the notion of extraterrestrial craft in our skies existed for some time, actually until quite recently, even though it is based on bad logic. If living entities exist within the craft, it is logical to assume they would sometimes land (as has been plentifully observed) and make at least occasional contact, accidental or otherwise, with human beings. Logic has not always ruled the UFO community.

As things stand, given conventional science's inability to explain some of the observed characteristics of UFOs, such as what would appear to be the use of antigravity and electromagnetism, and given conventional science's abdication of responsibility to pursue research that makes them nervous, perhaps because they cannot explain what has been observed, it is not unproductive behavior to indulge in some careful speculation to help fill the void.* We can attempt to sort out some of the problems which seem to be involved in sensuous and mechanical observations of extraterrestrial phenomena and, in particular, explore some of the more psychological aspects involved in many of the reported abduction scenarios.

It would seem somewhat persumptuous and perhaps self-defeating at this point in our knowledge to insist that the phenomena being experienced—which, together with abduction, must include phenomena in which the observer has participated—should be pigeonholed into either an exclusively extraterrestrial hypothesis or a predominantly psychologically/psychically-oriented hypothesis. The former inclination reflects an attitude which dominated the early days of UFO research and is still the inclination held to by MUFON and would seem to be the direction Budd Hopkins is heading. The latter inclination reflects the kind of thinking Whitley Strieber seems to be favoring and is reminiscent of the Borderland Sciences' and Jungian attitudes which preceded him. UFO phenomena may turn out, after all, to be both—sometimes physical, sometimes primarily psychic. Sometimes it may be both at the same time.

To be able to "blink in" and "blink out" of reality, at least as it is recorded by our scientific instruments and our human senses, may suggest that the phenomena, and whatever living beings are involved with it, is able to cross lines, cross dimensions, cross at any rate what we have rather arbitrarily demar-

---

*There is, of course, an assumption here which may be very wrong. It could be that some of the "conventional scientists" working for our government know much more about antigravity and electromagnetism than we have been lead to believe—knowledge gained, conceivably, from studying crashed extraterrestrial craft or by collusion with a group of extraterrestrials such as the "grays."

cated as a line separating what is substantial from what is intangible. That line may be really nothing more than a projection of the limitations of our senses, psyches and imaginations. We should not forget that the phenomena overall represents what would seem a broad spectrum of beings and machines *and states of reality.* The beings seem more or less substantial depending on the species represented and/or the situation. (Compare, for instance, the substantiality of Villas-Boas' abductors with the rather insubstantial consuming blobs reported to have attacked Hans Gustafson and Stig Rydberg in Sweden on December 20, 1958.) The same could be said of the machines or craft or UFOs themselves. (See Harley Rutledge's *Project Identification* and Trevor James Constable's *The Cosmic Pulse of Life* and *They Live in the Sky.*)

It is quite possible that some of this phenomena, including the beings which accompany it, represents various, distinguishable abilities. Some of it, then, may be able to do what some of it cannot. The living blobs that tried to abduct the two Swedish young men obviously did not look like the typical small "gray" extraterrestrials associated with the majority of reported contemporary abductions. Yet they could potentially be the same entities in another guise. We should not rule out the possibility. And we should never, as the evidence suggests, minimize the ability of some of these beings to manipulate the human brain into seeing or doing what they desire to be seen or done. This observation is relevant to all abduction, *and sighting*, reports—whether we are talking about the Book of Ezekiel, the Book of Daniel or what Whitley Strieber saw or thought he saw.

There is no doubt a great deal of difference between being offered a ride and being forcibly abducted. The entities who took biblical Ezekiel aloft several times did so by numbing his resistance (by hypnosis or thought suggestion) in a manner quite similar to methods reportedly employed by the "grays" today. In other books of the Old Testament, particularly the Book of Daniel (Dan 8:15), the Book of Zechariah (Zech 2:1), as well as in Genesis (Gen 18:2), these entities are sometimes referred to as "men" or said to resemble "men."* Did our extraterrestrial visitors do a job on these biblical observers, altering their consciousness in a way so that they thought they were seeing something quite different from what really was there? Were they being given an idealized image? It is possible. I have said elsewhere in *Extraterrestrials in Biblical Prophecy and the New Age Great Experiment* that I did not think the extraterrestrial visitors found in such great numbers in the Old Testament scriptures were the "grays" we are hearing so much about today. I could be wrong. According to some contactees, the "grays" have claimed otherwise. It is significant, however, that descriptions of the "grays" have been relatively consistent as to physical features, although there is some variation in size among them and, as Strieber points out, they sometimes appear to have attending robot-like forms accompanying them.

The "gray" problem(s) is almost overwhelmingly complicated at this point in time. It is also imperative, as I have already suggested, that even though we know so little now, we try hard to learn more. The "grays'" actions, as have been reported, are vastly different from the quality of contact humans have generally reported receiving from other extraterrestrial (UFO-occupant) types. And there is so much more of it to consider, as we have already made clear.

The first "gray"-type abduction which received large national attention was the Betty and Barney Hill affair, which was treated in detail in John Fuller's book *The Interrupted Journey* and was later cinematized and shown on national television twice. Several years later Betty Andreasson had "gray"-type experiences which have been recorded and analyzed by Raymond Fowler in two works, *The Andreasson Affair* and *The Andreasson Affair, Phase Two*.** There is a vast difference between the terror experienced by Betty and Barney Hill, as they were probed and examined physically by what appear to be "grays," and the experience of Betty Andreasson who, also having been physically probed, came away with the

*Also in Ez 40:3.
**And now in a new work, *The Watchers*.

feeling that these were angel-like creatures who had expanded her consciousness and religious perception.

Christa Tilton claims to have been repeatedly abducted by "gray"-like entities and taken to an underground base where she witnessed biological experiments being performed. She saw, she says, some rather weird bioengineered life forms in the lower levels of this massive underground laboratory. She, too, claims to have been repeatedly probed physically and perhaps has had her womb used as an incubator in a manner similar to what "Kathie Davis" reported to Budd Hopkins. Christa Tilton claims to have escaped once from this underground laboratory with the help of a guard. Both Tilton and "Davis" (a pseudonym) seem to have mixed feelings about their experiences, Tilton being perhaps more apprehensive about what happened to her than "Davis." "Davis" claims she was shown a hybrid child in the presence of the "gray" father and told that the child was hers/theirs.

It is remarkable in some ways that Betty Andreasson does not now feel threatened by her experiences. Both she and Strieber, who in the beginning was terrified by what was happening to him, have reached within their minds a kind of psychological accommodation with the "grays." The accommodations are not the same, but neither one now seems psychologically threatened by their past extraterrestrial experiences or future extraterrestrial possibilities. Strieber seems to be saying that his experiences are offering him a growth mode which can potentially "transform" the human creature into states of being and states of awareness that he probably would not have reached if not forced to break through his habitual responses to what he perceives as reality. This is akin to stress conditioning, whereby the subject is forced out of conventional habits of reaction and is made more receptive to the unusual by the pressure of unpredictable or unfamiliar circumstances. The positive side of such conditioning is a more open-minded and stronger personality. The negative side is that not everyone can take such pressure and a nervous breakdown can be the result. Strieber seems to be moving toward the hypothesis that the stress is only in the mind of the beholder, or percipient, and can be controlled, actually shed. We only fear what we do not know, do not understand, have not met head on—provided, of course, we become finally convinced that whatever we have met is not evil and does not have the intention to purposefully harm us.

Both Andreasson and Strieber have been told that they are special: Andreasson that she was a chosen one ('I have chosen you') and Strieber that 'You are our chosen one!'

Statements such as these raise all kinds of additional questions. Are the "grays" putting Andreasson and Strieber in a class among the "elect"? The language used is reminiscent of the language of biblical prophecy, especially the books of Ezekiel, Daniel and Revelation. Is that the intention? Are the "grays" telling us they are *angels* (literally, the word means "messengers") involved with the appearance of armies "coming on the clouds of heaven" during "end times"? It would be easy to interpret remarks such as these in such a way, even easier when we recall that they have told at least one contactee that it was they who created Jesus. Fowler also quotes Andreasson as saying that she was told '...you must release yourself of that fear *through my son.*'

Are these "grays" really the same group of extraterrestrials who programmed the Old Testament prophets and John in Revelation? I have already indicated that I have my doubts, but these doubts are only a hunch based on the prophets' own assertions that the visitors looked like "men." I am assuming that their minds were not hypnotized into seeing "grays" as "men." I have already indicated the strong biblical evidence found by textual analysis and careful reading which indicates that Ezekiel's, Daniel's and Zechariah's minds were acted upon, their consciousness unmistakably altered. The final questions become how much acted upon and what did the figures really look like who were described as "men"? Some people today would (and have) described the "grays" as looking like "little men."

If the answers to several of the key questions above are

"yes," then we would seem to have little to fear from the "grays" and much to gain. They become our historical morality teachers, our instructors and friends. Or could it be we are being bamboozled by sleight of hand and mind? Are they, perhaps, taking credit for others' work, supreme opportunists set on dominating us subtly before we have figured out we have been taken to the cleaners (or a specimen table in a round room with indirect lighting)? Could they be the sinister entities from Orion that some contactees have long been warning us about who, unscrupulous and seemingly amoral, are out to conquer the galaxy? If the latter sounds like Buck Rodgers fantasy, it is best to remember that human flight seemed ridiculous to most people at the turn of the century, and television and atomic energy had not been conceived.

Betty Andreasson Luca and her husband Bob Luca were speakers at the National New Age and Alien Agenda Conference which was held in Phoenix, Arizona in September, 1990. After I listened to her presentation, I had a chance to ask her a few questions.

"Could it be," I began, "that the large number of 'baby grays,' as you called them, that were shown to you within the spacecraft were not babies at all? What was it exactly the long-nosed taller gray said to you? Did he say 'babies' or 'little ones'? As I recall, you said you were told by the grays, 'We can make taller or smaller, wider or narrower.' Could it be these 'babies' you saw were really deflated or miniaturized mature grays?"

"I hadn't thought of that," she said. "It's possible."

"Then it occurred to me that they could transport tens of thousands at one time aboard one spacecraft, if they can affect proportions in such a way."

"I see what you mean," she said.

Perhaps she did. But I had not verbalized the last thought that ran through my mind. And that was this: What an effective way to transport an invading army, if the "grays" have that intention.

Paranoia is easy to come by if we let our imagination run

250

amok. However, there is now enough evidence to put us on our guard until we learn more about the "grays" themselves and their intentions. Certainly "gray" technology, as it has been observed, is beyond anything we now have, almost beyond anything we have even conceived of until recently. Yet other visiting life forms seem to be as far advanced as they are. Small consolation there, the pessimist would say.

The large edge in technology raises other questions. If the "grays" can change the dimensions of physical objects, including their own body sizes, this would explain why some abductees have commented on the fact that the rooms within the spacecraft to which they have been led have sometimes seemed larger than they should be, considering the estimated overall dimensions of the spacecraft themselves. If they do have this ability to alter proportions, and even time, no wonder our present science and its instruments have such difficulty trying to explain their demonstrations.

But if the "grays" are so technologically capable, why do they need to practice bioengineering experiments such as the "Kathie Davis"-Christa Tilton kind? Why go stealing sperm and artificially inseminating, which is low tech, when a capable bioengineer should be able to reproduce a clone, human or otherwise, from cells taken from anywhere on the body? Are these old-fashioned in vivo and other artificial insemination techniques really needed to produce a hybrid species, as some investigators have suggested? Both Villas-Boas and Strieber claim to have been raped by humanoid hybrids looking very much like us, or like us and "grays" combined. These episodes, by the way, happened with the three to four foot regular "grays" close by in attendance.

Questions generate questions, like cells growing in solution. What are the "grays" trying to accomplish genetically? Are they hoping to revive their own species which may be suffering from reproductive problems? Are they trying to create a new race of themselves combined with humans that can survive on an earth which has suffered great earth-change catastrophes and possibly a devastating nuclear world war?

They have warned some abductees about impending earth catastrophes in rare moments when they have deigned to communicate with their abductees. (The usual response to questions is "You will find out later.") Can we, dare we, believe these abductee reports?

Are the "grays" simply out to populate the earth with their own species? Are they thinking of sharing it with us in the future? They have claimed, according to reports, that they were here long before us. The questions keep multiplying maddeningly and definitive answers slip through the fingers of our minds like so many greased pigs. We have only recently started asking most of these questions. Is the hour already late?

Who are these taller, large-nosed "grays" who appear to control the shorter more common ones? Andreasson has noted them. Strieber also to some extent. Now Dr. Rauni-Leena Luukanen, chief medical officer of Finnish Lapland from 1975 to 1987 and presently retired in Switzerland, claims dozens of contacts with "grays," some of whom, she says, were of the large-nosed kind. She admits to having been medically examined several times and, like Betty Andreasson, seems to have no fear of her abductors or the exams they have administered to her. "I realize," she says, "that I am part of a huge experimental project." If there ever was a creditable witness, whose background inspires confidence, she would seem to be it. And yet the question remains, a huge experimental project with what ultimate objectives?

Strieber has written about observing several types of extraterrestrials other than "grays." One of these types is "blue" little men who are folded away in compartments, stored, when not needed by the "grays." When they are needed, they are, it appears, inflated almost like balloons. How alive are they? one wonders. Are they robotic or android in nature?

Are the short "grays" themselves really individuated beings with individualistic thoughts or are they perhaps clone-like beings with a group mind, taking their orders ultimately from the large-nosed "grays?" Ed Conroy, while researching

*Report On Communion*, interviewed Linda Howe, television journalist and producer now living in the Denver area, who has the award-winning 1978 documentary on possibly UFO-related cattle mutilations, *A Strange Harvest*, to her credits. On the subject of "grays," she had this interesting observation to make, 'One of the things that keeps occurring to me is that perhaps the large black-eyed gray things are like somebody else's worker bees. That beyond them, controlling them, is perhaps an intelligence we have yet to encounter.' This kind of thinking raises the idea of a chain of command that could go well above and beyond even the large-nosed "grays," who might, after all, hold only some kind of intermediate position of authority.

Leifur Magnusson, longtime student of UFO phenomenology, suggested to me, during the same Phoenix Conference at which I questioned Betty Andreasson Luca, that the small "grays" should perhaps be thought of as "dolls" with a group mentality. They have the cosmic life force within them but it is not nearly as differentiated as it is in us. "Don't assume," he said, "that they necessarily believe in a cosmic law that might restrain them from whatever their purpose may be." I have since filed his warning in an imminently retrievable zone of my consciousness.

It seems obvious from reports that the "grays" do not think very much like us. It is quite possible they do not think at all like we think and do not particularly care what we think. From a human ethical point of view, their abductive activity generally, and the particular methods they employ, seems inexcusable, if not execrable. There are not many acceptable explanations for forcibly kidnapping people, forcefully detaining them, forcefully injecting brain probes, stomach and anal probes and, as some victims have attested, inserting implants up the nasal passage and into other parts of the body. This sounds too much like the highhanded disregard for subjects/captives that we have come to associate with Dr. Frankenstein and his more modern equivalents, the Nazi experimenters such as the infamous Dr. Mengele and his many associates.

Is there any possible explanation that might justify the tactics allegedly used by the "grays" to capture their subjects and any acceptable rationale to the experimental procedures that seem to take place once these subjects are within the "grays'" laboratories, whether these be located on board spacecraft or found within underground bases? I can think of several, although they will not be acceptable to everyone and are not completely acceptable to me.

First, it is possible that abductees, either before entering this life, or subconsciously after entering it, have given explicit permission to the "grays" to be used as experimental subjects as long as they are not fundamentally harmed or destroyed. Such an idea is an intriguing speculation. Secondly, it is possible that, as the "grays" have claimed a time or two, they are responsible for eugenically transforming *Homo erectus* into *Homo sapiens* by bioengineering. In other words, they have created us and we are an ongoing biological experiment for reasons which we do not fully understand. Thirdly, the "grays" may have been given a mandate by a higher "god" to do the kind of experimenting they are alleged to be doing. The second and third alternatives offered here may be interrelated. In fact, all of the above possibilities could be operative at the same time.

At the worst, from a human perspective, this means we are "owned" or, at least, that those who bioengineered us feel that way, even if the subjects themselves feel rebellious. I have written elsewhere about prehistorical extraterrestrial bioengineering of *Homo sapiens*. I will sum up here by saying that I believe there is strong evidence it happened but I am not yet convinced it was the "grays" who are responsible.

Are we really the "property" of someone such as the "grays?" Are we being "farmed," as Charles Fort long ago suggested? The thought is a chilling one. It certainly deflates any human pretension that we are God's one and only intelligent cosmic bauble, his favorite creation. Are we, as some non-"gray" extraterrestrials are reported to have maintained, in danger of becoming slaves if we are not careful? Slaves to the "grays?" Another chilling thought.

And what do we make of the conversation reported by Whitley Strieber to have taken place between himself and the "grays" when he complained about an "operation" they were about to perform on him. He told them they had no right to do so. 'We do have a right,' he was told. Is that 'right' to be found under the three rationales I have offered—or somewhere else we have not thought of? Would we agree with it? The taciturn nature of the "grays," when it comes to offering explanations, is exasperating. No one likes to be treated as raw meat, as no better than a worm or bug stuck to a board. Where is the compassion we might expect from a superior intelligence?

Wherever the "grays" have come from, whether this galaxy, beyond, or from another plane or dimension makes no particular difference. If they have bioengineered us, in the first place, let them speak up. Let's see some proof. Even if this is so, there are some large questions, from a human ethical point of view, about their methods. We have already raised some of them in these paragraphs. Let's talk about them—"gray" and human together. A real dialogue. A real "communion." Strieber has said his initial title for *Communion* was *Body Terror* but that he changed it at the insistence of the "grays." Okay. Let's have real communion, which is a two-way street. Many of us are quite ready to walk it.

If the "grays" can prove convincingly that their motives are legitimate and acceptable to humans, I'm sure they would have no trouble finding volunteers for their research. We are all aware how humans love to volunteer for anything unusual or anything perceived as significant. But as things stand, there is too much misunderstanding among professional investigators and too much ignorance within the public masses. The time has come, it would seem, to raise the veil and behold the truth, whatever it is. Secrecy only binds in ignorance and undermines any real possibility for "communion" to happen.

The greatest problem so far is the unwillingness—as well as the tacitum aloofness—of the "grays" to tell their subjects/victims what they are up to. Even Whitley Strieber got the "We'll-explain-it-to-you-later" brush off when he tried questioning his captors as to their motives, more of a brush off, perhaps, than he's willing to admit. So did, for that matter, Betty Andreasson when she was told, 'I shall show you as time goes by.' This kind of disdain, this kind of superior attitude, is not acceptable to humans. It is offensive if not repulsive to us and unfitting behavior for anyone who says he wishes to "commune" with us. Surely the "grays" have studied us well enough to be aware of this. Or am I assuming too much?

If "gray" intelligence is superior, let it demonstrate itself to be so by its compassion and its willingness to explain itself. Otherwise, we may be right in assuming, under the circumstances, that we are considered meat on the hoof to be done with as desired. There is always the possibility, knowing as little as we do, that the "grays" may turn out to be a life form so totally removed from the human, so disinterested in human thoughts and feelings, perhaps so incapable of what we think of as compassion, that they don't give a damn about the suffering they have already caused and may cause in the future. A declaration of motive by the "grays" is now necessary. Let them clarify in detail to their abductees what is happening and why. Then these abductees must come forward, with clear memories unencumbered by brainwashing, to pass on publicly what they have been told. If the "grays" are really friends of humanity, let them say so. Then let them prove it. With "grays" as with man, they shall be known by their deeds.

As a final thought, we need to consider the idea, the possibility, that our government, or certain powerful groups either within or outside of it, may have in fact made some kind of secret agreement with the "grays," trading so many humans as guinea pigs, let's say, for so much hot new alien technology. The "grays" must come to realize that this kind of contract in our society, if it has indeed been made, is ethically unacceptable and legally and constitutionally illegitimate. It can only be maintained by deception and undemocratic force. No government or human has the right by international law, or by any national law now in existence, to trade humans as experimental guinea pigs or as slaves.

What is the human cosmic quester, that individual who would like to get to the bottom of things and understand better the creation about him, to do faced with the question of the "grays'" actions and motives? I can only offer some down-home practical advice. Keep your eyes open and keep an open mind. When Hamlet said, "There are more things under heaven and earth, Horatio, than thou has dreamt" he might as well have been talking about this New Age and all matter of strange and unusual phenomena associated with it that has raised its specter before us and must be recognized for whatever it is and dealt with as is appropriate. Or as we learn to deal with it. The "grays," and their attendant phenomena, among other things, would seem to apply here as well. An open mind is the only real hope we have to access these strange and unusual phenomena and to learn to understand them. It is through such minds that dreams often become reality and the seemingly absurd often turns out to have its own logical validity.

# CHAPTER EIGHTEEN

## World Government: A New World Order

World government is inevitable. The question is, When? And who will govern? And how? If it does not come soon, the civilization of man, such as it is, may erode further to the point where it is totally nonfunctional. It may cease to exist altogether. But present conditions, caused by learned habits of thought, make world government difficult to achieve.

What are these habits of thought that so threaten us all?

There are two special crosscurrents active in the thinking of men which are contradictory, if not mutually exclusive. One is the yearning for friendship, camaraderie, for a borderless world in which the human family can move freely about, intermingling in all its diversity. In this kind of world the members learn the educational value of differences while at the same time learning about the even more compelling similarites among all men. It is a world which recognizes that human subsistence problems, aspirations and yearnings are very much alike among all men; that You are a reflection of Me and, conversely, that I am a reflection of You—albeit sometimes with slightly different trappings of dress and certain negligible differences in color of skin, habits of behavior and personal preferences. It is a world which properly discounts, though respects, the differences in race and religion among us. These are seen for what they really are—minor biological variations and mental choices, interesting in themselves, but hardly essential in defining what is human and most remarkable about man. And what is that? Perhaps nothing more and nothing less than man's unquenchable determination to thoroughly discover himself, his cosmic origins and his reason for being. This determination, or self-determination, characteristic is crucial to any understanding of what man is but, unfortunately, it is one of the last things taught, and sometimes one of the last things perceived, by formal educators.

The other current which motivates much of human thinking and action, and which is at cross-purposes with the aforementioned, is far more insular and selfish. It is the drive within uneducated man, harkening back to his tribalistic roots, to proclaim nationalistic sovereignty and nationalistic differences. On a smaller, intranational scale, it is the same drive which encourages militant ethnic and subcultural groups to defiantly flaunt their differences, which they perceive as large, from the greater society of which they are a part. This current (drive) is not cohesive but divisive, looking for variances among men and falsely magnifying them, setting men against each other. Race, color and creed differences are made paramount. I look at You and see at best a stranger, at worst an enemy. It is not the way of psychological and physical fusion but of fission, and it is demonstrably explosive. It is the way of separation and often war and death. Megalomaniacal leaders, autocrats and other power brokers encourage the kind of thinking which gives birth to it. It is their bread and butter but a food that, to their followers, always, sooner or later, becomes a bitter loaf which neither nurtures nor satisfies.

What are we to think of the prospects of a world today which is desperately in need of social unity — with nuclear, biological and chemical weapons poised over its head like a sword of Damocles and population, pollution and food problems mounting daily — that perversely persists in extolling narrow nationalistic objectives? A world where political leaders and religious leaders pit nations and their peoples against one another for selfish motives. What are the prospects of a world in which individuals have been taught, or are driven by their baser natures, to put themselves first, their nationalistic prejudices second and to consider the commonweal of the world as a whole as an afterthought, if indeed the latter ever is brought to mind? A thinking man with some compassion would be led to believe they are poor, and he would be saddened by his conclusion in proportion to the amount of compassion in his heart.

A brief survey of some of the nationalistic drives alive and thriving in the world at present is not reassuring. The United States insists on playing world policeman but only when it is to its advantage. The Soviet Union, partially recognizing and reluctantly admitting the failure of its political and economic practices, is torn by movements for more democracy and freedom. Its satellites, and a majority of its own republics, demand home rule. At the same time separatist ethnic enclaves within and without the republics proclaim self-righteously a need to control their own affairs, often using democratic slogans as a screen to persecute neighboring and competing ethnic populations. Just a few examples among many draw a Goya-like portrait of pain and suffering. Georgians murder Ossetians and vice versa. Armenians spill Azerbaijani blood and vice versa. The bloody ages-old ethnic disputes continue now more violently than ever as the antagonists sense the weakness of centralized government. The satellite countries of Eastern Europe, such as Romania, Czechoslovakia, Hungary and Poland, all try to distance themselves as much as possible from direct Soviet control, as do the Baltic satellites Lithuania, Latvia and Estonia.

In Yugoslavia Titoism is almost dead but before it can be laid to rest, the six republics of the realm are busy devising how they can each separately profit from the demise. As central control diminishes, as in Russia, ethnic subcultures begin to persecute their enemies. Croatians spill the blood of their Serbian countrymen and vice versa. The *modus operandi* becomes, as it is found often elsewhere in the world, the anti-philosophy of an eye for an eye. Old grievances are disinterred and given new life so that new blood may be spilled as an offering to the ancient gods of vengeance.

Elsewhere East Germany reunites with West Germany.

The narrow-minded political optimist sees all of these developments as victories for greater freedom and budding democracy and, in a way, they are. Many New Agers see them as predictable harbingers of great world change, the necessary though unstable flux in a world that must change. Maybe so. But we had better ask ourselves if these changes, if this flux, is really leading us toward a more stable, friendly world. Or is it just flux? More of the same old thing packaged a little differently with a new address. Could it be we are seeing a "new" kind of self-righteous nationalistic fervor which will in the long run prove to separate men from men just as effectively as did the old kind of which we have become so familiar? Could it be it is all really just the latest budding branch of an old limb called nationalistic self-aggrandizement and, at a lower level, personal self-interest? Are we seeing an exchange of sweet potatoes for yams while being assured by the politically naive that we are watching something happen that is profoundly new and different, perhaps even the birth of a New World Order?

In a world which needs cohesion in politics and religion, attainable most probably through greater understanding and an abandonment of the search for petty differences, the trend is neither discernibly tide in nor tide out. There seems to be, however, as many nationalistic divisions in the world today as there were at the turn of the century. Actually more. At any rate, more have come to life recently, some having lain comatose or been in hiding for a long time.

The British Empire is gone. European colonialism is dead. Their passing unlocked in many parts of the world a suppressed regional nationalism that has been upwelling in the former colonies for some time now. We have all been spectators to its triumphs, its half-victories and its utter failures, often bloody ones and reprehensible from a traditional moral point of view but no more reprehensible, undoubtedly, than the colonial repressions out of which it grew. But the point to be made here is probably best expressed as an extended metaphor. If imperial, colonial nationalism (and we will include the Soviet Union here along with the more traditional empire builders) was the Mother of all Beasts, its demise has given birth to many little, inferior but vicious, nationalistic predators who are free to prey on a world (including themselves) which has become too crowded and too environmentally tenuous to accommodate their dangerous, uncouth behavior.

The depredations of the little beasts, however, seem in some ways minuscule (although still appreciable) when compared to those of the Mother(s) of all Beasts who helped create them. This mother or, more properly, these mothers are still alive and well and still carry the greatest weight and hold the biggest sticks in the world. We all know them, of course, by the name of the industrialized nations, the First World countries, international powers unto this day, although there is at any given moment a discernible pecking order even among them that changes only gradually over time. What is probably most remarkable about this family of "great" nations is that, not unlike their smaller brethren, they have never been able over an extended period of time to work together effectively enough to assure a peaceful world. They continue to squabble just as the new, smaller nations of the world do. They also continue to shed blood among themselves, just as ethnic subcultures are now doing the world over, often, ironically, within the very borders of some of these great nations.

Not surprisingly, it became obvious to some world leaders after World War I that the world needed a new kind of guiding hand, a world governing body. Woodrow Wilson's League of Nations was an attempt at such a reform but without his own government's support, and for a host of other reasons too numerous to mention, it was doomed to failure. And fail it did. But the idea of such an organization was perceived by many as a sound one. It did not die. Nor should it have.

The post World War II era brought us the United Nations. Here was undeniable further recognition that some kind of world government was desired and needed, if for no other reason than to keep nations from recreating the kind of colossal destruction that Nazi Germany and Japan had wrecked upon the world and that the United States, in particular, had unleashed against Japan by its use of nuclear weapons. The world generally was scared, and fear is often binding. The constituent nations of this new world body were, for the most part, ready to talk and act, as long as their self-interests were not jeopardized and their national sovereignties were supported. But, as skeptics well know, self-interests do frequently collide and, as cynics are want to say, one man's idea of sovereignty is often another man's idea of opportunity.

The Cold War that developed between the East bloc, China and the Western bloc shortly after the end of the hot war which had preceded it undercut the effectiveness of the United Nations from almost its inception. Real progress toward world peace became increasingly difficult. The UN did demonstrate for awhile during the Korean War that it could raise a large "police force." When, however, half the world supports and half the world refuses to support initiatives, policies and actions, the immediate potential for great accomplishments of a body like the UN is thoroughly diminished and compromised. This in fact proved to be the case. The veto power held by each permanent member of the UN Security Council further undermined the capacity of the body, considering its already inherent ideological splintering, to work cohesively and effectively together. The results the UN achieved in the decades following the Korean War were minimized, often paralyzed and periodically stultified by partisan politics, just as the Athenian League that preceded it almost 2,500 years ago, despite at times outstanding leadership in the General Assembly by such general secretaries as Dag Hammarskjold, U Thant and Perez de Cuellar.

The recent willingness of the United Nations to pass a strong resolution imposing an embargo on Iraq after Saddam Hussein's annexation of Kuwait and its further willingness to supply a peace-keeping force along the Kuwaiti border after his defeat and retreat, are encouraging signs that this body, or an international body like it, can reach consensus — especially in matters that threaten world peace — and work effectively in concert. How willing individual members will be to relinquish

264

nationalistic desires, which often are bound to conflict with consensus opinion, is debatable. How often they will do so is problematic. The predictable long-term, and even short-term, alternatives to effective collegiate action, principally world chaos caused by overpopulation, starvation, dwindling resources and similar social problems, as well as the threat to world peace caused by nationalistic and ethnic wars, are so horrible and life-threatening, that all those souls remaining with a shred of optimism must hope that the life preserving impulses of humanity will finally prove dominant and men will at last learn to work together for their own benefit and the commonwealth of all.

In the past, great world powers ignored UN positions when convenient. Even lesser powers flaunted their independent wills. If such attitudes and behavior remain commonplace in the future, political brinkmanship will hold us all hostage until one day we find we have been driven to the edge and over. The more level-headed among us would probably be correct in drawing the conclusion that world government is needed now. We cannot afford to wait. The need is too great. We must be willing to come to the international table and "play" together: *les jeux sont fait.**

Who will control this new world government reflecting the new world order once it is established? Hopefully, the members themselves, equitably, fairly. Every precaution possible must be taken to insure that one nation, or group of nations, does not gain hegemony over it. Or that a powerful group of allied individuals does not set up covertly an oligarchic interior control of it. Or that one individual becomes its dictator, promoting his own self-interest or the interests of those who may control him.

The fear of a powerful group of individuals, possibly a secret or semisecret organization, promoting its own selfish programs in the name of the common good is not paranoid thinking. It is real enough, just as is the threat of simple autocracy. History is filled with the accounts of one tyrant after

*A croupier's phrase: "The bets are (have been) made."

another imposing his will on those about him. We have spoken at some length elsewhere about the Sennacheribs, Alexanders, Caesars, Neros and their more modern counterparts. Some have been more despotic than others but they all have in common the suppression of individual freedom in the name of counterfeit, although sometimes impressive-sounding, motives and goals. The history of man is more the story of his enslavement to individuals and false ideas than it is the tale of freedom won and preserved.

It has been said that the greatest evil is the quiet kind that men never, or hardly ever, suspect. Few international cartels, other than the noisy and violent ones such as the drug cartel and, to a lesser extent, the Mafia, draw much attention to themselves.* The idea is to go about business unobtrusively, to gain objectives without fanfare, even without notice. Most of these objectives can be listed under two broad categories, categories with which human nature is already quite familiar: the assumption of greater power and the acquisition of greater wealth. The most convenient state of affairs to the cartelist is a "citizen" who has been made amenable to "reforms" without raising his ire or disapproval, ideally without him even knowing consciously, or caring, that "reforms" have been made. For "reforms," substitute the phrase "diminished freedom," and you will have a more accurate picture of the real world. "Reforms" may include, and often do, the devising of new ways and measures to control the flow of capital from one state to another, one organization to another, from the individual to the state or organization.... The net result, rather predictably, is the monetary and/or political manipulation of the individual to the benefit of the cartelist.

Never before in the history of the world have so many cartels of various kinds that are so powerful been vying so aggressively for the control of men's minds and pocketbooks. Many of these cartels pose great danger to the idea, and the implementation, of world government. As might be expected, if there is to be world government, they mean to control it or a

*And then only inadvertently as with the drug cartel(s) and the Mafia.

266

large piece of it. Needless to say, big money, big energy, big technology, big private "think tanks" with special ideological bents, must not be allowed to dictate to world citizenry overtly or covertly their own terms because they have individually or in concert, secretly or openly, usurped control of an international governing body.

The United States has many cartels and secret or semi-secret organizations wielding vast power. Some have very innocuous sounding names. How large a hand they wish to play in a New World Order and whether that hand is an action-positive one remains to be seen. Just a few examples, and a few questions, might further an open inquiry into the murky waters of their motives and intentions. Example number one: Why is the very large, private and powerful Council on Foreign Relations so secretive?* Rarely is mention made of it in the official news media. Few magazine articles have ever been printed describing it. Little is really known publicly about its professed goals. What are these goals? The Council seems in no hurry to enunciate them and gives the impression it does not want an investigation of any kind into its affairs. Yet this organization has been the main source for the last several decades, at least eight Presidencies, from which top future government leaders have been tapped. President Richard Nixon nominated and appointed well over 100 members of the Council to high government office (see Gary Allen, *None Dare Call It Conspiracy*).

Example number two: The Trilateral Commission and the Bilderbergers or Bilderberg Group. Outspoken former Senator Barry Goldwater has said, "The Trilateral Commission is international...is intended to be the vehicle for multinational consolidation of the commercial and banking interests by seizing control of the political government of the United States." Obviously Barry Goldwater is not a member but many other powerful, influential people are or were. Former Secretaries of the Defense Robert McNamara, Eliot Richardson, Harold

*Although the name makes the Council on Foreign Relations sound like an official government body, it is not.

Brown and Caspar Weinberger were, as is Deputy Secretary of State Lawrence S. Eagleberger, who is also a member of the Council on Foreign Relations, as is National Security Council member Brent Scowcroft. President George Bush is a "former" member. The list is a long one, including dozens of members outside of official government but in positions to mold public opinion, such as William Scranton of the New York Times Co., publisher Katherine Graham of the *Washington Post*, Sol Linowitz of Time, Inc., Joseph Kraft of the *L.A. Times Chronicle*, P.G. Peterson and John Sawhill of NBC/RCA and James Houghton and Harry Schacht of CBS.

The members, both past and present, of the Council on Foreign Relations are even more numerous. In the present administration, easily recognized names such as Secretary of Defense Richard B. Cheney, Chairman, Joint Chiefs of Staff Colin L. Powell, Attorney General Dick Thornburgh, Secretary of the Treasury Nicholas F. Brady, Director of the OMB Richard G. Darman, Director, Office of Equal Opportunity and Civil Rights, Horace G. Dawson, Jr. are all members.*

Is it very surprising that David Rockefeller is a former chairman of the Council on Foreign Relations and is North American Chairman of the Trilateral Commission?

Perhaps it is time to quote Senator Barry Goldwater again, "The Council on Foreign Relations is the American branch of a society which originated in England...believes national boundaries should be obliterated and one-world rule established...."

It should not surprise us to learn that there is an international organization equivalent to, and actually more powerful than, the Council on Foreign Relations. It calls itself the Bilderberg Group, created and led by His Royal Highness Prince Bernhard of the Netherlands. The prince makes no effort to hide the fact that the real goal of the Bilderbergers, other than financial manipulation of world markets, is the establishment of a world government. The Bilderbergers are the coordinators between various nationalistic interests, in-

*See Milton William Cooper's *Behold A Pale Horse*.

cluding American ones, who have the same ultimate program.

Besides the considerable influence wielded by the Council on Foreign Relations, the Trilateral Commission and the Bilderbergers, all of which seem interested in similar objectives — what are we to think of the aspirations, motives and goals of nongovernmental and quasi-governmental organizations such as the Group of Seven (G-7) and the Club of Rome? The Group of Seven, made up officially of the United States, Canada, Germany, France, Italy, Japan and Britain meets regularly to set economic policy that affects not only the West but the whole world. The international Club of Rome, though not ostensibly interested solely in economic matters, also is heavily involved in the initiation of policy that influences ultimately every human being alive. Are these organizations truly working for the common good of all? Are they selfless, nationalistically disinterested bodies or something else altogether?

The question returns to us like a boomerang: Who will rule us and how? We cannot escape it. To hide from it is inevitably impossible in the long run. If we do so in the short run, we jeopardize the quality of our future and the freedom of that future, and the kind of future our children and our children's children will have on planet Earth.

╳ History teaches us that private cartels and organizations, like nations and the individuals of which they are composed, have difficulty rising above their own vested interests, in fact sooner or later tend to become almost solely interested in themselves with little or no consideration for such abstract ideas as the "common good," "what is best for mankind," universal justice, fairness and equity of opportunity. The idea that no human being deserves to go without bread or shelter or needed medical attention is usually alien to their way of thinking, although they will sometimes pretend to support such humanitarian ideas, and even make use of them in advertising campaigns, if it is to their advantage. To those who would call such an indictment precipitous and patently unfair, we must ask, If nations and the controlling bureaucracies and organizations of which they are made did in fact value above all else

269

the welfare of each individual human constituent, then why is the world the way it is? If it is human nature that is at fault, then let us change human nature through careful educational practices, including above all else the teaching of the value of human compassion in all relationships whether they be between individuals, organizations and individuals or between the state and its citizens.

Do many of the cartels and organizations of which we have spoken have the best interest of humanity at heart? We must hope so, although there is much evidence at hand that they do not. Private organizations, even when pretending to speak for those beyond their own membership, tend to aloofness, elitism and presumptuousness. Will organizations such as the Council on Foreign Relations, the Trilateral Commission and the Bilderbergers working together (which they are) guarantee us in the future a humane, compassionate world government, a new world order that is "a kinder, gentler" order than what has preceded it? Will those who lead the new world government guarantee each human being a Bill of Rights similar to the one which was added to our own Constitution?

It is obvious that to bring all of humanity under the same umbrella, certain adjustments in law and enforcement of law will have to be made within cultures until they meet the new common ground. But any abridgement of freedom in any new world order that goes beyond what is guaranteed by the American Bill of Rights is unnecessary. Have those who are now planning out their own schemes for world government realized this simple truth? Do they care—enough? If they do not, we may find that our first world government is a beast that would devour us, and whatever we have, our freedom and our dignity as well as our material possessions, far more avidly and voraciously than the predacious nationalism that we now suffer. We must be eternally vigilant or else those who would secretly plot against our freedom, for whatever motives, will have taken it and made off with it like a chunk of choice raw meat, before we realize what we have lost.

Much of what has been said here seems obvious. Some of it

is not obvious at all. We seldom take time during our hectic individual lives to consider how dire the future may soon be if some form of humanly compassionate, workable world government is not quickly adopted. World population now stands at 5.3 billion. It is already at an unmanageable level, growing geometrically by the hour and projected to reach 6.127 billion by the year 2000 and over 10 billion by the year 2050. Present methods of nationalistic government cannot react adequately to the problems such increases bring about. The largest growth rate is where it can least be absorbed, in Third World countries. Every continent except Antarctica, and possibly Australia, has serious problems of poverty, hunger and starvation. Famine in the Sahel (the area south of the Sahara desert) of Africa, in the Horn of Africa, as well as in Mozambique, Angola, Nigeria, Malawi, Burkina, Faso and Liberia is a continuing problem, growing worse with time.*

Pollution of air, water and land has already darkened the future quality-of-life prospects in Europe. Many European forests, such as Germany's famed Black Forest, are slowly dying. The Eastern bloc industrial centers have severely fouled the environment, even more than their capitalist Western counterparts. But ecological problems are now worldwide, occuring from Haiti (where few trees are left standing) to Brazil (where the Amazon rain forest, with its rich and irreplaceable resource of flora and fauna, is being rapidly destroyed) to Calcutta (where overpopulation has created an exceptionally unhygienic situation, as it has in numerous places elsewhere). The world is rapidly running out of resources, deposits of raw materials which it needs to provide for its burgeoning population. Many of the resources which seem so abundantly available, such as oil, are being squandered or, as with coal, misused in a way which gives the appearance of increasing quality of life while in fact degrading it (e.g. coal used for the generation of electric power is a massive air polluter).

There is a great irony to these problems. We have men-

*Famine threatens 17 million people in the Horn area this year, an additional 13 million people elsewhere in Africa.

tioned it several times within other chapters of this work. It is the needlessness of many of them. They simply need not be. But for them to disappear or be significantly alleviated, several things must happen. Nations must learn quickly to forego nationalistic selfishness. Individual human beings, regardless of their country of origin or habitation, must be willing to forego *some* personal interests, if we are to have a world whose air does not choke us, whose water does not poison us and whose land is fertile enough to provide continuous sustenance.

One of the lesser ironies is a fact that the Environmental Fund underlined several years ago — the fact that there was then enough food in the world to feed everyone. There still is. Provided that those who have are willing to share with those who do not. And provided that more grain is used directly for food and not used to feed livestock which is itself intended for later consumption, a sequence which is notoriously ineffient and wasteful.

The idea of sharing, of course, is extendable to resources in general and all technology. Sharing is the key to successful world government, as it is to successful personal living. It is an idea which, if not emotionally and intellectually pleasing to some, has become, nonetheless, a necessity today. We are left finally with a simple, stark proposition: Either we learn to share today or we will soon be made to do so by necessity, by a world government forced to use harsh measures to insure that everyone receives an adequate portion of what is still available.

If we are to have a New Age controlled by men and women under the rule of a harmonious world government, we are going to have to go further than President Bush's rather fuzzy idea of a New World Order or financier Henry Kaufman's vision of "a supranational organization which would be responsible for setting international capital standards, trading regulations, and reporting requirements for financial institutions the world over." One cannot help but wonder if both of them aren't really contemplating pretty much the same old order with the major powers dominating affairs and business as usual.

All of us would do well now to begin to readjust our expectations about the future if we have not already begun to do so — our expectations that apply to food, resources, technology, all the necessities and amenities of life. We should start thinking about what a unified world governmental and legal system will really mean for the world and for us individually. World law means blending diverse legal systems into a workable new codification of rules and regulations. This can probably be done successfully while still guaranteeing each world citizen basic human rights, freedom and justice, but it does mean, most likely, that some of the lesser rights and prerogatives enjoyed by certain cultures, and members of certain cultures, will have to be surrendered. Many will resist losing their concessions, perks and privileges. It is predictable that some will try desperately to hang on to what they perceive as their higher standard of living, even in the face of an increasingly ravaged ecology.

What are some of the predictions we might make if a just and equitable world government becomes a reality? Many in the West will have to get used to having fewer material things. Even less money per capita. The trade-off is a world population which is on the average better fed, better housed and better doctored. It is a world free from the fear of war. A world where neighbors increasingly learn to share what they have and what they know. A world where the water is cleaner, the air healthier to breathe and the land more arable and wholesome. This kind of environment will not only nurtur the species in body but also in mind and spirit.

And what are the prospects if we fail to implement such change soon? One likely consequence is a world whose systems quickly atrophy. As one CIA scenario has it, the world simply runs out of raw materials and is so overburdened with population by 2050 A.D. or sooner that human civilization collapses in panic and misery. This, of course, discounts an earlier nuclear war which would cause similar, or even worse, suffering.

If humankind is unable to grasp soon enough the gravity of the situation, if it insists on discounting the enormity of the problems facing it and refuses to recognize how imperative it has become to work effectively together in an international forum which has been empowered to solve the global problems which face all of us, and which is sufficiently encouraged to do so, then our fate as rulers of our own individual destinies and as a species may be sealed. We have sent ourselves on a forced Bataan death march down Armageddon road. Whether we have a nuclear world war or not, the immensity of our problems will bury us unless we are extremely careful.

Many ancient prophecies, such as those found in our own Judeo-Christian and Hopi Indian traditions, graphically describe for us a troubled world which ultimately is able to come to terms with itself—but not without "outside" assistance. Some people take solace in that final scenario. In such a case, after much needless human suffering, when the very survival of the species is in doubt, we may be visited by the Great Nazarene returned or some other compassionate cosmic Overlord, the extraterrestrial solution to a great biological experiment having gone somewhat awry. A stopgap measure decreed from elsewhere (perhaps a Greater God) to guarantee that a new start for mankind is possible. Such, it would appear, is how cosmic affection is extended to those who care to those who haven't learned as yet how to care enough.

The above prophetic scenario may in fact come to pass, but in the meantime we must be very careful not to confuse some false predecessor, either hatched as a cabal in the minds of men or imposed by a group of opportunistic extraterrestrials working alone or in collaboration with human toadies, as the "real thing." Such a mistake will not only potentially enslave us, it may destroy the hope and self-determination found in human character which makes man so unique and valuable.

Whether we are finally ruled or not by direct extraterrestrial intervention—an idea given too little public currency these days—the stark reality remains. No matter who governs humanity, man, if he is to grow in all positive ways possible, must learn to live peacefully with himself or perpetually face the problems he claims so grieve him.

CHAPTER NINETEEN

# Money, Greed and the Equitable Distribution of the World's Wealth

"Money, money, money, money, money...." There is no question that some lyrics, such as the maddeningly repetitive example above, often reflect our human fascinations, compulsions and passions almost better than anything else. The passionate pursuit of money is well known to all of us with or without song. No doubt money is a universal sign of success, and this is nowhere more true than in our own country. It is often used, as we are all quite aware, to buy things denoting status and conferring prestige. Some people believe accumulating a goodly share of it assures happiness. Many of those who "have," whether they are happy or not, subscribe mentally to such thinking. Likewise, many of those who are "have nots" also believe the same thing. A small minority of both have learned better, and yet the knowledge that money is not happiness, no matter how firmly held, does not in itself guarantee happiness. Even democratic capitalism cannot assure us of attaining it, much to the chagrin of the compulsive accumulator. And democratic capitalism, despite its many virtues, has never been able to assure us of an equitable distribution of wealth or happiness. Truth is, it has never really tried.

If we are to have a New Age in this world of ours, if for one reason or another it is true that the old order of things is passing away and a New World Order is about to take its place, will we continue to use money in the ways we now do? Is it desirable to do so? Do we still need it as a form of payment for services rendered as well as for material needs? Might not there be a better way to imburse people for their work and for material necessities other than traditional currency, leaving us, perhaps, all better off individually as human beings and as citizens no matter where we call home?

Many thinking people are in agreement that world economic systems as they stand—with a mad scrambling by so many in most parts of the world to meet bare subsistence needs and a lavish display of material wealth, a conspicuous consumption, by others, the "winners," the "fat cats," in this life and death struggle—are not contributing to an equitable dispersal of payment for a days work or a fair sharing of the world's resources.

Is money really necessary? If we agree that the present system(s) of monetary dispersal is not very equitable and inevitably does not serve the best interests of a society (and world) which wishes to achieve "a kinder, gentler" civilization, then shouldn't we be willing to look for some alternatives to the way we are now doing things? People must be paid in some way for their labor. There is no question about that. They must be able to transact business. But as long as "money," currency as we know it, and the present acceptable means of its dispersal, are perceived as the best, or only, means to accomplish payment in kind for labor, services or materials, money and the system which now controls its delivery will reign supreme.

Obviously our highly technological civilization has become too complicated, in most cases, for a simple barter system to be effective. But there is another way. It is possible to institute under the auspices of a world government a new system based on merit-credit which could abolish many of the present excesses, and inequities, of today's world monetary system(s). For such a new system to work, we would have to change much of our habitual thinking. Indeed, it could be argued that unless we escape the present form of wealth sharing, including the present form of worker compensation, and change some of our present ideas of what is socially desirable and valuable, the world will continue to become progressively more violent as more and more people compete aggressively for a fair share, or a glutton's share, of the world's dwindling resources. A "kinder, gentler" world necessitates abandoning capitalism, as practiced in the West, and autocratic socialist communism, as practiced until recently in the Soviet Union and its satellites and, in its own peculiar form, in China.

How would this new merit-credit system work? Before that question can be answered, we need to recognize some of the changes in world opinion, particularly in social values, that must take place for such a program to be realized. First, men must come to recognize that most work is intrinsically good, not because it is proclaimed so by theological decree, reflecting the theologian's belief that he is preaching the will of God, or by state decree, reflecting the will of political hegemonists out for all they can get, but because it is action-positive and growth-positive. There is such a thing as work which is action-negative. This is work which does not contribute either to human growth potential or the well being of the planet. Two examples might be the political squandering of taxpayers money and selling drugs on the street corner. The kind of action-positive, growth-positive work we are talking about is work which, not surprisingly, is done by men and women who care about the implementing of a New Age and a New World Order, both of which are intimately related. It is constructive, fulfilling work and covers the spectrum from loving child care to finding jobs for the chronically unemployed and homes for the homeless. Action-negative work, on the other hand, because it contributes little or nothing to the welfare of the individual or society, should be, for those reasons alone, shunned.

Work which is action-positive and does contribute to human growth potential and the practical (and theoretical) well being of the planet would be in harmony with the cosmic law of interminable change. It would support positive, life-enhancing change. It would in no way support self-destructive behavior or even quiet acquiescence in atrophic decay. It would, however, tolerate for awhile the presence of some self-destructive behavior as long as strong evidence indicated verifiable steps were being taken to translate that behavior into a more positive life style. Neither a "thought police" or a KGB would be needed to bring pressure against sponsors of action-negative behavior. A public which was educated and increasingly enlightened about how fulfilling life could be on planet Earth, if only the eternal verities of cosmic law were used as guiding lights to direct that fulfillment, would gradually, perhaps more quickly than we might believe, bring this New World Order into being. In such a society self-reliance would be valued, tempered with the knowledge that much which is best and most fulfilling to human nature is related to the happy commingling, the social intercourse, of human beings.

If we are to support action-positive work and have an equitable merit-credit system of payment, we must reach the conclusion that all action-positive work is fundamentally equal in value. The street sweeper, truck driver and school teacher each deserve approximately the same, if not the very same, wages or merit-credits as the corporate chief executive officer, the US senator and the baseball star. The absurd disparity in wages that now exists in the United States and most other parts of the world must be radically altered. Statistics reveal a lot. The average school teacher earns $33,000 a year; the average postal worker $42,000 a year including benefits; the average corporate CEO of a major company $981,200 a year not counting stock options and fringe benefits; the average baseball player $891,188 a year. Without benefit of genius, it is not difficult to see that something is radically wrong here. Something is dreadfully askew. If wages are a reflection of social values and social priorities — and they most definitely are — then America, and much of the world, is very confused as to what is most valuable to the social welfare of its citizens.

Is the average baseball player's contribution to society really worth 27 times that of the average teacher? Is a CEO's value over 29 times as great? Does a baseball player really deserve a larger salary than a corporate CEO or a postal worker? We could carry this discussion further, but I believe the point is obvious. There seems little rhyme or reason to the way American culture, and most of the rest of the world, is dispensing earned wages for work accomplished. The system as it now stands is not only inequitable, it is destructive to the self-respect of the people who are a part of it, whether or not they actively support it or acquiesce in its existence.

The disparity in wages and earnings that now exists in the world within cultures, and from culture to culture, has hardly any basis in merit. Skill is often ignored. Education is often ignored. It is luck and greed and being in the right place at the right time that too often determines whether a man is rich in Manhattan or starving in Bombay. There is also truth to the old Marxist criticism, echoed by others, that raging bull capitalism, directed by owners, employers and exploiters of the working class, wrings from the sweat of the average working man excessive profits which are pocketed. We have seen, however, that the excesses of the Soviet system, which was offered as an alternative, also create a privileged class of favored party bureaucrats who use their positions to win for themselves a standard of living immeasurably higher than the workers they control. Historically, the favored few, because of positions of power based on politics and money, have expropriated to themselves an excess of profits. Lately in the West, a new technological elite has used their expertise to demand as much compensation as they can get, which, by the way, has been considerable. The yuppie syndrome, manifesting itself in a kind of middle-upper class materialistic imitation of the lives of the rich and famous, is one result of our increasing technological bent.

How would a merit-credit system function? And could it redirect the world away from a shallow, consuming infatuation with material things and material gain, from an acquisitive inclination toward an inquisitive mental and spiritual inclination? When we get tired of VCRs and camcorders, are we going to be willing to get on with the job of growing as points of universal light, of learning more about ourselves, of what makes us and our fellow man behave as we do? Are we going to become more interested in learning about what we don't now know about the vast array of flora and fauna that surrounds us on land and sea and, finally, about the untold revelations waiting for us as we investigate inner and outer space?

Here is a simple proposal—the rudiments of a large idea. I am sure it would need much fine tuning as a system to be practicable and functional. I am also convinced that the idea is sound and, in its basic structural bonework, will be similar to some system which we will see fleshed out in the near future. We may see it become a reality in our lifetime, provided we live so long and the excesses of the present system do not do us in first.

As a start, we take it as understood that all action-positive work is basically good and socially equal in value. The neurosurgeon in this new society, although respected for his specialized knowledge, is compensated the same as the primary school teacher and the corporate custodian. The baseball player's wages are the very same as those of the corporate executive and his the same as the postal employee's.

What? you say. An impossibility! People will never submit to such regimentation, such...equality of treatment. It is unheard of...outlandish...an injustice to the hard working and a sop to the lazy!

Before you go off half-cocked, my friend, hear me out. There are some safeguards built into the system to protect the less strong from the overzealous and even the hard working from being taken advantage of by the lazy and such types as the devious and the criminal-minded. Our system places a premium on *merit* and the recognition of it. No one will be kept from excelling. Indeed, people will be encouraged to excel at what they are best at and applauded for doing so. We are talking primarily about adjusting the inequitable distribution of wealth, not making everyone alike or destroying personal initiative or self-reliance. And as for anything being impossible, well, anything the mind of man can conceive of is possible.

Practically speaking, what is the world to do several decades from now when the population reaches 10 billion; how is it to feed and clothe and shelter its progeny as world resources continue to dwindle and even enough breathing space for each individual becomes a priority? We face these problems now, but they are nothing like they will be 10 or 20 years from now. The world's resources are strained, as it is, today. And war, famine, pestilence and death are with us. The four horsemen of the Apocalypse are riding now whether we like it or realize it, and they are taking a terrible toll, even this minute.

Twenty percent of the world's population cannot continue to consume 70 to 80 percent of its resources. As of this moment, the prospect for the future is the picture of an elite few dining, and living, well while those around them go hungry. This is not a new picture. But the consequences of continuing as we are, the stakes involved, will become much greater as the inequity becomes more disproportionate. Numbers, simple numbers, if nothing else, make a profound difference. Even with better contraceptive use, world population growth will most likely remain out of control. When does the day come — and it will most surely come — when those that have been grossly shortchanged by this old system, along with the starving multitudes, out of hunger and desperation, decide to take by force their fair share? That is the inevitable backlash. And it is close at hand. Pretending it will not happen, putting the idea out of mind, will not make it not happen.

We have no choice, then, but to restructure ourselves socially and economically — as a nation, as a world. For such reasons as the above, I offer an alternative. For no other reasons than practicality and reality, I ask that it be heard. Hopefully, it will also strike a human chord of compassion and justice in the hearts of men and give birth to an awareness, if it does not already exist, that something new and benevolent and fair must be created by men to save us from our selves.

Here is how such a new system might work. Our new world society, under the auspices of a just and benevolent world government, establishes by mutual agreement that all jobs, all positions of employment, whether held by owner, manager or worker, are equal and worth approximately 100 merit-credits per year. One hundred merit-credits, it has been decided, are enough to insure each world citizen ample credit to live per annum a relatively comfortable life—enough to afford an adequate residence, adequate food and clothing and other necessities and still not overstrain world resources. There would be sufficient credits left over after meeting these needs for some travel and entertainment.

As each individual reaches the age of forty, and after he (she) reaches each successive decade of life, he is allotted an additional 5 merit-credits until he reaches the age of 70, at which time no additional credits will be added to his total in the future. Any individual may retire after the age of 60, although he will not receive, if he chooses to do so, the 5 extra merit-credit points he would normally have been allotted at reaching 70 years of age. He will, however, in his retirement continue to receive the same number of merit-credit points he received up to, and including, the age of 60.

Citizens would be allowed to pass on to others some of their merit-credits as gifts or for barter purposes. No citizen, however, could give away as gifts within a year a sum of merit-credits which would leave him with less than 50, it having been agreed that a minimum of 50 merit-credits was necessary to insure the well being and independent functioning of each citizen. Thus poverty is avoided. And most social welfare programs, with which we are now familiar, are not needed.

Citizens are guaranteed in two ways by such a system that no con artist will talk them out of their ability to provide for themselves. First, they can dispense freely for life's extras or for gifts only those credits which they hold beyond the minimum 50. Secondly, firm laws would exist, and be rigidly enforced, to discourage bilking the unwary and infirm. In fact, it would be hoped that in such an evolving, more compassionate society that the very idea of cheating one's neighbor, or ostentatiously desiring, acquiring and flaunting excess wealth, would become, if not unthinkable, at least a rare occurrence in reality. Such social attitudes can be learned and become, after a time, second nature if citizens are properly educated and sufficiently encouraged to adopt them.

To protect each citizen from catastrophic loses such as might be caused by chronic physical or mental disease, universal health care would be offered to everyone at a minimal yearly fee of several merit-credits. How can any society maintain it is just and compassionate if it turns away the sick and needy because they do not have the money to be treated? No Great Society is worthy of the name if even one of its kind must go hungry or untreated because that person does not have coins in his (her) pocket.

As a protection against some individuals amassing large numbers of merit-credits, it is established by law that no individual may add more than 25 additonal merit-credits to his yearly allotment from any source whatsoever. This provision of the law further discourages the accumulation of excess wealth and its concomitant materialistic values and attitudes.

As a protection against the lazy and slothful who are healthy and fit to work but refuse to do so, the law provides the basic 50 merit-credits and 50 only, until the individual decides to become gainfully employed. Each citizen has the right to refuse to work and contribute to society and his own growth, but such behavior would be rare because education, training and public attitudes would discourage it.

What would motivate human beings to excel in a society of this nature? Public commendation and recognition. Awards for admirable performance of duties and excellence in craftsmanship would be created. They would be commonplace but not so commonplace as not to be greatly desired and sought after. They would be coveted for the right reasons. The public would be taught, educated to believe, that the most worthy occupation of man is a determined effort to improve himself spiritually, mentally and physically to the best of his abilities; that the most admirable attitude a man can have is the desire to share, if and when possible, whatever he has, whether it be his knowledge, his discoveries or inventions or simply his hearth and his heart.

In such a society questing inward and outward would be a spiritual and intellectual priority. Those who had made great gains in their development would be recognized and applauded. Those who were not quite as far along in their development would be encouraged and continually helped to proceed with their development. There would be no spiritual or intellectual elite. Smugness, egocentric behavior and flaunting of any kind would be considered in bad taste and discouraged. Each citizen would be taught that all grow in time, some a little more quickly, some a little less so, but that relatively speaking, we are all travelers on the same road, only differing in the way stations we have met.

You say you don't think such a world will ever exist here? I wouldn't bet on it, my friend. If not here, surely elsewhere. There are many way stations in the heavens. Each traveler-quester will find his own and pass on.*

*The Great Nazarene put it another way, 'In my father's house are many mansions.'

# CHAPTER TWENTY

## Possessing Demons, Guides and Gurus

Several years ago, during a bus trip, I listened to a young man talking out loud to a negative, disembodied entity he had somehow contacted. Or the entity had contacted him. It was night. The coach was dark. Fear was almost palpable. I could feel but not see the petrification of the people sitting around me. As the saying goes, you could have heard a pin drop. I couldn't hear anyone breathing, and I assumed they were holding their breath.

I'm sure no one was asleep. The conversation was noisy and disturbing, even the one side of it that we could hear — terrorizing, I'm convinced, to all those within earshot, most of whom probably thought the young man was just crazy and potentially dangerous.

And dangerous he probably was. Potentially more so than your average ambulatory citizen. He was, it was obvious, being given advice and instructions by the corresponding entity. This advice, though I won't go into details, sounded violent, vindictive and uncompromising. I do remember clearly it had something to do with getting even with someone who had crossed the young man in some undefined way.

It is not unusual for weak or weakened personalities — such as those who have let their defenses down because of negative thinking, drugs, alcohol and the like, or those who have had their defenses unwillingly undermined, such as by severe illness — to make contact with negative entities of some intelligence.* A few of these entities are of great intelligence; that is, they are extremely shrewd and clever. There is a great difference, however, between being intelligent and being wise. The wise entity is always compassionate and would never think of using, or trying to control, another human being for his own selfish reasons.

The kind of negative entity that we are talking about is a disharmonious, unbalanced type of intelligence. It reflects little of wisdom or true understanding, tends to be extremely ego-centered, and is hardly ever truly compassionate, although it sometimes pretends to be. It can pretend to be many things, claim many powers. It will often lie, connive and cheat, when it is not being subtle. It can also be quite subtle when it wants to be, when subtlety serves its purpose, and as hypnotic as the proverbial cobra.

Whether this type of negative entity dwells solely on the astral plane, except for excursions into our plane, is debatable. I suspect the cosmos is filled with embodied and disembodied entities which are capable, under certain conditions, of making contact with man. Some are friendly, wise, even benevolent; others self-centered, manipulative and corrupting. I also would guess that there are many which fall somewhere between these two poles. Whatever you can conceive, you can be fairly certain exists sometime somewhere.

It has been suggested by quite a few writers that many mental patients have been influenced, even possessed by these negative projectors. I believe that may well be true. Cases of

---

*Criminologists tell us that over 80 percent of the people incarcerated for violent felonies are either using drugs or alcohol, or both, at the time their offenses are committed. There is no telling, however, how many of these people are under the temporary (or perpetual) influence of a negative entity. For examples of invading entities taking control of people, we have such various and interesting scriptural and literary accounts as the Great Nazarene driving out demons in the possessed, Goethe's Faust succumbing almost completely to Mephistopheles and the American literary classic "The Devil and Daniel Webster." What is most remarkable today is the great number of thoroughly nonfictive examples of people exhibiting symptoms of either whole or partial possession, people who now flood the offices of psychiatrists, psychoanalysts and psychotherapists and are probably most often misdiagnosed.

multiple personality probably are, more often than we think, cases of multiple invasion of the personality by a foreign host. Modern science, including modern medicine, knows little of the reality, much less the metaphysical mechanics, by which these entities influence and invade the personality. Only folklore and the occult traditon have kept knowledge of such things alive. Most of the time, the Catholic Church and Protestant sects seem embarrassed by the very idea, although occasionally we hear of a Catholic priest somewhere performing the old rites of exorcism. The average contemporary scientist has had any potential interest in such matters trained out of him. To him it is all hokum, pure misuse of the imagination (which he doesn't much understand either).

The cosmic quester, in his inward and outward journeys to enlightenment, will sooner or later encounter some of these entities. Christianity calls them evil spirits and demons and has assiduously persecuted in the past individuals suspected of being them or being contaminated by them. It has been estimated that between 300,000 and 9,000,000 suspected witches were killed in Europe between the 11th and 18th centuries. Dozens were put to death in the early American colonies. This included, we might assume, the innocent, the falsely accused as well as those who resisted contact but, because of some reason such as illness, which was outside their control, were contacted, admitted contact (rather foolishly) and paid the price for their honesty. Whatever we decide to call these negative entities — incubi, succubi, devils, Satan, evil spirits, elementals, dark-side extraterrestrials — it is best to be prepared for meeting them accidentally come now or tomorrow.

Helen Blavatsky, that great inquirer into the ancient wisdom religions and the founder of Theosophy, was quite aware that the world "demon" was derived from the Greek *daemon* or *daimon* and that its early definition did not always suffer from negative connotations. The early Hermetic works and some ancient classics reserved the word for "god," "angel" or "genius" (the latter of which has the same root as our contemporary word "genie," as in "My Little Genie"). Socrates' *daemon* represented the incorruptible part of man, the true inner man. Much later the term was used by the Alexandrine school and by some philosophers to identify a whole melange of good and bad spirits. Confusion arose. Then some philosophers and early Church theologians tried to draw a line, and the word "demon" came to represent a class of negative, generally disembodied, beings. These are the lesser and many of the greater devils of contemporary Christianity, excluding the Devil himself, Lucifer or Satan who is conceived of as Supreme Evil. A good example of such a contemporary "demon" would be the entity which drove the infamous Son of Sam murderer to his actions.

Whatever term we decide to use to designate these negative energies, it is advised to be forewarned about them, to gain some knowledge of them for protection and peace of mind. They do exist. Gautama Buddha said most demons were created by the mind of man. And that is correct. Most of the time we make our own Hell. But Gautama never said there is no such thing as intelligent, negative, disembodied energies. They do in fact make occasional contact with us — or try to. More often than we think. Often when we are astral projecting while asleep. It is very important for mental health reasons that the cosmic quester (or potential cosmic quester, and that means all of us) be aware of their existence, especially if he (she) is to make any attempt to contact his ethereal "guide" (Christians say "guardian angel") or any other positive disembodied intelligence. It is also important from the point of view of the knowledge-quest itself. It does absolutely no good (and can do much harm) to get faulty information or drivel when we are seeking something more accurate, more helpful to ourselves and others.

Once contact is made, this new communicating intelligence must be tried and tested. No positive entity who is concerned with your well being or humanity's welfare will ever give you false advice — advice that would injure you or others or any of earth's life forms or the general ecology. Truly, positive entities are not malicious; they do not gossip about others or revel in small talk. Usually, they will refuse to speak of others unless it concerns your well being or humanity's at large. They should be thoroughly questioned as to whom they are, where they come from and what their motives are. If they are really intent upon positive service, they will not hedge their answers.

Do not allow yourself to be set up by a communicator who seems positive in the beginning, only to find out later that "it" is not what it pretends to be. If any advice from this entity at any time suggests you perform a negative action, drop contact immediately. And do not resume contact with it at any time in the future for any reason. Consider yourself lucky. You escaped a potentially disastrous situation without injury, with your sanity and life still intact.

Negative energies feed off of positive energy. There is no need for anyone to become victimized or controlled in any way if caution is used. As has often been said, negative thoughts and negative living attract negative energies—just one more good reason to put your life in order and to refuse to indulge in negative thinking of any kind.

It is important during the kind of communication of which we have been speaking to always try to ascertain as best as possible who is saying, or hearing, what. It is easy to let human emotions intrude. And human emotions, above all else, can make you mishear. When in doubt, check and recheck with your communicator. Get it, whatever the message, accurately or forget it. It is also very easy to hear one's self when we think, perhaps because we want to, that we are receiving the message from elsewhere. Accurate communication depends largely on the human subject being in a thoroughly relaxed mental and physical state. Agitation of the emotions, the mind and even the body can cause false readings of great variety.

Much of what has been said in the previous paragraphs applies as well to relationships between students and their earthly, embodied gurus. It would be wonderful indeed to have a living, breathing teacher such as the Great Nazarene, Gautama Buddha, Confucious, Socrates, Plato, Pythagorus, Krishnamurti or even a Henry David Thoreau walking through life beside us and imparting nuggets of pure golden wisdom. Of course, if we are not ready for it, this much cherished wisdom may pass right by us like a whipporwill in the night and we will never know it was ever so close by. Too many Westerners have too great a faith in finding a magic bullet, or at least a quick fix, to personal or even world problems — just as Easterners often rely too heavily, even slavishly, on a chosen guru, expecting him to all but live their lives for them. Westerners, however, seldom stay with one mentor very long. They are a restless lot, attaching themselves for awhile to a perceived teacher of wisdom with great hopes that the experience will change them greatly for the better. When results are not immediate, they soon move on, a little more frustrated, a little more confused about the whole process, as they conceive of it, but fundamentally the same person they were in the beginning of their quest.

Most Westerners have forgotten, or more likely have never learned, that the learning experience progresses more from within outward than from outward to within. Americans, Canadians and most South Americans, for instance, are almost totally outward-oriented people.* The spiritual life, even the mental life, is not given great priority. North and South American culture generally, while giving tacit acknowledgment to the existence of the spiritual life (especially in the form of conventional religious worship) and the mental life (for one to become a professional, such as a doctor or lawyer, is considered, rather irrationally, by the public to be involved in "mental" affairs), really does not understand either. Consciously or unconsciously, these cultures have arranged their life styles so that they will be as little burdened with the pursuit of real spirituality and true mental development as possible. Television, popular music, drug-induced euphoria, sports' madness and other "entertainments" are, contrary to Marxian thought, the real opiate of the people, the Roman circuses of our day.

*Which, needless to say, helps keep them earthbound-oriented and impedes their cosmic-oriented growth.

Governments either directly support or encourage these entertainments or look the other way when they become uncouth and harmful to the welfare of the public, which most of them, having become addictive long ago, surely are. After all, an entertained citizenry is a busy one, unlikely to think too much and involve itself in the profitable business of government which has been expropriated by bureaucrats disguised as elected representatives or, as in the case of many autocratic South American regimes, as "competent" statesmen.

For the student to get the maximum benefit from the knowledge imparted by a worthy, capable teacher-mentor, he must be well enough along on the inward journey of discovery for the imparted knowledge to fully register. We are assuming that the imparted knowledge is truly useful. Otherwise, the student is wasting his time and should seek another teacher. But nothing avails, nothing happens unless, and until, the student is ready. It is he who has to do the preliminary "work." It is he who must make the field ready and receptive to the seeds. The old saying, When the student is ready, the master will appear, applies here as well. There is no point expecting a blind and deaf man to hear a shot fired or to see the shooter. When the student is ready, he will see and hear, intuit and understand. His circuits will be open and receptive. The messages will be received, duly noted and stored in his growing consciousness, messages reflecting the immense variety and intimate interrelatedness of all creation.

Strangely, almost magically, the true student, the intent cosmic quester, is never let down. What he needs, when he needs it, will always appear, if his motives are selfless and unimpeachable. We do not understand adequately the Guiding Energy of which we are a part. But it does exist. And it is eternally active. We are continually given glimpses of its greater possibilities but most of the time these glimpses pass us by unseen because of our figurative, self-imposed blindness and deafness. We have plugged our ears and put on blinders and then complained because we cannot see or hear the truth.

Whether it is certain specific knowledge, the company of

enlightening friends (or strangers) or simply special experiences that the student needs to continue his journey, he will find that "it" appears, "they" become available to him when he needs them.* Our student-quester must learn to recognize those provisions for what they are and to make beneficial use of them. He must be vigilant and clear-headed, like the lookout in the crowsnest of a clipper ship of old, if he is to be ready for the many unexpected vicissitudes of life that await him, no matter how prepared he may imagine himself to be. If he remains clear-headed, hopeful and aware, our mariner-quester stands a much better chance of reaching his next port of call relatively unscathed and wiser for his experience on the seemingly endless cosmic voyage of individual unfoldment. To have a good captain, that is, a worthy teacher-mentor, is reassuring. However, no one but the student-quester himself can be the steersman of his fate.

*The Supreme Intelligence that guides us all, provides us with whatever provisions we need, when we need them, in the way we need them. We are never denied access to those provisions, not ever, although our nearsightedness sometimes makes it seem so.

# CHAPTER TWENTY-ONE

## You Are Gods

We are star stuff. We are composed of the primordial matter and energy and spirit of the cosmos. Thus, we can properly say that we are made of God stuff, as is everything in creation. We are god but not God inclusive. Little bits of God, you might say, but significant ones nonetheless. We have, however, unlike most portions of creation, a higher mind and an intuition of possessing a spirit, an intuition which goes beyond the simple recognition that we are inflated with a life-force called by some the "divine fire" or *divinus inflatus*. We intuit this spirit as directly linking us with the Spirit-Force out of which came all creation, including ourselves. Most encouraging of all, perhaps, we are imbued by this spirit with a need and an ability to discover ourselves thoroughly and completely, which becomes, finally, sooner or later for every man-spirit, a constitutional necessity. All these recognitions are part of the Grand Scheme of which we must become more aware before we can go further in our observations and discoveries — our growth.

We are also godlike from another perspective. We are, as we have seen elsewhere in these pages, potential gods, gods-in-the-making. If we continue to insist as we have in the past that the intellectually and spiritually advanced extraterrestrial entities that landed in ancient times were "gods" (or God) — those beings who, as the evidence suggests, bioengineered us and programmed us with their morality — then we need to become thoroughly aware that it is within our will power, within our potential growth parameters, to intellectually and spiritually metamorphose ourselves to their level of development. They are waiting for us to join them. And if the reports and rumors are at all accurate, they will be overjoyed to see us do so. We have the biological equipment and the spiritual capacity to achieve such a victory; however, unhappily, much of it is not now being used in a way which will assure it.

Those who are discovering that they are cosmic-oriented, our searching cosmic questers, are already well on their way to unraveling the mysteries of being which fascinate the open-minded individual. It is important, needless to say, that latent, "sleeping" cosmic-oriented types be awakened or awaken themselves as soon as possible. They will then be better able not only to help themselves but those around them, earthbound-oriented and cosmic-oriented alike, all who are willing to listen, look honestly inward and outward and learn.

The exhortation to awaken and to serve is as old as the first Wise Ones who walked the earth. Whether it came first from intuitive man or was brought to him by cosmic visitors, it makes no great difference. It makes a large difference, however, whether or not the exhortation is heeded and acted upon. It cannot be reiterated enough. It needs to be repeated interminably until everyone everywhere understands what it means. Once understood, a renaissance in the spirit of man is possible, a world can be reborn. A few active cosmic-oriented individuals carry the seed from which a new garden may bloom. Even though they are a small lot in number, their influence is great, their power to enhance the quality of life is large. How great, how large depends on how many hear them and heed their message or begin carefully listening to that "still small voice" within themselves that carries the same message and offers the same hope. Then ten thousand gardens may bloom and the earth will flower as never before.

We are told that when the Jews approached the Great Nazarene and threatened to stone him for blasphemy for making himself God, he said, 'Is it not written in your law, "I said, you are gods?" If he called them gods to whom the word of God came (and scripture cannot be broken), do you say of him whom the Father consecrated and sent into the world, "You are blaspheming," because I said, "I am the Son of God?"' He thus confirmed the idea of the godliness of man to his disbelieving auditors. They proceeded to try to arrest him. Any man who dares to tell his fellow men of their godliness today risks the same kind of outrageous disbelief, if not bodily harm, or the very opposite kind of reaction that springs from the twins apathy and indifference. Men have been brainwashed and programmed to think otherwise.

A few other similar examples concerning the Great Nazarene are revealing of a greater truth. Two especially. In the Gospel of John (from which the above quotation came), we are also told, 'Truly, truly, I say to you, he who believes in me will also do the works that I do; and greater works than these will he do, because I go to the Father.' Never has a statement of scripture been so misunderstood and so bruised by man-handling.

In Matthew we hear, 'For truly, I say to you, if you have faith as a grain of mustard seed, you will say to this mountain, "Move hence to yonder place," and it will move; nothing will be impossible to you.' Remember in Genesis the extraterrestrial commander commenting on the future abilities and capacities of the builders of the Tower of Babel? '...and this is only the beginning of what they will do; and nothing that they propose to do will now be impossible for them.'

How many Christians, how many individuals the world over, really believe that the powers inherent in human beings are as large (and glorious) as those spoken of in Chapters 10 and 14 of John and Chapter 17 of Matthew? And Chapter 11 of Genesis? The extraterrestrial commander of Genesis meant exactly what he said. The Great Nazarene himself meant literally what he said, this carpenter-entity from Nazareth, this healer-king of men who, so much evidence now indicates, was an embodied extraterrestrial visitor on a great and special mission. He appears to have been one of those ancient astronaut "gods" humankind so admires and so despairs of ever imitating much less emulating. And yet...and yet he was telling mankind all along that they, too, were "gods" who *could do* as he had done, if they only had the faith and the will power. This is the great message of Jesus Christ, the one he cared most about, and it has been misunderstood, this message which was intended as primary, and relegated to an inferior position while the man himself has been raised to the status of Primal Cause. This he never desired. Instead of giving us the Master's message to contemplate and uplift us, theologians have given us the man-god Jesus to worhship rather than emulate. If there is true blasphemy, perhaps it lies here.

People have been taught that the Great Nazarene's language is figurative, metaphorical speech. Theologians fear the idea that his followers, their parishoners, will believe his message and take it literally, as it was intended to be understood. The idea that meer fallible man can, with adequate spiritual growth, equal the "miracles" of Christ is distasteful to them. So fouled are many of them in their understandings and interpretations, that the very possibility makes them blanch and tremble. So little faith do they have in God and the spirit of God which dwells in men.

Sadly, Christians and humankind the world over have not been taught the true potential of man. Often they have been taught just the opposite: guilt, sin, doom, death and hell-fire.

When the Great Nazarene said that men who have the proper understanding of faith, even the minutest amount, can move a mountain, he believed it. He knew it to be true. They did not believe it or did not believe it enough. And they have now been convinced it is a metaphor, to be taken seriously but not too seriously, otherwise the hope might go to their heads and invigorate them. Then they might cast off their false shepherds who would find themselves jobless and unhappy in a world which had happily found its true direction and meaning.

Even the most fundamental of fundamentalists has a hard time putting the truth of the Great Nazarene's statement into perspective. He would be much happier if he did. We all would be. And we must all learn to do just that. In other words, when a cosmic-oriented being reaches a certain state of development, when he has come to understand natural and cosmic laws as Jesus did, and as we have yet to do, then he will be able to move mountains, even on voice command. No "miracles" here, just a better understanding of cosmic law. To achieve that understanding, we must put ourselves in greater harmony with cosmic law. Then our present achievements as individuals and as a civilization will pale compared to what we will be able to accomplish. What will we think, then, of our present prideful contemporary science and its accomplishments in comparison?

When we reach adequate cosmic understanding, when we have the ability as indicated in Matthew, we will be capable far beyond our present dreams. And rightfully so. By then we will have become consummate cosmic questers. We may well have passed far beyond this world, but, wherever we find ourselves, we will know that we have earned our status through proper spiritual growth. We will not have become misguided black magicians trying to tap powers we do not fully understand for the wrong reasons. We will be able to use our new-earned prowess at the right time for the right selfless reasons. We will have become like many of our extraterrestrial visitors of today and those of yesterday, who were often mistaken as angels and gods and worshiped accordingly. By then we also will have become extraterrestrial cosmic travelers, worthy to be accepted among cosmic life forms everywhere as compassionate, knowledgeable space souls, probably to be mistaken ourselves somewhere sometime as "angels" or the Godhead Itself. How we will react then will have much to do with how much we have learned in all of our Ultimate Game adventures.

When Jehovah, a commander of the *Elohim-Nephilim* cosmic visitors, observed early earthbound-oriented man attempting to build a launch tower for spacecraft (the Babylonian and Hebrew word of Genesis 11:4 for spacecraft is *shem* or "that which goes up," rocket ship, unfortunately offered in many texts by a much later derivative definition, i.e. to "make a name") so that he could imitate the cosmic visitors and reach the heavens, he was rightly appalled. 'Behold, they are one people, and they have all one language; *and this is only the beginning of what they will do; and nothing that they propose to do will now be impossible for them.*' His remarks indicate that he and his followers were very aware of the potential of the new man. It is also obvious that he considered this attempt (probably aided by a few rebellious extraterrestrial visitors under his own command) to rival the "gods" an inappropriate and presumptuous action by a spiritually and morally underdeveloped specimen. Man wasn't ready for such projects. Is he ready today? More than half of his space launches to date concern deploying military hardware of one kind or another. Is he, as aggressive and warlike as he has remained, a fit emissary to the stars?

Jehovah and his band threw a glitch or two into early man's attempt to use a technology he did not really understand. He blocked the way temporarily to dangerous exploits that would undoubtedly have ended in tragedy. But there is really no incontrovertible evidence that our extraterrestrial visitors of past ages wished then, or wish now, to stand in the way of humankind coming to a greater understanding of its potential, that is, literally coming of age.

Our early visitors, it now appears, were our partial progenitors, and they kept a paternalistic eye on our early development. But once they understood the full potential of their creation, it appears they stepped back, observing and monitoring from time to time, it is true, but relaxing most overt control and allowing the new species to develop on its own. This story can be read in the Hindu Vedas, in the Venidad of the Mazdeans, in Buddhist scripture, in the Mayan Popul Vuh, in the Koran and elsewhere. It is a great story now seldom told and too little appreciated and understood for what it really says.

Our ancient cosmic visitors did offer, periodically, laws, moral instruction (e.g. Mosaic law and the Great Nazarene's teachings), advice and warnings. Much of this in its Judeo-Christian version can be read in the books of the Old Testament prophets and in the Gospels and the Book of Revelation.

The dissemination of this "advice," it must be reaized, was a worldwide project long ago carried out to completion, if not fruition. Every mass of mankind on the face of the planet received the promptings and teachings in one form or another. The overall influence of our visitor-teachers was, and remains, uplifting and encouraging. They fathered us but at metaphorical puberty, they let us begin to discover the world and ourselves by ourselves.

If the extraterrestrial visitors to earth have had our best interests at heart, can the same thing be said for the organized religions of the world which were given birth, or at any rate much of their impetus to formation and elaboration, by extraterrestrial contact? What kind of judgment can be made of Christianity's attempt to shepherd her flock? Has it been all that successful?

Regrettably, the answers to the above questions, where applicable, would seem to be "no." As time passes, original teachings—even if they are recorded accurately in the beginning, which seldom happens—are turned into dogma. If there are certain flaws that are resident in the original transcriptions (original errors) caused by transmission difficulties (or failures) between the receiver and his divine (or extraterrestrial) source, these flaws are nothing compared to the warping of exegesis and interpretation and translation that follows in time. What we get finally are emendations of interpretations of interpretations. Much of this is done in good faith, as the phrase goes, but it does nothing for the accuracy of the original Word.

The problems involved in the successful conveyance of the original Word are huge ones, but when even the main idea of the message fails to get through, it is a very dark day. And that is the case with orthodox Judaism and conventional Christianity and with the other major religions. The main idea, humanity's potential divinity, has been smothered where and when, infrequently, it has been recognized at all. It is the primary message of the Old and New Testaments. It was the Nazarene's (and Gautama Buddha's) great message. He was to be the great exemplar, the living example of what human potential (Jesus) could achieve (the Christ state). He came to demonstrate and to prove. Instead of a grateful acceptance of his inspiring message—a message which, you might think, should have caused jubilation in the minds of men—the focus was changed (not surprisingly, by theological politicians) to worshiping him as God, a practice he did not at all encourage. That focus has remained to this day.

Because earthbound-oriented man didn't (and still doesn't) want God or a potential god traipsing around and butting into his earthly affairs, the Nazarene was killed. It is much easier to worship a god or God when he isn't standing before you, reminding you inadvertently of your own inadequacies. Close up the exemplar, as perfected man, is too embarrassing. But it is convenient to have him at one's disposal as long as he is at a distance, where he becomes useful. Then the idea of him, the design of him, can be woven to one's advantage, just as the weaver chooses the colors of his woof and warp to please himself.

The Christian Church from early on kept man as a child. The mold was set as early as the first several centuries of the new era. The dogma had jelled in the mold by the time of the Nicene Council of 325 A.D. and had thoroughly solidified by the Nicene Council of 787 A.D. This misdirected and intrinsically pernicious paternalism denied man the encouragement he needed to use his self-determination, his will power, to learn all he could about everything—himself, his Creator, his reason(s) for being, about life and its meaning(s), about the world in all its multitudinous diversity, about the beauty and order of the solar system of which he is an important part and even about the complexity and mystery of the cosmos which surrounds and enfolds him. He was kept ignorant, encouraged to remain so and threatened whenever he departed from dogma. And the dogman over time grew apace with bureaucratic mysticism, which created it and nurtured it and whose roots had little to do with original scripture. As a reminder of how to present the dogma in an invariable sequence, ritual came into practice. It in itself had several advantages. It invested the arcane with a solemn pomp; it bedecked the once simple, original scriptural messages with magnificent accounterments, turning into complicated symbolism what was once unadorned naked truth intended originally for everyone to understand without effort. In such ways is the sacred made profane and inscrutable.

Christianity has not taught effectively the inherent glory of man. It has discouraged, even persecuted those who would deviate from its prescribed formulas with great worldly inquisitions and littler neighborhood inquisitions which have taken place in the smallest parish. It has frowned upon the idea of soul-exploration or any other kind of exploration. It has been in its practices for centuries a thoroughly reactionary institution. Once its dogma was in place, it became like a Medusa, attempting to devour any questers traveling along the road of self-enlightenment. Specifically, it has fostered a great tragedy for almost 2000 years; it has encouraged its followers, more often than not, to feel ashamed of their shortcomings rather than hopeful about their indigenous godliness. Guilt has not improved humanity, it has, however, been used to control it.*

What was the "original sin?" If it is a term conceived to explain the idea that primitive earthbound-oriented man wished to understand the nature of the real world, both the negative and positive aspects of it, however imperfectly he understood the idea of the "real world"—wished to know what was beyond the confines of the biogenetic laboratory, the Garden of Eden, in which he was created—then the term "original sin" is surely a misnomer and should be buried whereever terminology which is grossly inadequate is buried. By the definition given above, he qualifies not as a "sinner" but as a burgeoning cosmic quester.

Early earthbound-oriented man may have broken the restrictive, paternalistic orders of the extraterrestrial being who bioengineered him, but that kind of behavior should not necessarily be considered sinful. The *Elohim-Nephilim* were

---

*As has fear, for which, also, nothing positive can be said.

303

neither perfect and infallible nor above acting in their own self-interest. Once realizing the self-determining drive of their creation—and after much initial anger at having their orders broken which, in their view, had been established for the good of their fledgling product—once convinced of the fact that this new man insisted on the independence of his own existence, they cut him loose. Twice. First, he was expelled from the protection of the Garden-Laboratory (Gen 3:23-24). Then he was later scattered over the face of the earth (Gen 11:8-9). They knew he would make a myriad mistakes becoming whatever he would become, but they cut him loose *and eventually wished him well.* They finally realized his potential, admitted to it (Gen 11:6) and decided in a limited way to help him achieve greatness (Gen 12:1-3) if he would accept their tutelage.

Organized religion in the world has only one legitimate function: to encourage continually the individual in his quest for cosmic understanding and his desire to perfect himself. In this regard, it has failed miserably. Instead of encouraging ideas such as the spiritual bond among men, the spiritual likeness of all men, of essential brotherhood, it has through adamant, inert dogma and dangerous dabbling in international politics, set men against men, irrationally proclaiming and celebrating perceived differences in creed and ritual, pretending to understand the Godhead and cosmic law when it did not, all the while maintaining a pose of self-righteousness which has pretended to be above criticism because it was, or so it thought, divinely inspired. But this kind of religion is not inspired by God. It is the product of men's minds. And it carries within its bosom all the weaknesses and excesses of human nature.

The consequences of such nearsighted religion is sacred irrelevance, secular smugness, spiritual provincialism, intellectual parochialism and hate-mongering. The major faiths of the world today do not elicit confidence or respect from the cosmic-oriented temperament. Tribalism of the spirit is as dangerous to self-growth as political tribalism is to world peace.

With such an existing state of affairs, what is the cosmic quester to do? Where is he (she) to go? Where is refuge in this world?

Refuge can be found in only one place, the original place. That place is within the individual spirit. No program of development, no panacea, no magic talisman, no guru, guide or teacher can take its place, plumb its depths for you or replace it in any way. The truly self-reliant person, and the only thoroughly aware soul, has learned to take refuge there, where the beginnings and endings all conjoin, where the true man lies. Few have ventured so far inward, which is why so few can honestly say "I am that I am, and I know who and what I am."

The cosmic quester must learn to do as countless aspiring seekers before him. He must remember that inevitably his fate, his spiritual fate—which is ultimately the only enduring fate—is his responsibility and no one else's. No one can live his life but him. No one was intended to. No one can bring into existence the unique chord of the cosmic song that is his alone to offer. Once sounded it becomes instantaneously orchestrated and added to the great cosmic symphony that plays interminably about us. But the chord which is his, is his alone. He must live it. He must write it. He must offer it up. Then, somewhat in amazement, after all is done, he can perhaps stand back for a moment, frozen in cosmic time, and hear his chord blend in that song we are all in the process of making and discovering.

The ancient Gnostics knew that to write that chord well, at least the chord that pertains to the song of this particular life, was, first and foremost, an intensely personal affair. One had to step back, so to speak, out of the pack and away from the turmoil of men (if doing so meant only mentally removing oneself) to successfully explore our fundamental relationship with creation and the Creative Force. By stepping back or to the side of life's mad rush, out of the way of everything which is geared and oiled to distract us, we can get a more objective perspective as well as the peace and quiet necessary to look inward. Paradoxically, we come to understand the Pleroma, the plentitude of creation, by understanding first our individual relationship to the whole. This by stepping back. Otherwise, most probably, we will be swept along with the noisome crowd which is too busy and too exhausted to ever discover consciously what it has missed but what, invariably, its sleeping subconscious mind and its shackled spirit so long for.

The cosmic quester, the cosmic-oriented soul, will find at the beginning of his quest great terrifying moments of aloneness — and loneliness. He soon discovers that he does not "fit" the contemporary scene as well as those about him. This may cause him to doubt himself. He may even feel like a pariah. But what he is after, after all, is not what the crowd of earthbound-oriented mortals about him is after. They are busy with "eating, drinking, marrying and giving in marriage...." He is pursuing a different path and the goal, the horizon of understanding which he seeks, seems to be forever escaping him, perpetually receding before his eyes, even, sometimes, it would seem, at the very moment he has caught a clear, quick glimpse of it. It seems cruel to strive so hard and then to be left empty-handed.

As time goes on, the cosmic quester will begin to feel less alone. He will become convinced, and rightfully, that the difference between himself and the others around him isn't, in fact, so great. He will more fully recognize that they, too, are embarked on a unique journey, although most of them are only vaguely, if at all, aware of its uniqueness and dimly, if at all, conscious of its meaning. At such moments, he should take heart. He is extraordinarily fortunate to have made his present personal progress toward the greater enlightenment that our (and his) intuition tells us awaits us at some future supernal moment of the Ultimate Game. His progress to date, as he has come to realize, is not by accident. It has been occasioned by the use of will power and the help of loving friends both earthy and extraterrestrial. It is at moments of recognition like these that the quester will feel less alone and become more thoroughly convinced than ever before of the inextricable interrelatedness of all things and the need, when possible, of those "things" to communicate to one another, even...especially to love one another.

Thus is the song written. Thus does the orchestra come to play. Thus do we begin to hear, at first almost inaudibly, then with more clarity, a music of almost unimaginable beauty and variety that beggars the use of poor words such as these.

## DISCOVERING THE LOST PYRAMID
### G. Cope Schellhorn

*The true story of an archeological quest leading ultimately to a spiritual initiation. A young man searches for the fabled lost records of Thoth (Hermes Trismegistus) rumored since ancient times to contain the history of Lemuria, Atlantis and early Egypt and to be buried near the Great Pyramid of Giza. His relationship with Hugh Lynn Cayce, then director of the A.R.E. and also interested in locating the records, is explored. After early despair, he triumphs over material and spiritual obstacles and pinpoints the location of the records.*

*"He wondered who it would be who would finally raise the records to the light of day. Would it be some virtuous Percival among men who had yet to make his appearance, someone more faultless than he? Or would it be some flawed Lancelot who, at last finding a greater perfection in himself, would come to the rescue and raise up the story of ancient man, more ancient than most men dare dream? Who would be so bold? he wondered. And who so worthy as to succeed?"*

*"The objective of our quest, strangely, marvellously seems to recede before our eyes and is replaced, most appropriately, and in good and proper time, by a larger vision, a promise of even greater understanding as we continue to grow apace."*

*205 pages*

---

# Index